Developing Lean Leaders at Northeast Georgia Health System

Copyright © 2014 Jeffrey Liker

All rights reserved.

Dr. Jeffrey K. Liker

with George Trachilis

Thank you to Carol Burrell and the team at Northeast Georgia Health System for recognizing the value of the book, Developing Lean Leaders at All Levels, and making it their own.

Jeffrey K. Liker copyrights the following document. All Rights Reserved. Reproduction of any part of this document, mechanical or electronically, beyond that permitted in Section 107 or 108 of the 1976 United States Copyright Act is unlawful without the expressed written permission of the copyright author and publisher. International copyright laws also apply.

ISBN: 978-1-948210-00-3

Published By: Lean Leadership Institute Publications
V.P. of Publications: Daniel J. Stanley AAP
Published in the United States of America
First Edition – English

Table of Contents

FOREWORD *by Carol Burrell*	iiv
FOREWORD *by George Trachilis*	vii
ABOUT THE AUTHOR	xiii

CHAPTER 1

LEAN AND LEAN LEADERSHIP — 1

Overview of Lean Leadership and Recommended Learning Approach	1
What is Lean Leadership?	8
History of The Toyota Way	10
What is Real TPS?	13
What is the Real Toyota Production System?	17
Lean Processes as a System	22
Developing Exceptional People through Problem Solving	29
Lean is now redefined	31

CHAPTER 2

PROBLEM SOLVING, IMPROVEMENT, & A3 THINKING — 33

Problem Solving your way toward an Ideal State	33
Toyota Business Practices: One Company, One Improvement Process	37
Toyota Business Practices: Experimentation and Learning	43
Toyota Business Practices for Warranty Reduction	45
Driving to the root cause through 5 Whys	52
Countermeasures and Problem Solving to Develop People	56
Why is PDCA so rarely followed?	61
Why do so many companies miss the PCA from the PDCA cycle?	64
A3 Thinking to Slow Down Problem Solving	67
The other A3 Stories	72
The Improvement *Kata*, Another Approach	84
Lean Leaders Strive for Continuous Improvement	89

CHAPTER 3

STANDARDS, STANDARD WORK, AND VISUAL MANAGEMENT — 93

Standard Work and Visual Management	93
Standard Work Document for non-cyclical Work	96

Standards and Continuous Improvement	99
Lean's Core Leadership Model	102
Visual Management to See the Gaps: Standard vs Actual	105
A Non-traditional Lean Case: Menlo Innovations	109
Visual Management and Teamwork at Menlo	113
Visual Management Supports a Collaborative Culture	117
What did we learn about Visual Management?	120

CHAPTER 4

COMMIT TO SELF DEVELOPMENT   123

What are you trying to Self-Develop?	123
How do you work to become a Lean Leader?	129
Leadership Self-Development Learning Cycles (PDCA)	131
How do Lean Leaders develop and get promoted?	134
Deep Expertise through *Shu-Ha-Ri* Stages	137
Do senior executives still need to self-develop?	140
Important Factors for Leader Success in an Exceptional Company	145

CHAPTER 5

LEARNING TO COACH AND DEVELOP OTHERS   149

While self-developing begin to learn how to develop others	149
Beginning the Steps of Coaching and Developing Others	153
How to Coach and Develop Others at the *Gemba*	158
Using *Kata* to Coach One Person at a Time	161
Three-Part Recipe for What Lean Leaders Must Learn	165
How can this Apply to Developing Others in Your Organization?	168

CHAPTER 6

SUPPORT DAILY KAIZEN   173

Bringing Lean Leadership to Work Groups	173
Toyota work groups are at the heart of Continuous Improvement	176
Visual Controls and the Andon System Support Improvement	179
Creating a teacher who creates a critical mass of Lean Thinkers	182
Role of B-labor at Toyota to Supplement the Work Groups	184
Creating a Material Flow Revolution (Minomi Case)	185
Minomi Project Results	190
Standard Work to Support Kaizen in Work Groups	191
What is Leader Standard Work?	198
Tying it all Together	204
What is the Current State in your organization?	207

CHAPTER 7

CREATE VISION AND ALIGN GOALS THROUGH *Hoshin Kanri*   211

   Create the Vision and the Capability   211
   Hoshin Kanri to focus energy on aligned learning cycles   213
   Hoshin Kanri at Toyota   215
   Align people horizontally and vertically   220
   How *Hoshin Kanri* and Daily Management Work Together   222
   Philosophy in *Hoshin Kanri*   227
   Comparison between MBO and *Hoshin Kanri*   229
   Radical Lean Transformation: Dana Chassis Parts Supplier   232
   With the Right Philosophy it all Comes Together   247
   Final Feedback: Deliberate Practice is not Fun   251

CHAPTER 8

CONNECTING STRATEGY TO OPERATIONAL EXCELLENCE: The Scion Example   255

   Every Improvement Starts with a Challenge   255
   Scion Sales-Marketing Approach   257
   Connecting Purpose to Results   261
   Relationship between Strategic Innovation & Operational Excellence for Scion   262
   Toyota Way Principles in Action   264

DEVELOPING LEAN LEADERS: For Further Reading   267

DEVELOPING LEAN LEADERS

FOREWORD *by Carol Burrell*

Dear Reader,

With so many changes in health care today, it is key for leadership at Northeast Georgia Health System to have a full understanding of our organizational focus on continuous improvement, our Quest for Excellence. The understanding, support and fostering of our Quest for Excellence is necessary as we strive to better serve our patients, families and visitors through exceptional service. Quest for Excellence is our goal to be better tomorrow than we are today and is a direct reflection of our core values and mission to improve the health of our community in all we do.

As we continue on our lean journey, we have identified books, articles and pertinent information to personally support and educate staff at a variety of levels. Focus is placed on our Daily Management System as we empower staff to be successful problem solvers, escalating issues as necessary. *Leading Change Through Problem Solving at Northeast Georgia Health System* is a book that I feel truly embraces this lean methodology and our Quest for Excellence. Utilizing a lean toolset is extremely important, but the unique characteristic of this book is the emphasis and importance placed on key leadership elements that are necessary to successfully implement and sustain process improvements. Respect for people is fundamental in lean, beginning with a commitment to self-development to spending time in the workplace to engaging front-line staff and problem solving.

I am sure you will find, as I did, the value within this book and will be able to immediately see areas of opportunity both personally and professionally. We are pleased to present this copy to our leaders with the intent to read and revisit key chapters as you continue to grow in your lean journey at NGHS.

Enjoy!

Carol Burrell
President and CEO
Northeast Georgia Health System

DEVELOPING LEAN LEADERS

FOREWORD *by George Trachilis*

My name is George Trachilis and I am a professional engineer in Canada. After many years of implementing Lean Thinking tools and techniques in many different companies, locally and globally, it became very evident to me that there was one common theme that stood out above all others, "Lean rarely worked as we expected." Before you close the book in validation of your thoughts about Lean, read a little further. You will not be disappointed.

I feel I have to justify my comment. Sure, Lean works, and I have seen amazing transformations in the initial year of implementation, or while I am there. These transformations are usually physical in nature, like cleaning up the place, moving machines close together; organizing the office for better communication between people, and the list goes on. All of these things add to the efficiency of a process, and in some cases to the efficiency of the company as a whole. Often a company is in crisis mode when they start "Lean." The crisis ranges from having to reduce costs or they will not be in business in one year's time to there is so much business we cannot take on any more work until we fix our process deficiencies. In both cases, I do my best to help, and lean works beautifully in the first year. What is the problem? My big Aha came when the government in Alberta, Canada asked me to create an online course that educates companies in Lean Thinking. They required me to focus on the "Leadership" in the organization - the president, the directors, and senior managers - only. They realized that the companies in their Province of Canada must strive for *sustainable change* and not initial quick wins by applying Lean tools.

In June 2012, Dr. Liker came to my home town of Winnipeg, Canada to speak at our Lean conference. I had made arrangements to pick him up at the airport, take him on a boat ride on the Red River, then take him to the conference where he would do a keynote speech for just over one hour, and then drive him back to the airport, all in the same day. I had a few great conversations with him, but two of them stood out for me. The first was when we were on the river and started discussing the Canadian Museum of Human Rights (unfinished at the time) which was well over budget, coming in at a total cost of $351 million, and two years late in its construction. We talked about how Lean applies to all industries, including construction. The second came after his speech. Many managers were waiting in line for Dr. Liker to sign his latest book *The Toyota Way to Lean Leadership*, when one of the managers asked, "Dr. Liker what is it that prevents Lean thinking from being sustained in many companies?" Jeff looked the manager in the eyes, and said, "In one word, Leadership." The conversation that then ensued had me thinking about this missing link. I do not know about you, but when I receive clarity in my life, I capture it by setting a new goal around that new focal point. In this way, I start moving towards it, hopefully in the right direction. This was the right direction, and I knew it.

In the following months, I established and developed a friendship with Jeff to the point of having him do some webinars for my organization. These later became a new online course on Lean leadership, www.ToyotaWaytoLeanLeadership.com. We later decided that this information was too valuable to leave in video format alone, where their access was limited to those who could afford to pay for an online course and coach. We decided that the best way to spread the word is through a book. That book is now in your hands, *Developing Lean Leaders at all Levels*.

In my 20 years implementing Lean Thinking I had not come across this kind of contribution to the Lean world before, that is, until Dr. Liker's speech in my hometown. I just had to share it with others. Whether you know anything about Lean or you are a 25-year veteran of Toyota (its origin) you will learn what you need to know from this book. I always knew it was about the people, but "What was it about the people that made Lean work?"

Jeff deeply describes the core skills, values, behaviors, patterns, and the prescribed process a manager/leader must have and follow for long-term success. He compares this success with that of an athlete or musician who, using a coach, develops while performing their skills. He describes how a coach identifies their weaknesses in a systematic way so that the student can improve their form and accelerate their development on the way to reaching their goal, or target condition. Outside of the workplace, everyone should use a coach if they are serious about their craft. It turns out this is also true inside the workplace.

This book and Jeff's contribution to the Lean world is nothing short of stellar. While we are living in a world that bombards us with information, Jeff builds on his 32 years of research and knowledge of the Toyota inner workings to get to the point so that you, as a student, coach, manager, or CEO, know what to do to succeed in the workplace regardless of the industry in which you work. As an example of the power of this learning, I have converted my own approach to implementing the physical part of Lean to one of developing Lean Leadership. I start with the core values of the organization and just as I have been learning about Toyota; I coach the organization to clearly define their core values. Then, I move to the first step of the *Lean Leadership Development Model; Commit to Self-development.* With leaders in the organization reaching out for help, and recognizing the need for self-development, it is easier to guide them up the mountain. What a novel concept; help those that wish to help themselves. The four steps of the Lean Leadership Development Model are:

1. Commit to Self-development
2. Coach and Develop Others
3. Support Daily *Kaizen* (improvement)
4. Create Vision and Align Goals

As a Lean Leader myself I have not stopped learning. I have a vision of my ideal state that I am working towards every minute of every day of my life. I learned from Dr. Liker's books in the past, and most recently from Jeff as a friend, that after you strip away all of the obstacles, one by one, that prevent you from reaching your target condition, one day you will look back on how far you have come. Join Dr. Liker and myself as we greet students and coaches from all around the world in our online community at www.LeanLeadership.guru/Community.html. Understand when you get to your target condition there is always another one in front of you, which is why this will always be a Lean journey for me. I have enjoyed my journey thus far. I look forward to hearing your stories once you connect with this book, and our online network of Lean practitioners.

Initially I made the statement, "Lean rarely worked as we expected," and for many companies it may never work, without the leadership and the process in which they must go through to develop their skills and those of their subordinates. That is why this book offers a contribution like no other. It gets to the core of the matter, you! What can you do to develop yourself? What can you do to develop others? How can you develop a culture of Continuous Improvement to achieve breakthrough goals and stay ahead of the competition? All of these questions are answered with great insight in this book. All are substantiated with case studies.

I thank Dr. Jeff Liker for this gift, and for allowing me to join him in spreading the word.

George Trachilis, P.Eng.

President & CEO, Lean Leadership Institute Inc.

www.leanleadership.guru

Author, *OEM Principles of Lean Thinking*

Winnipeg, Canada, 2014

ABOUT THE AUTHOR

Dr. Jeffrey K. Liker is Professor of Industrial and Operations Engineering at the University of Michigan, President of Liker Lean Advisors, LLC, and Senior Advisor and Partner in Lean Leadership Institute, Inc. He is author of the international best-seller, *The Toyota Way: 14 Management Principles from the World's Greatest Manufacturer*, 2004 and has coauthored seven other books about Toyota including *Toyota Culture* and *The Toyota Product Development System*. His most recent books from 2011 are *The Toyota Way to Continuous Improvement* and *The Toyota Way to Lean Leadership*. His articles and books have won eleven Shingo Prizes for Research Excellence. In 2012, he was inducted into the Association of Manufacturing Excellence Hall of Fame.

DEVELOPING LEAN LEADERS

The leader wonders about everything, wants to learn as much as he can, is willing to take risks, experiment, try new things. He does not worry about failure but embraces errors, knowing he will learn from them.

Warren Bennis, *On Becoming a Leader*, 1989

CHAPTER 1
LEAN AND LEAN LEADERSHIP

Overview of Lean Leadership and Recommended Learning Approach

This book is a live, spontaneous discussion of Lean leadership as I have come to understand it over the last 30 years and learned from my collaboration on The Toyota Way to Lean Leadership with Gary Convis, former head of North American manufacturing and Managing Officer for Toyota. Since that book came out in the Fall of 2011, my colleagues and I have been teaching courses and working with individual companies interested in developing Lean Leaders. I have learned a good deal about how to apply the leadership development approach I learned from Toyota. This book reflects that additional learning and speaks to those focused on excellence, who want to develop highly capable leaders who share a common philosophy and desire to create a coherent corporate culture based on continuous improvement and respect for people.

We started with an online course. We decided to write this book either as a complement to the course or as a standalone for those who do not take the course. We wrote it as a practical guide modeled after the course. To get the full benefit, you need to find a coach and practice the leadership concepts as you work your way through the chapters. There are suggested exercises throughout.

Our goal is to facilitate Lean Leadership, which we believe is based on a sound and tested set of principles that apply in any type of organization. Lean Leaders do more with less. They realize challenging goals that at first may not seem possible, develop teams and individuals, and adapt processes to meet the high uncertainty of the environment. We wish you the best on your journey!

Background to the Book

I would like to begin by telling you about my collaboration with Gary Convis on the original book this one builds on. I have been a professor at the University of Michigan in industrial operations and engineering for over 30 years. During that time, I have been studying the differences between US and Japanese management systems, specifically Toyota, which led to my book in 2004, *The Toyota Way*, and a series of books on more specific aspects of The Toyota Way. Most recently, Gary Convis, and I wrote *The Toyota Way to Lean Leadership*, which extracts what we learned about leadership development from Toyota and summarizes it as a four-stage model. I re-created that structure for this book.

Gary began his automotive career at General Motors for a brief period and then joined Ford Motor Company in quality control, engineering, and production for about twenty years. While at Ford, he displayed habits that were a bit unusual for a Ford manager. He spent more time going down to the shop floor compared to most Ford managers at the time, talking to workers and trying to get to the root cause of problems. He then developed countermeasures with those workers. Gary did something that was unheard of for Ford back in the 1980s—he actually stopped the line because of a quality problem. This resulted in the operations manager coming to his office and kicking his trashcan through his plate glass window. This violent reaction happened because stopping the line was a fundamental sin at Ford at the time. Gary was advancing rapidly at Ford, but he knew there had to be a better way. What he was doing naturally was similar to The Toyota Way; however, it got him in trouble at Ford. Frustrated by his experiences at GM and Ford, he decided to interview for a job at the New United Motor Manufacturing, Inc. (NUMMI) facility. NUMMI was a risky start-up automobile manufacturing plant in Fremont, California, jointly owned by General Motors and Toyota. Gary moved his family to California fully aware of the risks.

At NUMMI, he was developed as a Toyota leader. Toyota ran the plant in California based on the Toyota Production System. NUMMI offered the first opportunity to experiment with the Toyota Production System in an American assembly plant, as it turned out, working with the United Auto Workers union. After that experience, Gary rose through the hierarchy at NUMMI and then was offered a position at Toyota's Georgetown, Kentucky facility. He became the first American president of that plant. Then, he continued to rise within the Toyota hierarchy and retired as the head of operations for North America as well as a managing officer of Toyota in Japan.

When he left Toyota, he realized he was not ready for retirement and took an opportunity to become a temporary CEO, Vice Chairman and ultimately, advisor for the Dana Corporation. He helped Dana survive the crisis of emerging from Chapter 11 bankruptcy during the Great Recession. Eventually, with Gary and his counterpart Chairman John Devine's leadership, Dana became healthy financially. We use this story as a case example of another type of Lean Leadership. Gary then moved on as COO of the Bloom Energy Corporation—a high-tech start-up focused on environmentally friendly energy—and has retired for a third time.

I met with Gary while he was considering retirement from Toyota and he asked if I would collaborate on a book. He wanted to share his Toyota learning experiences with people in many different industries throughout the world. We soon concluded that the key to success at Toyota—as well as other companies that were trying to learn Lean, Lean Six Sigma, and The Toyota Way—was leadership.

The Learning Model of the Book and Course

When we began this endeavor, George and I developed lofty goals. The purpose starts with our desire to teach the true philosophy of Lean Leadership. The philosophy, as Gary and I learned it in different ways, is different from the techniques. It is the reason why and the principles of what you are trying to accomplish as a Lean Leader. Gary and I both saw organizations that were struggling to create the kind of culture needed to foster Continuous Improvement. We saw many tools being implemented with marginal success, and usually these results were not sustainable. The missing ingredient, we concluded, was Lean Leadership. Lean Leadership must extend from the executive suites down to the supervisors and to what Toyota calls team leaders, who are production workers on the floor given leadership roles.

We want to spread this understanding globally, and there is a limit to the scale of face-to-face courses. This book, and the online course, are intended to accelerate true lean transformation. True lean transformation means following the philosophy, developing the people, and developing the culture. Ultimately we are striving to develop an organization that is able to react to the environment in appropriate ways towards achieving business objectives on an ongoing basis, and at the same time, get a little bit better every day at serving customers.

Teaching Lean Leadership is a challenge, particularly en masse, but we believe it is possible to combine concepts through a book or online (preferably both) with actual hands-on work at your workplace. The Toyota Way philosophy is that most of the important self-development is learned by doing with a coach, not listening to me talk in video clips, looking at PowerPoint(™) slides, or reading. To simulate the Toyota method of teaching, the course requires a project with a coach. The key is practice, which in this case means leading a real improvement project at the *gemba* (where the work is being done or where your product or services are being used). Practice must be guided by a strong coach—the quality of the coach and the relationship that develops between the coach and the learner are critical.

George and I have been evolving a network of highly developed Lean Coaches for the online course. Our requirements are a minimum of 10 years' experience and that they have developed the skills; studied the book; and with the help of a mentor, perhaps in their company, become a Lean Leader. Some might call them master black belts. Their role is to provide learners with one-on-one mentoring. For those reading the book who are not taking the course, we recommend you find similar people to coach you through stages of self-development. You need to have the dedication to find one.

Learning to Live True North: The Lean Leadership Development Model

When I first began studying Toyota in 1983, there was nothing called the "Toyota Way." Fujio Cho finally introduced it as president of Toyota in 2001. He spent many years in America as the first president of the Georgetown Kentucky Plant, and it was there that he identified a need for making The Toyota Way explicit. People in Japan learned it on the job and almost always spent their entire careers working for Toyota. Those outside of Japan, who did not have the intense understanding within their management team, needed a more explicit way of learning. The deceptively simple model has only two pillars: Continuous Improvement and Respect for People.

Toyota recognizes that the ideal of everyone, everywhere continually improving their processes and themselves is really a dream. They call this dream "True North" because it offers an unattainable vision of what should be happening in an ideal world. You are never going to be perfect, but you can strive for perfection.

Fujio Cho described The Toyota Way as "an ideal, a standard, and a guiding beacon for the people of the global Toyota organization." He talked about one Toyota. What that really means is everyone in Toyota is guided by the same vision of True North. The foundation consists of a set of values that form the center of our leadership development model, which I will talk about next. We realize that any type of development of people has to begin with values and a stated purpose. For example, the purpose of the company might be to satisfy, surprise and delight customers in a continually changing environment and be healthy as a business.

In the case of Toyota, that set of values begins with **Challenge**. Toyota believes that people need to be challenged, or they will not improve to the extent they are capable. In addition, they need the skills and confidence to welcome the next challenge with enthusiasm and energy.

The next value is the development of a ***Kaizen* Mind** - you think naturally in terms of improvement. You reveal openly any imperfections –any waste, anything that does not fit the ideal. A related belief within Toyota is that continuous improvement depends on managers **Going and Seeing** first-hand. You need to go to the *gemba* to get the facts. That is where the work is being done, where the customers are using their product, and where your suppliers are making your product. You need to build a clear picture of the current situation through systematic observation.

Toyota believes in **Teamwork**. Toyota has a complex view of teamwork, which includes both individuals who are developing others and individuals who are being developed working together. The team will be stronger than the individuals will, but the team will be stronger as individuals learn. Team development and individual development go hand-in-hand.

Finally, **Respect** has to be present in everything you do and everybody with whom you interact.

These five values are at the center of our Lean Leadership model. There are four stages in evolving an organization to develop these values to be the very fabric of the culture.

In order to work toward our own perfection we need to be committed to developing ourselves. That is Stage I. We need to learn, step-by-step, to live True North Values. We cannot go from being an amateur violin player to a virtuoso overnight. In some organizations, leaders are sent to courses in universities for a week or two. They go to off-site meetings and are given a range of challenges working in different departments to get a broad view of the company. None of the time is structured around specifically developing the skills they need to both continuously improve and respect people.

As you begin to develop yourself, you may begin Stage II, coaching and developing others. Developing others is key to being a leader. Your goal as a Lean Leader is not to force people to follow your way, but to develop them so they have the capability of contributing in the right way to your organization. They deeply understand the values and will strive to develop themselves.

Over time, you are striving to reach the level of daily *kaizen*, continuous improvement, Stage III in our model. As group leaders and team leaders develop, the workgroups become more independent.

In Stage IV, you can set difficult goals in a way that is aligned across the organization and from top to bottom. In Japan, the method for that alignment is called *Hoshin Kanri*. Toyota is not the only company to use this method. It is part of total quality management and is the method Toyota has adopted to align goals company-wide year after year. You cannot align goals and expect to get results unless you have an organization of people who have the skills, knowledge and motivation to achieve those goals.

With that, I have given you the background on the course and some of the background on the leadership development model we will be teaching. Students will be asked to go through these stages to develop themselves and others.

Using a Coach to Self-Develop

Those reading the book but not taking our course can think about how you can simulate the process. The starting point of the course is for you, as a student, to have a very clear understanding of the characteristics of a Lean Leader. You also have to have a conceptual idea of what it takes to develop a Lean Leader—what it takes to develop yourself as a Lean Leader. Then you need to begin your process with the stage of self-development, the major focus of the course and this book. This provides a foundation for developing others, supporting daily *kaizen*, and eventually having your organization aligned through *Hoshin Kanri*.

To learn by doing you need to lead an actual improvement project at the *gemba*. Using a structured problem-solving process, we are going to ask you to focus not only on the improvement project and achieving the goals, but also on your own leadership process. What are you doing on a day-to-day basis? How are you interacting with people? How are you gathering information? Are you giving assignments to the right people? Are you ensuring that the team itself is progressing, both in their learning and the project? For that, we are going to ask you to keep a diary. Just jot down short daily reflections on your leadership experiences. That diary should be shared with your coach. This record will help you diagnose how you are doing in your process of developing as a Lean Leader.

A key tool for sharing the progress of your project with your coach is the A3 story. A3 is simply the size of the piece of paper, 11" by 17." The idea is not the size of the paper, but rather that you can tell a story from start to finish on one side of one piece of paper. The story does not get written out in one sitting, but evolves with your coaching box-by-box as you progress through the process. In problem solving, we go through the entire Plan-Do-Check-Act process. The first step is to define the problem. This could then be reviewed with your coach. The coach will ask you challenging questions, as well as suggest some additional assignments to assist your development. The coach will provide feedback and follow up with you to see how you did when you tried out the new approach. This will evolve to a very important relationship between the coach and you.

The coach will lead you through a process that we have defined. You will follow the problem-solving process, starting at a high level grasping the situation. Then, with your coach, you will define a project that is appropriate for you. It has to be possible to complete within a few months. It must be meaningful to you. It will be a vehicle to develop your leadership skills. The content of the actual project, or even the results, are less important than what you learn about leadership.

Define the Problem

In the first stage of defining the problem, you stay at a high level of abstraction. The next step is to put together a team with whom you are going to work to carry out the project. This will also include identifying an executive sponsor - someone to help break down the barriers that might stand in the way of what you intend to accomplish. They will also provide an additional source of feedback on how you are doing as a leader.

Toyota's problem-solving process is known as Toyota Business Practices. This eight-step process provides one model for all levels of Toyota. You do not have to use Toyota's process, but you will need to include its key elements. For example, your approach to problem solving has to carefully define the problem and you have to work toward understanding the root cause(s).

Finally, the coaches should focus most of their attention on your self-development. You will be getting started on the other three phases of Lean Leadership, but you primarily will be leading a problem-solving process. **That** is self-development. That is where most of your energy will be spent. In the process of carrying out this project, you will lead a team of people; you will be in the role of coaching and developing those people.

At some point, we are going to ask you to develop a rudimentary visual management system and the cadence of problem solving at regularly scheduled meetings to sustain what you do at the *gemba*. We also want you to identify key performance indicators and the next step plans for further problem solving. It will be a mini version of *Hoshin Kanri*.

The Principles of Lean

Before we can define Lean Leadership, we have to define lean and its principles. We are going to use the Toyota philosophy as a model. We are not going to go into detail about the tools. There is a *Principles of Lean Thinking* online course (www.Lean101.ca) at the Lean Leadership Institute that covers the basic tools as well as a plethora of books, some of the best, at the Lean Enterprise Institute.

After you learn what lean is and the history as it evolved within Toyota, you will understand the principles. In Chapter Two, we will provide a toolset for your project, including problem solving and the A3 reporting method. There are additional tools that are necessary in any good Lean project, including standard work and visual management (Chapter Three). You visually represent the standard to make it clear whether you are on track. Where there is a deviation from the standard, there is a problem that needs your attention.

Then we go through the four-step model (Chapters Four to Seven): Commit to self-development, develop others, support work groups, and align goals toward a common vision.

Finally, in Chapter Eight we tie the key concepts together through the story of how Toyota developed the Scion brand, which was designed to bring young people in America, an underrepresented group, into the Toyota family. Toyota started what became Scion at a strategic level. They spent time understanding the customer. They defined the core requirements of the Scion brand necessary to satisfy young people in America. Then they had to define the operational features and Lean systems, as well as put those in place to deliver on the promise to their customers. We will see how the whole process was integrated from strategy to operational excellence.

That is what the book covers, but as far as we are concerned, you will still just be beginning the journey to becoming a Lean Leader. We hope to give you a good start in the right direction. We cannot force you to continue sustaining that effort any more than a personal trainer can force you to work out and eat right every day for the rest of your life. We sincerely hope that you take this opportunity and all of the resources at your disposal to seriously start or continue your development as a leader. We need many more of you in the world so that the entire world can continuously improve.

We look forward to continuing to teach you. There will be a variety of resources available to you even beyond the coach and beyond the online course. One of those resources is our online network of consultants and practitioners at the following link: www.LeanLeadership.guru/Community.html.

We are also going suggest you read a second book, *Managing to Learn* by my colleague John Shook, who worked for years for Toyota in Japan. He learned the A3 problem solving process by being mentored in the traditional Toyota Way. Another approach, which provides a very structured framework for practicing to learn, is in *Toyota Kata* by Mike Rother. We also host The Toyota Way group on LinkedIn and have a public Facebook page. We have discussions within these groups and you can also send in your comments. We look forward to you taking advantage of all of all these resources.

What is Lean Leadership?

The central question we address in this book is "What is Lean Leadership and what does it take to develop it?" As background, I am going to provide an overview of *The Toyota Way* and its "4P Model" as introduced in *The Toyota Way*. That will provide a context for understanding Toyota Leadership.

Figure 1-1. *The Toyota Way*

Figure 1-2. *Good to Great*

At the very end of *The Toyota Way,* there is a reference to Jim Collins' work. What we talk about in that short summary is what he called "Level 5" leadership. While I was writing that last chapter of *The Toyota Way* (see Figure 1-1), a PhD student called me and asked, "Have you read *Good to Great*?" (see Figure 1-2), and I had not. He said, "You've got to read about Level 5 leadership, because it sounds exactly like Toyota leadership." I read it and added a little part in the last chapter. Later I had a chance to read the whole book in more detail. It was a revelation for me. I cried out, "Oh my gosh, he is talking about Toyota!"

In fact, Jim Collins had not studied Toyota, or even Japanese companies. He was describing great American companies and how they financially outperformed their competitors, decade after decade. Moreover, he asked the question: "What makes them great? What is the difference between the companies that do okay and the great ones?"

He synthesized a list of characteristics from that book. I realized they fit well with what I was trying to communicate as the principles of The Toyota Way. Toyota begins with a focus on customers. Jim Collins talks about a passion for delivering value to customers. He says that the great companies start there. They do not start with, "How much money did we make this quarter?" They do not start with, "What is our next product that is going to be a smash hit?" They start with, "Who is our customer and what can we do to solve their problems, to add value to them in a way that they do not expect, in a way that is superior to our competitors?" The customer is always the focus!

Internally, great companies create core values that go beyond short-term profits. Of course, the number one value is satisfying customers – the reason for the business. Number two, "What environment are we creating for our team members to grow and have a good quality of life? We should make our team members better when they leave here than they were when they came into this company."

Then, they have a passion for excellence, starting with the CEO, who in the great companies was often the founder. For example, Walt Disney as the founder of the Disney Corporation was obsessed with the question, "How can I build something great that will live way beyond me and be my legacy?" For Walt Disney, that had a lot to do with turning his dreams into reality. "I dream, I test my dreams against my beliefs, I dare to take risks, and I execute my vision to make those dreams come true." He built much more than a business; he built a legacy, a great enterprise to far outlive him.

To continue their legacy, they develop leaders who can succeed them who are as passionate as they are about the enterprise, the customers, and the culture they have created. It is very hard to develop that level of understanding, passion, and commitment if you simply purchase that CEO from another company who has a track record of driving up stock prices in the short term.

Senior leaders need to commit - through their lives - to their business. It does not mean that they cannot have a life outside of work, but you probably notice that as you move up in the company, people spend more time at the office, more time in the business, and somewhat less time with their families.

They are obsessive about studying and adapting to the environment. The work of studying is very important. If you are at Walt Disney, for example, you have competitors like other theme parks in your industry. Thus, you know everything about them. You know what they are thinking, how they are thinking and probably what they are going to do next. You do not care about the auto industry, you do not care about semiconductors, and you do not care about hospitals. You care about your business. You are not a generic plug-and-play CEO who could go anywhere and run anything.

Collins also uses the term "AND" thinking as opposed to "OR" thinking, a Toyota Way concept that is key to *kaizen*. If you suggest to your boss at Toyota, "we can either have productivity OR quality", your boss as the coach is going to ask, "Why not both? What makes you think that you need to trade off quality for productivity?" That leader knows it is possible to achieve both because they have done it many times in their own career. Walt Disney was perhaps most famous for his quote: "If you can dream it, you can do it."

Collins' great company characteristic of innovation by experimenting and learning blew me away, because the standard paradigm of innovation is the lone inventor. The lone inventor has a eureka moment that leads to a prototype and then brings the product to market through the commercialization process. The starting point is always one brilliant idea that one genius dreamed up. What Jim Collins is saying is that the great companies learn by doing, by trying, by experimenting. Walt Disney also said, "The way to get started is to quit talking and begin doing." In lean, we believe that most important breakthroughs come from the *gemba*, through rapid experimenting to gain a deeper understanding of what works and what does not. The world is too complex in most cases to expect abstract eureka moments to provide all of our great innovations.

Great companies have an unwavering belief in the value of capable and motivated people. What Toyota says is that people are your only appreciating asset. In other words, people are the only part of the company that gain value instead of depreciating. Every other part of the business, like equipment and even intellectual property, will depreciate and we will have to renew it. People can actually get smarter; they can acquire a higher level of skill. A ten-year person is generally more skilled and knowledgeable than a one-year person. What that suggests is that you need to invest in people for the long-term because you do not get the exceptional ten-year person unless, one, you can keep them around, and two, you invest in developing them. They do not naturally develop wonderful skills on their own.

Finally, the result is a strong, coherent, cohesive culture. By strong, we mean that the culture, the values, and the beliefs are shared at all levels across the company. Coherent means that it is clear and understandable, that if you talk to different people you get a similar story. Cohesive means that people feel bound together like a team, even if they do not know each other – because they all work for this great enterprise and serve the same customers. J. Willard Marriott, founder of another of Collins' great companies, said, "Great companies are built by people who never stop thinking about ways to improve the business." He also said, "Take care of your people and they will take care of your customers."

History of The Toyota Way

When I study the thoughts of leaders of great American companies, the parallels to Toyota culture are stunning, which suggests great leadership is universal. Let us look at the history of Toyota that led to its becoming a great company.

Figure 1-3. Picture of an early automatic loom and its inventor, Sakichi Toyoda

Where did the Toyota Way of thinking about a company, about how to improve processes, about the role of leaders begin? It started with Sakichi Toyoda, who was the founder of Toyoda Automatic Loom Works, Ltd (see Figure 1-3).

Some of you may know the story of Sakichi Toyoda's wood looms and the motivation for their creation. He was the son of a poor carpenter in a remote rice village. He observed that women were working their fingers to the bone making cloth for their families to sell, and all after a full day of work. His mission was to help them by reducing the amount of labor required to make this cloth.

He was able to invent the loom because he was a carpenter and understood wood , he had deep craft knowledge, he was imaginative, and he could think of clever solutions and then, with his own hands, put them into practice. The first loom he created was very simple, and used gravity. He was watching these women push back and forth a shuttle of thread (the weft). Then with their hands they would have to push a piece of wood to tighten the threads (beating). That was the action, push the thread back and forth, and then tighten the cloth. He thought that perhaps the action of pushing the shuttle of thread back and forth could be done by gravity. He created a wood chute and a system with foot pedals. With the foot pedals, you could make the shuttle slide down the chute back and forth eliminating at least half the labor, and it turns out women were three times as productive as a result.

This was good kaizen, and notice, it came from a real need. It came from someone who had deeply invested in wood working skills, studied looms, had craft-based knowledge, and as a result could actually do it with his hands. Then he improved upon it, and improved upon it, and improved upon it. He had a vision of making a fully functional, automatic loom. A full 38 years later, the rights to produce the "G Type" loom, the first fully automatic loom in the world, was sold by Sakichi Toyoda to the Platt brothers in England, one of the rare instances at the time of Japan exporting innovation. The G-Loom was light years ahead of its time. (See it in action at http://youtu.be/1SBxxlbeMgU)

Everything he invented was the solution to a specific problem, and it was all done through rapid experimentation—what we now call PDCA. Moreover, he iterated from nothing to the first fully automated loom in the world. It was not due to brilliant insight, but rather to solving thousands of problems and working with teams of people. He did not know how he was going to get beyond that one problem to the fully automated loom, but he knew there would be a next problem, then another problem, and over time he would get closer and closer to that vision.

One of his best-known innovations came from one of those problems. As the looms were powered and semi-automatic, people played a smaller role, mostly watching for the thread to run out or correcting a problem when the loom broke down. If a single thread broke on the warp, all the material from then on would be defective. When a person noticed, they would shut down the machine, tear out the bad cloth, and fix the machine. People needed to stand by a machine and babysit it, which Sakichi thought was a terrible waste of the person's precious time.

His countermeasure was what we now call jidoka. When a single thread broke, a weight would fall and shut down the machine automatically. This freed the person from the machine so that one person could watch a number of machines and respond to machines that shut themselves down. The human was a problem solver, not a baby-sitter. This became the foundation for Toyota's famous andon system: pull a cord and stop production in any out-of-standard condition. Then think about why the problem occurred and what can be done about it.

The core values lived by Sakichi Toyoda are still at the foundation of Toyota today: contribute to society, then prioritize the customer over the company, respect for people, know your business from the inside out, get your hands dirty, hard work, build-in quality, discipline, teamwork, and constant innovation toward a vision.

Sakichi tasked his son with doing something great for society beyond looms. Kiichiro picked automobiles, a major challenge since they were starting from almost nothing and American auto companies like Ford were world dominant. In a Seminal Speech by son Kiichiro, he said:

> *I plan to cut down on the slack time in our work processes….As the basic principle in realizing this I will uphold the "Just in Time" approach.*

He could have said that today and had an army of consultants behind him, and he would have my book and the LEI (Lean Enterprise Institute) books and everybody would know exactly what he was talking about with Just-in-Time. However, this was 1939, and the concept of Just-in-Time had not been invented. He made it up. It was a vision he had no idea how to achieve, like the automatic loom. The person who led the people who made this vision a reality was Taiichi Ohno, a manufacturing genius (see Figure 1-4).

Taiichi Ohno

Taicihi Ohno and his team accepted Kiichiro Toyoda's Challenge by laboring non-stop to develop the Toyota Production System...through adaptive problem solving like Sakichi Toyoda.

Figure 1-4. Picture of Taiichi Ohno

He and his team accepted Kiichiro's challenge to achieve Just-in-Time and also a "stretch goal" to catch up to Ford's productivity in three years when Ford was about nine times as productive building over a million vehicles a year. Toyota was building a few thousand with a lot more variety.

What is Real TPS?

One of Taiichi Ohno's early experiments was creating a U-shaped cell in machining. His goal became to get equal productivity at any volume level and to be able to adjust flexibly to customer demand. He learned to run the cell of different machines with one person or two people or six people depending on the demand. However, he hit a wall. He asked team members to learn multiple jobs, to run a lathe, to run a drill, and they did not want to. They were happy being an expert on one kind of machine.

This advanced Ohno's education on how to influence and motivate people. He realized that he had to be on the shop floor with the people, watching them struggle, asking them questions, challenging them, and learning to be a coach. This was the beginning of the Toyota Production System (TPS), (see Figure 1-5). He later learned that in order to have a reliable cell you need standard work. You also need a way to teach people. He later discovered and adopted the job instruction training method from the American system called Training Within Industry (TWI).

Then you had to connect that cell to other processes that were some distance from the cell. He needed to hold a small amount of inventory and replenish it using a pull system. In addition, the foundation of a stable cell and pull system was a stable operation to achieve a leveled schedule (*heijunka*). Again, over time, over decades, pieces of the Toyota Production System started to fall in place. Finally, it was written down, initially over the objections of Taiichi Ohno.

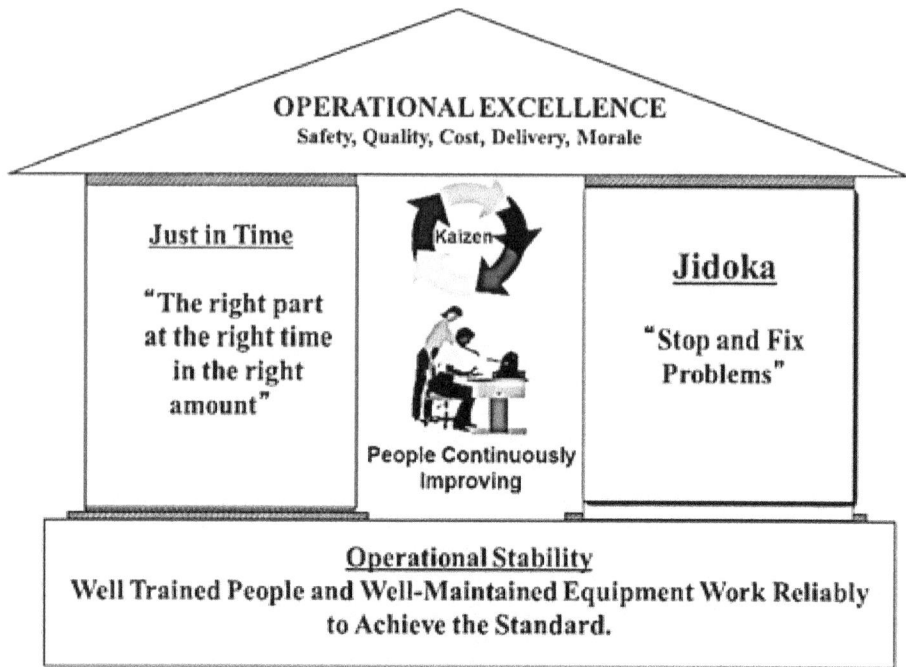

Figure 1-5. Visual of the Toyota Production System (TPS)

Why would he object to a simple diagram? From Ohno's viewpoint, the Toyota Production System was a living, breathing, evolving body of knowledge. It was the ideas of people as they were at the *gemba* discovering weaknesses, learning to overcome those weaknesses through the improvement process, and developing their own capabilities. He was afraid that written down it becomes a static picture and *kaizen* ends. He was known to see somebody drawing some sort of image of the Toyota Production System, tear it up and say, "If you write it down you will kill it!"

Later in life, Ohno grew more laid back and allowed people to represent it as a house, because a house is a system. If you take away the structure that holds up the roof, the roof will collapse. If the roof is weak, the roof will leak. If there is a poor foundation, the whole house will collapse. Every part is necessary for the system to function. At the center of the system are people continuously improving.

You might recognize the two pillars now as the contributions of Sakichi Toyoda and Kiichiro Toyoda. Sakichi Toyoda introduced *Jidoka*, which is translated today as "Stop and Fix Problems" or "Surface Problems and Solve them." For Sakichi it was a loom with human intelligence that stopped itself when there was a problem. Then we have Kiichiro Toyoda's "Just-in-Time:" The right part, the right time and the right amount to the customer with minimum waste. The ideal is one-piece flow with perfect quality to the customer, which really is an impossible dream if you think about it. If you can imagine any type of service that you get on-demand that works 100% of the time, you have something better than anything I have seen.

The goal was *not* to implement Just-in-Time. The goal was for Just-in-Time to be a vision, an ideal, and for *Jidoka* to also be a vision, which would be zero defects. Everything you do, you do perfectly. This vision is what drives *kaizen*. *Kaizen* is striving for perfection and it never ends, because you can never reach perfection.

At the base of the house, the foundation is operational stability. This includes disciplined people following standardized work. It requires well-maintained equipment, which also requires much-disciplined people who are doing their preventive maintenance and learning from each machine shutdown to solve the problem. Production control has the function of working to create a leveled schedule, *heijunka*, leveled in volume and mix. However, *heijunka* is really another vision that must be achieved through constantly working to reduce variation in the schedule, in people, and in processes. To make this all the more challenging, the standard for the system keeps on getting tougher and tougher

You can see why people are at the center. People must have the drive and discipline to strive to achieve every aspect of the system through *kaizen* and then follow the new standards. If people stop thinking and simply execute what some expert says, then the system will fail because conditions change. People at the worksite are the only creative force to continuously adapt the process.

As an example, imagine a pilot having a plan before the plane takes off and the pilot is instructed, no matter what happens, do not adjust, just follow the plan. If you run into a storm, just follow the plan. The plane is going to go down! You need the pilot to follow the standards in most circumstances but adapt in any out of standard condition.

People are at the center of TPS and need leaders who help motivate them to be diligent in following and improving the standards. Very few people have the self-discipline to constantly push themselves to get better and better.

Lean today has become a global movement. There is Lean, Six Sigma, and Lean Six Sigma, and unfortunately what we see most often is a shadow of The Toyota Way or the Toyota Production System. For example, we can walk into a factory, an office, or a hospital and see posters, charts, systems for pull replenishment—and in cultural terms, these are mere artifacts. It would be like finding a vase from the first century and trying to interpret what this vase means. If we get to dig down to try to understand the meaning behind these artifacts and behaviors, we get to norms and values.

The norms and values are too often translated into "Follow the Rules, Meet the Targets." These are created and enforced by experts who have black belts leading projects. This represents what we call bureaucracy. Rigid bureaucracy is what Frederick Taylor was creating in his scientific management. He was very clear that the only thinkers should be the industrial engineers and the management should be telling the workers to follow the standards set by the industrial engineers. From that system, with people not thinking, there can be no adaptation unless the industrial engineers come up with all the ideas. They are spread too thin, often across multiple factories, to continuously improve anything.

The underlying assumption that leads to this misinterpretation of the Toyota Production System is that the most important part of Respect for People is respecting shareholders. They are the owners of the business and should expect quarterly returns. This means you have to drive up stock prices and any development of people and process improvement must have a clear return on investment (ROI).

If you do not get the ROI, you should not do it. This means you are going to cherry pick only those projects that have a clear, direct cause and effect. Spend the money to get results and report this in dollars saved to the shareholders. The most clear-cut dollars saved are labor savings—bodies out the door. This is very different from building up a strong capability and striving toward a vision of perfection. What Toyota would say is that if you strive for perfection you are constantly improving products and services, providing more products for less money, and keeping your customers satisfied, and the profits will follow. On the one hand, satisfy customers and you get revenue. On the other hand using the same *kaizen* methods you will reduce costs. Of course, there are also targets for safety, quality, and human resource development. Eliminate defects, eliminate waste, and reduce cost. Eliminate safety issues, eliminate waste, and eliminate cost. However, if you jump ahead and just say you will not do anything unless that improvement can be cost justified, you will never make the investments in people, process and product, you will not have satisfied customers, and eventually you will run out of steam and your organization will go out of business.

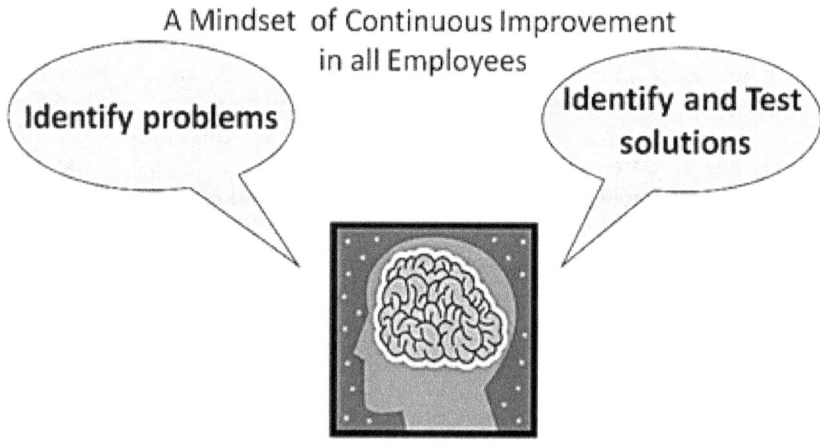

Source: Michael Balle
Figure 1-6. The Thinking Production System (TPS)

What are we really talking about with the Toyota Production System? When we think of TPS we may immediately think of manufacturing, tools, and machines, but really, that was never what TPS represented. One of the students of Taiichi Ohno said, "We at Toyota made a mistake. We should never have called it the Toyota Production System. We should have called it the Thinking Production System, because the real point of everything is to make people think." Even with a simple kanban, a visual signal when we are ready for more product or information, there is an underlying thought process. We have a kanban on every container and if I see that there is a container without a kanban then I have to think, *why did the container move without a kanban*? If I have 10 bins of inventory and I take out one kanban, and I now have nine bins of inventory. Now my processes are going to shut down more quickly if I have a problem. Again, that forces people to think. Really, the essence of TPS is on the one hand to identify problems, and on the other hand, to identify and test solutions so you can learn and continuously improve (see Figure 1-6).

What is the Real Toyota Production System?

The Toyota Way 2001

Unlike Jim Collins, who looked at a sample of companies and compared the great to the rest, I looked in depth at one company and built up a model from observation and learning to apply lean concepts. What is it that makes Toyota tick and makes them great? The starting point is the company philosophy, which has many of the same characteristics that Jim Collins talks about: passion for customers, wanting to build a great enterprise, deeply valuing your people, and developing them for the long-term. All of that requires, as an underlying core value, that you think long-term about the business.

Figure 1-7. *The Toyota Way 2001* (Toyota Motor Company)

The philosophy was first written down by Toyota in 2001, before my book came out in 2004. *The Toyota Way* 2001, (see Figure 1-7), summarized earlier, has the two pillars of Continuous Improvement and Respect for People. They say that these two pillars are completely intertwined; you cannot have one without the other. Continuous Improvement literally means we are improving all the time in everything we do. If you are packaging parts, you are improving how you do that. If you are developing the next Camry, you are improving the process by which you develop the next Camry. This includes improving the process by which you get customer feedback, the process by which you turn that customer feedback into design characteristics, and the way you engineer the product so that it is easy to build in manufacturing.

Every function in the company—accounting, finance, sales, and information technology—is continually being challenged to improve. The philosophy is that we want to be continually reflecting on how we are doing. Are we getting better? Who is going to do the hard thinking so that we can improve? We do not have a supercomputer that can do that. We do not have a robot that can do that. Only humans can do that. To get Continuous Improvement you need a team of people who share the values and identify with the company. That takes **respect**.

Now in Toyota's view respect means a little bit more than 'we will treat you nicely, we will not yell at you, we will not hit you, and the work environment will be pleasant'. It actually means 'we will challenge you to keep on improving yourself because that is how you will be valuable to the company and that is how you will be a better person'. In return, that is how the company will be able to provide you with good pay and job security. The foundation is the five core values I already touched on. I will elaborate on each.

The first is **Challenge**. Every part of the company from the senior leaders to the shop floor worker, is regularly challenged to continuously improve themselves and the process. The challenge comes from specific targets or goals. It comes from a very clearly understanding of where we are trying to go compared to where we are. On a minute-by-minute basis ideally, or an hour-by-hour or day-by-day basis, it requires an attitude that whatever the challenge is, we will somehow find a way to meet it.

When the worst earthquake in Japan's recorded history struck in 2011, 500 parts were not available to Toyota, and many supplier plants were in rubble, Toyota had to stand up to the challenge and go through the process of finding out what the problems were and how to help suppliers solve the problems. One by one, they had to help bring the plants back online to get parts. In the meantime, they had to figure out how to ration the parts to plants around the globe. In the aftermath, they asked what they could learn from the disaster leading to kaizen in the supply base. For example, they realized that these were suppliers to suppliers and in some cases there was only one location making critical parts. They realized they had to manage deeper into the supply base and asked those suppliers to develop a second location in a different geographical area.

There is a distinctive process for **Kaizen** which Toyota calls problem solving. Toyota's view of a problem is not just something that went wrong that day, but a gap between the desired state and the actual state. Problem solving is aspirational—to achieve a higher level of performance then the current state. We will talk in Chapter Two about Toyota Business Practices, an eight-step problem-solving process. It is interesting that a problem-solving process has been elevated within Toyota to its core business practice. That is because any part of the organization working to improve, to adapt to changes in the environment, to better satisfy customers, and to work more cooperatively with the community should be following the thinking pattern of Toyota Business Practices.

At a high level, it is modeled after Deming's Plan-Do-Check-Act, and you will hear PDCA constantly around Toyota. The structure of PDCA prevents you from jumping to hasty conclusions about where you want to go, what problem to attack next, and what countermeasures to try. It forces you to reflect on what happened compared to what you expected to happen and what you learned from that experiment. In *Toyota Kata*, Mike Rother points out that problem solving may imply too much running around fixing things instead of striving toward an aspirational goal through an improvement process. At Toyota, problem solving is very much about improving your way toward a clear vision.

Genchi Genbutsu is very closely related to *kaizen*. *Genchi Genbutsu* means the way that you understand the problem is by going to the actual place where the actual thing is happening. It could be where people are designing. It could be where customers are using the car. It could be the test track where the vehicle is driven. Wherever the thing is happening, you go there, you study the current condition and try to understand the strengths and weaknesses, and that is the starting point for improvement. That is not enough. You need a vision of where you want to go, but the vision should be grounded in reality so you can see the gaps between where you are and where you want to be. *Genchi genbutsu* literally means the actual part, the actual place, which sometimes more generally is termed the *gemba*.

Respect details what Respect for People means. This includes respect for stakeholders, mutual trust and responsibility, and sincere accountability. Accountability is described as, "We accept responsibility for working independently, putting forth honest effort to the best of our abilities and always honoring our performance promises."

Teamwork is teamwork. The only thing that is a little bit unusual is that when Toyota talks about teamwork they do not separate individual development from teamwork. They believe that the best team has individuals who are constantly being challenged, they are growing and becoming better team members and then they are working together toward a common goal as a team. If you are putting together a winning team, you are going to go through a selection process. You are going to want your team members to go through many training drills. You want the best players, and you want those best players to work together cooperatively. Individual development and team development are intertwined. As stated in *The Toyota Way 2001*, "We stimulate personal and professional growth, share the opportunities of development, and maximize individual and team performance."

What does this house mean to Toyota? Is it a recipe to be implemented? Is there a set of tools associated with each of these, and measurements to see how good you are in each? They do have measurement systems for these five foundational values in some parts of the company and they use that for judging people, but really, the most important role is to provide a True North vision, an ideal, a standard and a guiding beacon.

They are fully aware that Continuous Improvement is an impossible dream. There is always going to be some time of the day when you are not improving in some part of the company. You also realize that Respect for People is an impossible dream. There is always going to be somebody, especially when you have hundreds of thousands of people, who at any point in time are doing something disrespectful. It is not possible to eliminate variability, but the goal is to reduce the variability and get closer and closer to the True North vision.

When we talk about lean, what are we trying to accomplish? With lean, unfortunately, the perception is often a very narrow and specific goal. For some in might be to lower our cost structure by reducing labor costs. For others it might be to reduce our inventory costs to free up cash. For still others, late deliveries are a big problem and needs to be solved. If you are in a hospital, you might look at the patient traveling through the hospital and be asked how long it takes from the time the patient enters until the time the patient leaves. If we reduce that, we have more satisfied patients, we have systems that are more efficient and lead-time is often associated with lean.

These are all legitimate challenges and when properly used, the improvement process of lean can achieve these goals. Nevertheless, we view lean in a broader context. What we really want to do is strive to completely satisfy customers in many different ways, lower costs in many different ways, and provide a good quality of life for our team members. In Figure 1-8 we show some examples that are little different from the usual thinking. Engineering products that solve your customer's usage problems is a legitimate lean goal. It is not lead-time, nor cost reduction. It is really about innovation and creativity. If you can engineer and manufacture defect-free products, what we might call designed-in quality, this will help satisfy customers. Below are examples of the broad range of goals that can be worked toward by engaging people in Continuous Improvement.

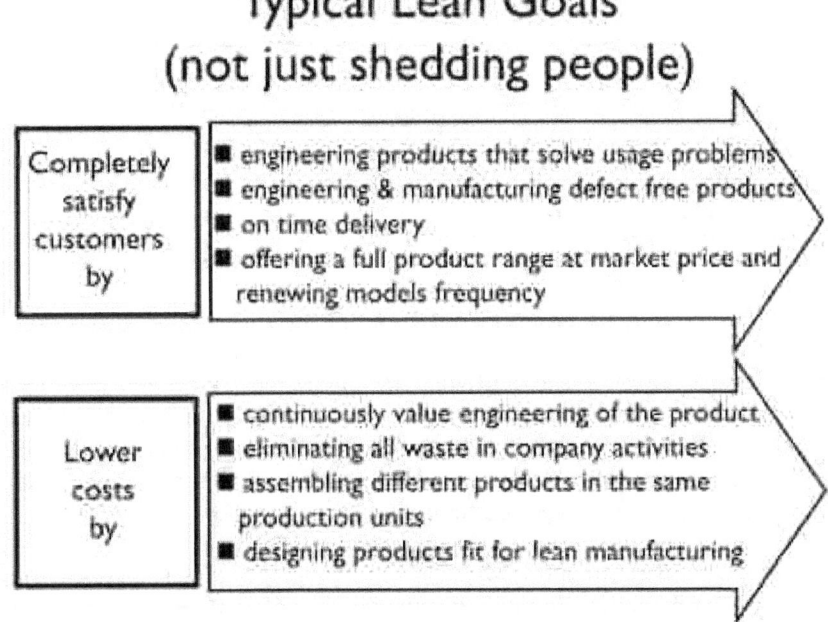

Figure 1-8. Typical Lean Goals – Satisfying Customers and Lowering Costs

If you look at these examples, you see why I identified with the Jim Collins' findings about great companies, which is a much broader picture of lean than simply the idea that we shorten the lead-time by eliminating waste. It really touches every part of the company and the company's capability to add value to the customer.

Unfortunately, lean too often is reduced to a waste reduction tool kit. It leads to a vision of eliminating things. Eliminate wasted steps; eliminate wasted activities and move on to the next waste. Is that what Sakichi Toyoda was doing? Did Sakichi Toyoda invent the best loom in the world by going through the shop and finding waste and eliminating it? This is obviously not the case. He was creatively innovating toward a vision.

The 4P Model Connects Philosophy, Processes, People, and Problem Solving

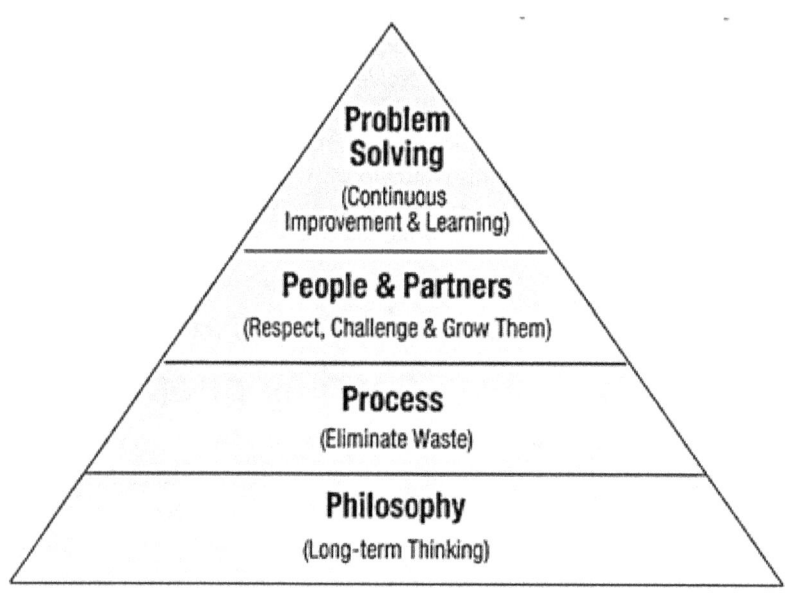

Figure 1-9. Liker's Pyramid (4Ps) of The Toyota Way

Toyota has a house to represent The Toyota Way. I developed a pyramid (see Figure 1-9). I started with a foundation of the way you think about the company—the philosophy. It is long term. You are building something great as an enterprise. You are doing it through great processes that cut across departments and focus on what the customer wants. The Toyota Way 2001 in its totality is the philosophy of Toyota.

The processes, contrary to some common beliefs, are not physical things that run themselves. Even if you have a much-automated process, you need to constantly be monitoring, checking, adjusting that process and improving how it operates, and that requires ingenuity and that is where people and problem solving come in.

Lean Processes as a System

The philosophy is a very broad picture of what it will take to make our company great for the long term where it will outlive us and continue to be great. Then we have an idea of satisfying customers, and now we need a way to do that. We need a delivery mechanism, and the delivery mechanism is a whole series of processes in your organization – whatever organization you have, whatever your customers' wants are.

In healthcare, there are many different processes that directly affect the customer, that add value to the customer. Examples include getting a blood test taken and then quickly getting the results of that blood test leading to a diagnosis and then being operated on if there is something seriously wrong requiring surgery. Other patients are seen and treated in rooms by generalist doctors. In addition, there are many supporting processes. There are people who have to prepare the operating room for the surgery, move the blood to the lab, run complex diagnostic equipment, clean the uniforms of the doctors and nurses, fill prescription drug orders, and so on. All of the value-added and support processes can be improved. They can be improved by reducing lead-time. They can be improved by reducing variation and making a more predictable product. There is a process, and there are some tools in the toolkit of Lean that will help you to improve that process so it better delivers value to the customers.

Vertical and Horizontal Processes

To make life more complex these processes typically cut across departments. In a vertical organization, life is good. I am the boss. I know what I want from you. I am the purchasing boss. You are a purchasing agent. I want lower cost components, that are high quality and delivered on time. That is a given. I want my suppliers to perform, but I want them to do it at a low cost. I could then measure that very easily, and I can judge you as a subordinate based on whether you are delivering that. You, as the subordinate, know exactly how you are measured and what you need to do is within your control. You need to get a lower piece price, and you know how to negotiate with suppliers.

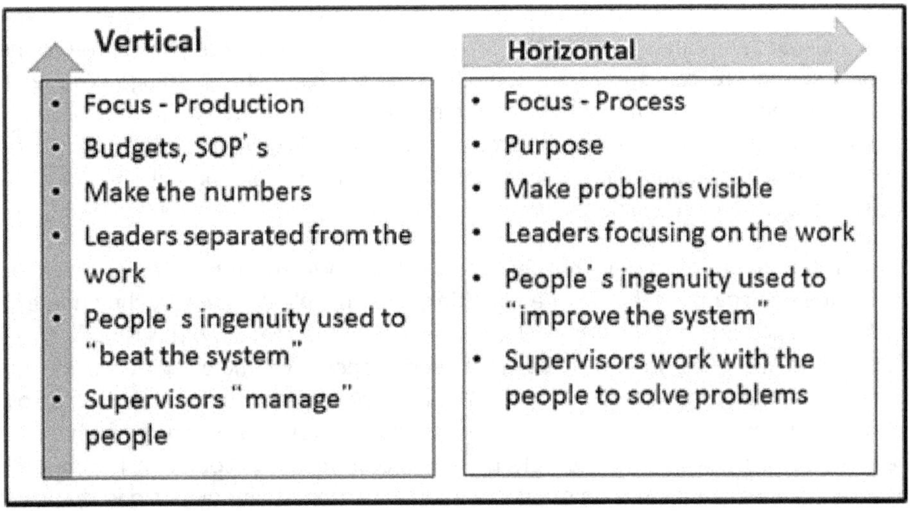

Vertical	Horizontal
• Focus - Production	• Focus - Process
• Budgets, SOP's	• Purpose
• Make the numbers	• Make problems visible
• Leaders separated from the work	• Leaders focusing on the work
• People's ingenuity used to "beat the system"	• People's ingenuity used to "improve the system"
• Supervisors "manage" people	• Supervisors work with the people to solve problems

Figure 1-10. Vertical versus Horizontal Organizations

The supervisors are matching people to specific functional targets within that chimney, and they feel in control because they are measuring just a few simple things they control. The people know the game that they need to play to make the numbers look good (see Figure 1-10). Now this is actually a type of culture. It is a culture of making the numbers, of rising in the hierarchy, and it becomes a purchasing culture or a sales culture. The customer, frankly, does not care. The customer could care less what kind of games you are playing with the suppliers. The customer cares about the product you deliver to them, the cost, the quality, and innovation in the design of the product, how well they are treated when they have a problem, and the overall service. They care about what impacts them.

What affects customers is not only happening in one department. Often what affects them depends upon collaboration across departments. For example, purchasing may be trying to get the lowest price possible for each piece and engineering is trying to solve a specific customer problem, which requires extremely tight tolerances that only a small number of suppliers in the world can achieve consistently. Engineering is going to be in conflict with purchasing because purchasing wants the low cost producer and engineering wants the high quality producer that is capable of making the special part. What you start to find horizontally is conflict across the value stream in the measured objectives that will negatively affect the value delivered to the customer.

The horizontal focus cuts across departments with a purpose in mind, and the purpose is to satisfy customers. It is overall quality, cost, and delivery, and of course safety. You have a bigger set of variables to try to manage to, and you have to work with other people who do not report to you and suddenly life is not fun and easy. You have to think. Thinking is not fun. It is hard work. You have to talk to other people and cooperate with them. That could be painful, particularly if doing the right thing for the customer conflicts with how you are being measured and rewarded.

Now you want the same people, who for years figured out how to play games in the vertical system, to collaborate horizontally. This is a big cultural change. You want people's ingenuity to be channeled. The same ingenuity that allowed them to make the numbers look good even though the process was terrible is going to be used to make a great process. The supervisors, instead of just controlling people through the numbers, are going to work with people to solve problems.

You can see that this is a dramatic change in mindset. We are turning the organization on its side and changing the way people think, what people do, the way they relate to each other, and the way they think about their role in the company. This is not a trivial thing. Tools like value stream mapping, if used properly, can help a group of people understand the current condition, how badly they are working together across organizations, where the waste is, and then develop a future state picture of what they need to do to work more effectively to satisfy customers. Of course, a future state picture is still only a picture unless translated into action at all points along the value stream.

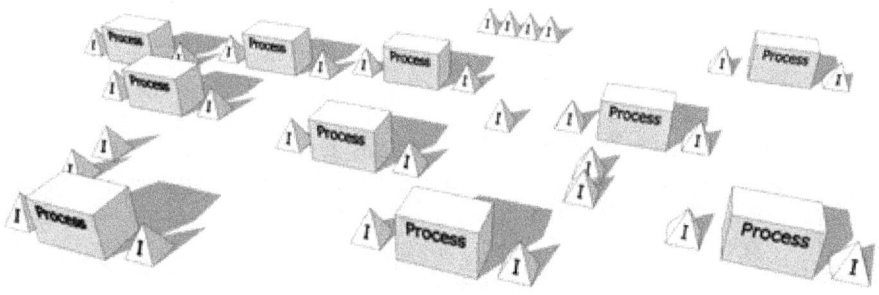

Source: *The Toyota Way to Continuous Improvement*
Figure 1-11. Disconnected processes and inventory hide problems.

Disconnected Processes Hide Problems

Here is a way of thinking about Lean. We start out by asking – what is the process? We take in some things, and we put out some things. There are inputs and outputs. In a traditional process, the inputs are in the form of a bundle of inputs, a batch, that is inventory, and that could just as well be information inventory. I have a large number of email items in my inbox or I am getting batches of reports from engineering or batches of test results from the laboratory. Then we keep on producing based on our own logic, what we have available to us, what our priorities are, and then we push out stuff – information, products, service – and it waits for somebody else to pick it up and use it. It is inventory in, inventory out of a process (see Figure 1-11).

What really happens in a company is there are many processes. They are all more or less independently working based on their metrics, based on what they do. Purchasing is purchasing. The stamping department is making steel parts a certain shape. The painting department is painting them. The accounting department is generating reports. You have disconnected processes, and they are all working from inventory and they are all building to inventory.

One thing we know about inventory, as we learned from Taiichi Ohno, is that inventory hides problems. He said "the more inventory you have, the less likely you will have what you really need." As long as I am busy and I am not directly connected to my customer, I can be happy, and ignorant. I do not have to know that I am not providing the information in a good form and they are struggling to figure out what I was really trying to say and where in this report it is hiding. I can be ignorant of the waste I am creating and think I am doing a great job as long as I am keeping busy and making my productivity targets.

I am fighting fires. I am working, and I am a good person because I am doing a lot of work. The inventory and the disconnection between these processes allow people to stay within their silos. The bigger that buffer – whether it is a time buffer, a physical buffer, or a buffer of many different reports or many different analysis results – the more breathing room to solve the problems, to get behind without negatively affecting your direct customer.

Connected Processes Surface Problems

Literally, when you get to one-piece flow, you are generating exactly what the next process needs, when it is needed. As an internal customer, you are getting exactly what you need, and when anybody stops, everything stops. It is immediately visible, and suddenly everybody is looking at you because you stopped the process. That is when the problems are visible. In Figure 1-12, we are not showing one-piece flow, but rather small buffers controlled by pull systems. I pull one and you can build one to replace it. The smaller the buffer the more quickly problems surface.

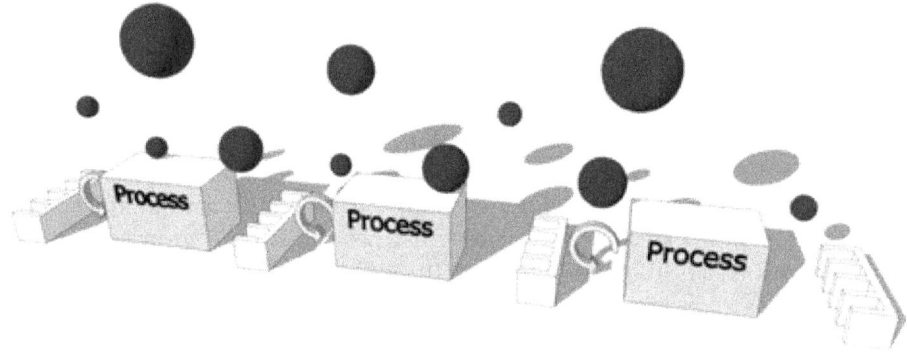

Source: *The Toyota Way to Continuous Improvement*
Figure 1-12. Process connected together surface problems.

There are too many problems so we have to focus

The problems could be small, medium, and large. Large might be a basic problem in how we schedule the whole operation. At the smaller process level, it could mean that the parts are not oriented right and then I pick them up wrong and I position them in the opposite direction. There are many problems, and then you have to prioritize those problems. Part of prioritizing is not simply focusing on big problems and ignoring the little problems. It is also an assignment process.

We assign priority to the problems as well as who works on each opportunity for improvement. The little problems can go to the work groups. The bigger problems might have to go to senior management and to specialty organizations like planning and scheduling. You are sorting and you are assigning, and then people have to take on the responsibility and go through the problem solving process (see Figure 1-13).

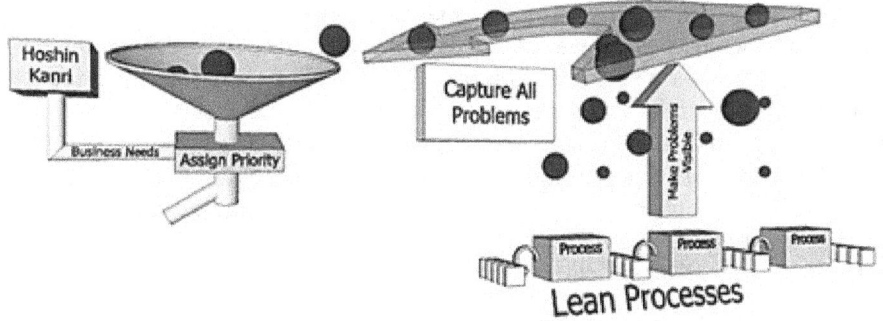

Source: *The Toyota Way to Continuous Improvement*
Figure 1-13. Capturing, Sorting Problems and Assigning Priority

At a higher level of maturity, we can prioritize problems to support our overall business strategy using *Hoshin Kanri*, which we will discuss in Chapter Seven. It provides all levels of the organization with their goals for the year. It is the annual plan that helps me to decide what I should focus on, so I know what is more important. When we get to a priority item, we drop it into Plan-Do-Check-Act cycles shown by the PDCA discs (see Figure 1-14). We will need to set aside some problems that are low priority unless they directly relate to delivered quality or internal or external safety. We are intentionally ignoring problems in order to focus on our priorities.

Source: *The Toyota Way to Continuous Improvement*
Figure 1-14. Priority 1 (PDCA) Issues and Priority 2 Issues

Plan-Do-Check-Act is the Engine of Continuous Improvement

The next step after that is Plan-Do-Check-Act, which does two things. First, we are improving the processes themselves to make them leaner, more consistent, higher quality, on time, and second, we are developing people. People are doing the problem solving. If there is visual management, (see Figure 1-15), people are seeing the same information which clearly separates performance into red (behind target), yellow (behind target but a countermeasure is in process), or green (on track). Then it is clear where there are problems, and the right people with the right leader can then start to use a systematic problem solving process to understand the current situation, plan and test countermeasures, check what we learned, decide what we should share of what we learned, and work to sustain the improvements.

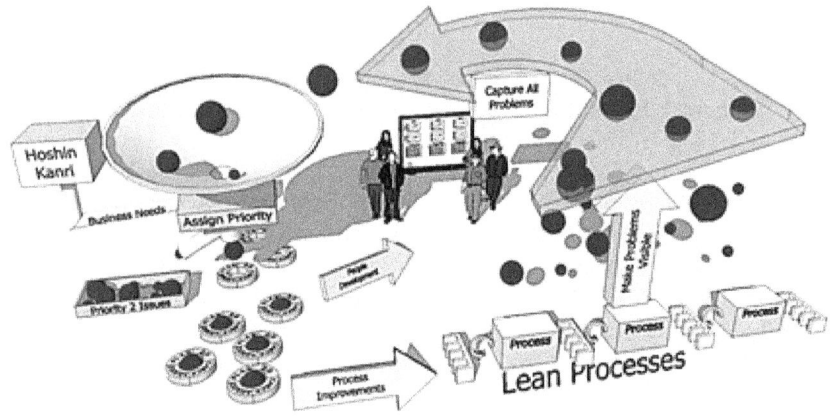

Source: *The Toyota Way to Continuous Improvement*
Figure 1-15. The Complete Lean System

At some point, the system will be relatively stable and fewer problems will bubble up. Then we are going to stress the system by reducing the inventory, making the processes even more connected, so a larger number of problems will surface.

Now you have a day instead of a week to deliver this. When you can do that comfortably you are going to have a half day, and at some point, you are going to have an hour. As you compress the process, the steps become more tightly linked, and the problems, even smaller problems, will come up fast. What we most often see is lean projects focusing on the big problems, the low hanging fruit, and the smaller problems are ignored. You need to persist down this path of Continuous Improvement. As you solve those big problems, you get into smaller and smaller problems. For example, standardized work gets to a very detailed level. It is dealing with very small problems, whereas overall scheduling is dealing with a very big problem, but you eventually need to get down to those little problems to really get the precision of delivery lean companies strive to achieve.

Developing Exceptional People through Problem Solving

I originally had made those 4Ps with people as the third level, and then a Toyota executive looked at it and he said, "Where are our partners?"

I said, "Well they are people too."

He said, "We have a really special focus on how we deal with our outside partners, whether they are parts suppliers or equipment vendors or lawyers or dealers. There are independent businesses, and they are just as important to our success as the people who work in our company."

His suggestion was to set apart partners, in addition to the people who you think of as your employees. What you are doing with both is respect, which, as I said, is challenging and growing them, not simply treating them nicely. That suggests you should be helping your outside partners get better.

I give an example in *The Toyota Way* of a lawyer who had been selected as Phoenix Man of the Year when I interviewed him, and his legal company was growing and performing wonderfully. He personally won Man of the Year because he also worked to build a not-for-profit foundation to research new treatments for cancer. He gave Toyota all the credit in the world for how he rebuilt himself as a person by learning from Toyota leaders. He said he never really understood how to be a lawyer until he worked with Toyota. Toyota asked so many questions nobody had ever asked so he felt like he was starting law school over. Even a lawyer learned from that interaction. You need to invest in people and partners to a degree that I find very unusual in most companies.

Investing in People and Partners

George asks – "You said it was unusual for most companies to invest in developing people as Toyota does. What do you find unusual about it?"

Liker responds – Good question. Doesn't every company want great and exceptional people who are committed to the company? The answer is yes. I do not think you can find a mission or value statement that does not say that. Then you need to look inside the company at what they actually do, and really that is part of the story of the Toyota leadership book is what does Toyota actually do to invest in people.

What the typical company does is they send them to training, and they count the investment in people in units of training. If you have 40 hours of training, you are four times better trained than if you have 10 hours of training. I remember the union at Ford fighting with management to increase the number of hours of training.

In Toyota, they never believed that. They always believed that what really matters is not the hours of classroom training, but what people have learned which turns into a demonstrated skill. What they need to learn is a new way of thinking that is rigorous, and they need to learn skills. One thing we know about learning is that you do not learn skills, and you do not fundamentally change your way of thinking, by sitting in a classroom. The worst possible environment for developing skill is in a classroom. The best possible environment is at the *gemba*. If you want to learn golf, you do not sit in a nice air-conditioned hotel and watch the instructor swing a club. You go to the driving range or the golf course – the *gemba* – and you hit many balls.

Toyota's view is that almost all-important learning happens on the job. They use the term OJD or on the job development. To give people a framework they will do a little bit of training in a classroom and then immediately hit the *gemba*. Then you have some intensive learning. Of course, just doing at the *gemba* is not useful if what you are doing is wrong. It is critical for skill development that you are monitored and coached until you master pieces of the overall skill set to be developed. You practice until you master one lesson then move on to the next lesson, the next skill. Learning itself becomes a continuous process.

What I hear too often in other organizations I visit are things like: "we have a Lean department and we have hired these people or we picked people from a company and they have gone to some Lean training that a university or association offers. They are certified and they have black belts." My response to this is that almost all the learning that matters is the on the job training. They have to actually do projects and the bigger the scope of the project, for example if it is a value stream, the more skill they will need. It is probably more effective to start learning with a smaller scope such as developing standard work for an individual process. Even developing the standard work for an individual process is a big skill. You can get deeper and deeper in understanding standard work. You have to learn those individual skills, and also learn the bigger picture of how you get a group of people together, get them to work collaboratively, coach the leader to where they could lead a cross-functional cooperation process. There are so many technical and social skills to master and that is why it requires a lifetime of learning.

Then I ask, "Let's do a little bit of training, but instead of doing forty hours in five days is it possible to do two hours a week and spread it over the year?."

Executive - "No, that this is not possible."

"Why is that not possible?"

Executive - "Because we cannot get people together for that short a time in a cost effective way."

"Well, what if we go to where they are? We can work with small groups in their area, then they will work on projects, and we will come back and check."

Executive - "Well, that is too expensive because we have to pay for your time and travel. "

"What can we do?"

Executive – "Can you do a five-day course?"

"Well what if we do a two-and-a-half day course and they will do something at the *gemba* on their own, and two weeks later we will do another two-and-a-half day course?"

Executive - "Okay, we can manage that."

You end with a major compromise compared to what we know is the right way to learn. We end up with a fire hose of information in a short time that cannot possibly be absorbed into long-term memory, let alone turned into actual skills. There is no ongoing coaching, doing, trying, reflecting, and learning.

Problem Solving is the Dynamic of The Toyota Way

The final P is problem solving. As discussed earlier what Toyota calls problem solving is striving toward a clear goal. The goal is defined as the gap between the desired situation and the current situation. You are here (current situation) and you want to get to their (desired situation). The creative focus for everybody in the company is how we can use the improvement process to achieve challenging goals whether you are designing the next generation fuel-efficient car and trying to figure out how to make cost-effective hydrogen fuel cells or trying to eliminate some wasted motion.

I call problem solving "the dynamic of The Toyota Way" because the way you get from the current state to a better state is through problem solving. The underlying philosophy of problem solving is what is often credited to Dr. Deming called either Plan-Do-Check-Act, or Plan-Do-Check-Adjust, or Plan-Do-Study-Act, but it is a wheel – it was called in Japan the "Deming Wheel" – meaning it continually rotates. It continually moves. What you are doing continually is planning in advance of doing, understanding the current condition, defining targets, identifying causes, developing countermeasures to be tested, trying out the countermeasures, then checking the process and reflecting on what you learned and what to do next. You *"yoketen"* or share with others what you learned that might be useful to them. And one PDCA cycle leads naturally to identifying the next problem to work on which leads you to planning again. For the smallest or largest goal, you have to solve a series of problems through multiple iterations of PDCA. Chapter Two elaborates on this critical core of continuous improvement.

Lean is now redefined

How will we define Lean now? I have discussed Good to Great, excellent companies, problem solving, philosophy, people, and good processes. It is one thing to say Lean is waste reduction. That is very easy. We find and we eliminate waste, but will that get you to excellence?

We have all experienced a poorly organized company where people are not communicating well with each other, where there is not a clear vision of what the customer wants, where people are trying to beat the system and make the numbers. Let us say we do some individual projects to eliminate waste – we fill out forms, redefine the process, write new standard operating procedures. Have we really fundamentally changed the company to better deliver value to the customer at a better price while making a healthy profit? The answer is no. You cannot "waste eliminate" your way to being great.

> **Lean is**
>
> A Strategy for Operational Excellence based on Clearly Defined Values to Engage People in Continuously Improving Safety, Morale, Quality, Cost, and Productivity.

The vision for Lean, I believe, should be achieving operational excellence based on a clearly defined value system and a way of engaging people in Continuous Improvement. The goals can generally be summarized as Safety, Morale, Quality, Cost, and Productivity. If you achieve those things, you are going to be more successful as a business, you are going to satisfy customers, and you are going to get more business.

You have to do all those things. It is not as simple as saying lean will focus only on the cost side and we have a safety program for the safety side. Underlying all of these targets is the same basic core concept of problem solving, of challenging assumptions, of coming up with countermeasures creatively, of trying them, of learning as an organization how to improve safety, how to reduce quality problems, how to reduce cost, how to better satisfy customers. The underlying dynamic of PDCA is really at the core of learning your way to greatness.

CHAPTER 2

PROBLEM SOLVING, IMPROVEMENT, & A3 THINKING

Problem Solving your way toward an Ideal State

Welcome to what may be the most important chapter in this book. I will be talking about problem solving and also a way of visually representing problem solving which is often called A3 reporting or A3 storytelling. I am going to talk about it as A3 thinking. That is, it is more a way of scientific thinking about improvement rather than a way of documenting information on a piece of paper. I will also summarize a more recent approach to improve toward a challenge—Toyota *Kata*.

The reason this is the most important chapter is that, in *The Toyota Way*, problem solving is the driver for Continuous Improvement and Respect for People. It is captured in all the core values, most directly in challenge, *kaizen*, and *genchi genbutsu*. This is really the core skill of a Lean Leader and the skill where most leaders are not terribly strong. You will see as we go through it that problem solving, in the Toyota Way, is different in important ways from what we typically think of as solving a problem.

For example, try brainstorming words that come to mind when you think of problem solving. You might say firefighting. You might say we have a crisis. You might say something is broken and needs to be fixed. Whereas, in Toyota when they hear problem solving, they hear **we have a gap between the desired state and the current state.** We want to be the best quality and the safest automaker in the world, and the competitive gap is closing with other automakers. We need to increase that gap by getting better. For them, problem solving is aspirational, and it is improvement. It is not simply reacting to the problem of the day through firefighting. This is made clear in Mike Rother's Toyota *Kata* who has chosen to drop the phrase problem solving and replace it with the improvement *kata*.

Problem solving your way to an ideal state is the way that Toyota practices Continuous Improvement. It could be as tiny as we need to reorganize this cart containing parts for the assembler to reduce some waste, some reach time, some walk time, or it could be as grand as we want to start a new brand, like the Scion brand (analyzed in Chapter Eight). It could be that we need to innovate. We need to reduce, by half, the time it takes for us to design and build a die for stamping out a body part. Thus it incorporates both small improvements (which some call *kaizen*) and breakthrough improvements (which some call *kaikaku*).

We can think of problem solving as taking a series of steps – what we talk about as Continuous Improvement – toward a target on the way to an ideal state, and you have to define the ideal state. Toyota has their ideas for the company as a whole as represented in The Toyota Way 2001. For a specific problem it could be – in the case of Scion – to bring the youngest buyers in the auto industry into the Toyota family.

I will start by building a model of how you go from where you are at the current state to the purpose. The purpose should be both a **business purpose** and a **people purpose**. In other words, getting the best financial returns to ensure financial stability and reward shareholders is a business purpose. When Toyota says we want to improve quality and safety for our customers that is a bit more inspiring to team members, but still a business purpose.

Then they have a more internally focused people purpose, which is, we want to develop people at all levels to be better problem solvers, to be better at Continuous Improvement, to have more confidence in themselves, to take on challenging targets that they have no idea how they are going to achieve, and to contribute to their personal growth and wellbeing, for they and their families. There is also an external people purpose of contributing to society and the communities in which Toyota does business, including philanthropic activities. **The business and people purpose is very general.** This is the overall purpose for the business, people in your company, and your outside partners and society.

Then you define the ideal state. What would it look like if we achieved perfection? We know we cannot achieve perfection. We have to set challenging but achievable targets to move towards the ideal state. It can be the True North for the layout of a workstation or for the creation of a new brand or for the company as a whole. Interestingly the True North for some things is that they are no longer needed. For example, kanban is a way of managing an inventory buffer based on pull but the True North is no buffer and no kanban.

The gap to the ideal state must be broken down to a more concrete and achievable challenge. Later, I will talk about an example, one where Gary Convis was asked to lead an effort to reduce warranty costs in the United States by 60%. At that point, Toyota was already the best in the industry, having the lowest warranty cost. It seemed like an impossible challenge, but Gary said, "Yes, I will take it on," and he began the problem solving process.

A specific target is both the result and it could also be defined as a target condition, as Mike Rother defines in *Toyota Kata*. For example, as a result, we may want to launch a new highly flexible plant on time, on budget, and with specific quality and productivity targets. As a condition, we might want a mixed-model assembly cell, which can be adjusted to the customer demand rate, the takt, without any change in the productivity level. It is something visible that you can measure, that you can observe, and it gives you a process condition to strive for which you theorize will lead in the direction of the result you want. Some have talked about management by means rather than management by objectives. What they are referring to is thinking about the characteristics of the process needed to achieve the desired results, rather than jumping right to results. To be actionable the more abstract ideal state must be broken down into concrete challenges, which must be broken down into even more discrete, short-term target conditions that we can work toward through rapid experiments.

Plan-Do-Check-Act is the Problem Solving Process

Once you know the direction you want to go, you need to understand your starting point, the current state. In Lean, we emphasize *genchi genbutsu* or go to the *gemba*. We emphasize go and see and deeply understand the current condition. That includes looking at data. It includes collecting some data that you may not have. It includes direct observation of facts. It includes talking to the people within that area and spending time observing, more than the usual one or two-minute tours as you blast through the facility.

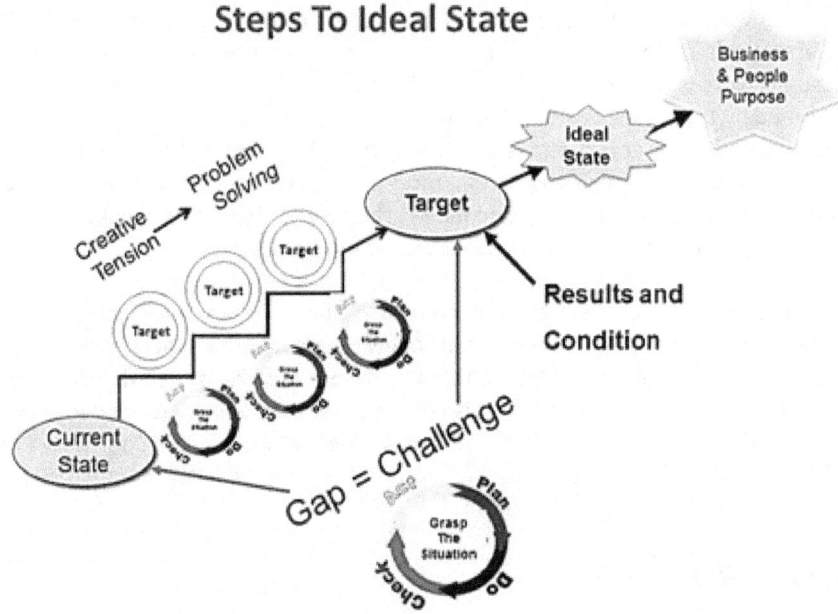

Source: *The Toyota Way to Continuous Improvement*
Figure 2-1. Problem Solving your way toward an Ideal State

When you understand your target, compared to your current condition, you have identified a gap that becomes your challenge (see Figure 2-1). The way you are going to achieve the challenge is through Plan-Do-Check-Act (PDCA), which we will be talking some more about in this chapter. Plan-Do-Check-Act is the scientific method for innovating and learning. It is the way of thinking. It is the philosophy. It suggests that we are going to start with a plan, which eventually leads to countermeasures. Toyota calls these "countermeasures," rather than solutions, because they do not know if they are going to work until they do something and check their assumptions. Based on the check and what they learned from that, they decide what further action to take.

We are going to PDCA our way from the current state to the target, and we are going to do that by setting intermediate target conditions. What do I believe the process needs to look like to achieve the desired result? If I am on an assembly line, I may have a goal to reduce quality defects by one-half by the end of the year. I am going to spread that target over the period of a year. I am going to pick a job, one at a time, and for each job, I am going to cut the defects first by 25% of the target, then 50%, then 75%, then I will get to the 50% –100% of the target. In the improvement *kata,* I will go even farther and study the patterns of working setting target conditions for the new desired patterns of work to produce the lower defect rate. Then I will move to the next job. I am spreading out the problem solving process into steps over time, as I would if I had an ambitious weight loss target.

The distinction between PDCA, learning your way step-by-step to the target, and coming up with a 14-step roadmap and detailed plan that people execute exactly as they are told is huge. It is the difference between *The Toyota Way* of thinking and philosophy versus traditional Western thinking, which is follow the detailed plan established by the experts who are presumed to know more than we do. In *The Toyota Way*, we need the people who are in the area, who know it best, with their local leadership, with some guidance from more senior leadership and subject matter experts, to experiment every day and move gradually to the target condition and then the next target condition and ultimately to meet the challenge.

This may be the reason why there is confusion about *kaizen*. The confusion is that Continuous Improvement or *kaizen* means many little changes. Then I get the question, "What about big changes?" Sometimes it is called *kaikaku* rather than *kaizen*. My strong belief and experience is that it is very unusual that *kaikaku* is done in one-step. The 60% reduction in warranty for all of North America was a *kaikaku* for Gary Convis, but the way he achieved the *kaikaku* was through a great deal of *kaizen* – many small steps, PDCA-ing at every step of the way.

Learn your Way to the Target

PDCA-ing is both the big process – there will be one overall PDCA from the current state to the target – and many small PDCA's to get there. When we have a target, which seems out of reach and is much more aggressive than our current situation, we get creative tension. This tension is what leads to innovation, but only if the learner who accepts the challenge has a defined process for improvement, confidence, motivation, and a good coach.

Think about the goal of John F. Kennedy of putting a man on the moon before the Russians. That created a huge amount of creative tension. NASA not only achieved that challenge but they invented many things that we use today in our lives, including cordless tools, tire treads that last longer, lightweight fabrics that resist both heat and cold temperatures, UV coatings for glasses, and on and on. All of those inventions, or all of that creative energy, was caused by the tension between a challenge we understand, we relate to, and we are desperate to achieve, and our understanding of the current state of where we are.

George: "Jeff would you say that the big PDCA cycle and the three little ones could be called a mother A3 and three baby A3's?"

Jeff: That is an interesting way of thinking about this which is that the big PDCA could be considered the mother and then the small PDCA's could be the children, and as a metaphor that is just fine.

As an example, let us say that Toyota has started the process of developing the next generation Camry. The entire process of developing the Camry at a large scale is a mother PDCA. It is a big, huge PDCA. There is a process of defining what the customer wants, what the problem is, our vision for the vehicle, and then moving to some of the features that will be in that vehicle – the countermeasures – which will surprise and delight the customers and put the Camry ahead of competitive vehicles. Then, that is executed, it is checked, and there is learning – reflection – so that we can do even better on the next vehicle.

At that level, it is one huge PDCA loop that takes several years, but then that gets broken down. If I am the engineer who is responsible for the bumper of the car, then I am going to go through many PDCA loops for the bumper – again, one large PDCA from start to finish, and many small PDCA's to design features of that bumper to improve strength and crash protection.

Toyota Business Practices: One Company, One Improvement Process

Four Phases of PDCA Problem Solving

The four phases of PDCA start with Plan (see Figure 2-2), beginning with defining the problem. Again, the problem should be based on a gap between where you want to be and where you are currently. You then find what you believe is the root cause of the gap. Next, you need to formulate countermeasures. We make this plural because you should have more than one that you can select from, and you should be creative and get a lot of input at this point.

You now know what you want to do, the possible countermeasures, and then you need to do it. To do it, you need to develop and implement a plan to begin the experimentation process, which includes knowing who is going to do what and when. You need to communicate the plan. You need to execute the plan. You need to monitor progress of the implementation, the first step of the Check. As you are checking, in reality, you are also acting. You are adjusting the plan as you are checking, and there are many PDCA loops as you are doing, checking, and making adjustments until you get to a level where you believe that you have achieved the objective.

Figure 2-2. Plan-Do-Check-Act Cycle

In the Act stage, you do a final evaluation of the results. Whatever is working that led to the results, you want to now standardize, stabilize, teach and practice so it becomes routine. In some cases, you might decide you failed and you have to start over, or in other cases, you will do both. You will standardize some aspects, and you will start over with other aspects. The Act also should be communicating what you think you learned, that others should know about, that they might be able to use and you should be planning the next PDCA loop for the next challenging problem.

George: "Do the employees at Toyota actually say the words PDCA? Do they use the terminology? Are they looking for these steps? The bullet points that you have underneath these steps – are they actually calling those one, two, three as you have them described, or is it just natural?"

Jeff: Toyota is actually using the concept of PDCA the way I have it laid out here in a deliberate way, and for more advanced problem solvers it is also natural. They may do it without talking about it this way. What I will cover later, Toyota Business Practices, is a series of steps that go through Plan-Do-Check-Act that are a little bit different than the way I have stated in the very generic case here. And it is used formally for significant improvements. You will not see, for example, every time a line stops and every time a group leader solves a problem that they think, what is the Plan, what should we Do, what should I check to see what happened and what did I learn? They may be solving many daily problems just naturally to bring the system back to the standard condition, and as you follow PDCA enough times, it becomes a natural way of thinking.

On the other hand, they will do projects intentionally, where they document them on an A3, and one reason for that is to deepen their understanding. You have to refresh your knowledge and practice because we slip into bad habits. Just like learning any skill, to maintain a high level, you have to go back to the basics and practice.

The Trap of Taking on Too Much

One common mistake is that of *not* having a clear understanding of the needs of the organization and how that relates to a logical next step for improvement. Many companies want to jump to end-to-end improvement at the enterprise level before having the competency or stability needed at the process level.

I was working with a major Russian company, and they processed a raw material from mining to processing for power plants. They had been working with a Toyota sensei. Toyota provided them with a sensei for free, one of their best people. This was an agreement at the president-to-president level.

Their Toyota sensei, on one visit, was meeting with the CEO, who was showing off a macro value stream map from mining all the way through to the power plant. It was massive, and it was complicated. The CEO had done it with a group of people and was very proud that they were doing Lean as an executive team. The response of the Toyota sensei was a little surprising. He said, with subtle sarcasm, "Oh my! So many problems, so many problems. Where are you going to get started?"

Of course, the CEO and the staff were a little bit offended – "how can this guy be criticizing us? He is a Lean guy, and we are doing Lean, so it has to be good." What this sensei was concerned about is that by taking such a broad swipe at such a macro level, they did not understand, in detail, any problems. They did not have any way of prioritizing problems. They could look at the longest lead-time, but that may not be the biggest business concern. You will often hear from a Toyota sensei, "How do you know this is your biggest problem? How do you know that if you solve it, it will actually benefit the organization, both in business terms and in people-development terms?" What the sensei chose to do in year one was work in one processing plant on one product line developing a model they could learn from to understand TPS as a system. Until leaders in the company had that understanding, he did not believe any projects they took on would be effective.

Toyota Business Practices (TBP): Plan Stage

Toyota Business Practices (TBP) is the one formerly sanctioned improvement process. Again, you do not have to do this with every little problem you face each day. You should be doing PDCA mentally, but if you go through a formal project, perhaps it is a three or six month project, perhaps it is the project to cut quality errors in half, and you may have several A3s, maybe one a quarter, and TBP should be followed religiously.

Let me again emphasize that Toyota is standardizing on the process of improvement, not on specific solutions or "best practices" as they are often called. There is a lot of concern within Toyota about over standardizing, over specifying, and therefore killing *kaizen*. One thing that they are happy to specify, in detail, is the improvement process. The specific content of what you improve is going to be different in every part of the company. Nobody is going to copy a best practice blindly without going through the improvement process and identifying countermeasures that work for them.

Toyota Business Practices is an eight-step process (see Figure 2-3). One might ask why would an eight-step improvement process be called the Toyota Business Practices? Why is it not simply called a problem solving process that you learn in a workshop?

Shortly after Fujio Cho introduced *The Toyota Way 2001,* he introduced Toyota Business Practices as the concrete method to put The Toyota Way into action. The Toyota Way is a set of principles. It is not actionable. Toyota Business Practices is the method for making The Toyota Way, including the foundational values, a living reality in Toyota's culture.

Continuous Improvement is one pillar of the Toyota Way and needs to be done with respect for people, the second pillar. This reflects a strong and basic assumption of the company that the only way to deal with a very challenging environment, that is always changing and always throwing new challenges at us, is through constant adaptation and improvement using PDCA in every part of the company. Toyota Business Practices is the pattern for improvement that allows this to happen. That same pattern of improvement will apply to any size problem, from the largest earthquake in the history of Japan that led to severe parts shortages to making one workstation more efficient.

Plan	STEP 1: Clarify the Problem vs Ideal State [Clarify the problem and True North]
Plan	STEP 2: Grasp the Present Situation and See the Gaps [Ground problem in reality to further clarify]
Plan	STEP 3: Breakdown Problem and Set Targets [Breakdown problem to manageable focus and set targets and metrics]
Plan	STEP 4: Analyze Underlying Causes [Ascertain root causes]
Plan	STEP 5: Develop Countermeasures [Identify what, when, and who]
Do	STEP 6: See Countermeasures Through [Follow the plan and note deviations]
Check	STEP 7: Monitor both Results and Processes [Check the results vs targets]
Act	STEP 8: Standardize and Spread [Take actions to sustain effects and yokoten learnings to other areas]

Figure 2-3. The Eight Steps involved in Toyota Business Practices (TBP)

The Plan-Do-Check-Act is shown alongside the eight steps as shown above, and this is Toyota's definition. PDCA appears repeatedly in Toyota figures and models.

STEP 1: Clarify the Problem vs Ideal State
[Clarify the problem and True North]

Figure 2-4. Plan Step 1

The first step (see Figure 2-4) is to clarify the problem versus the ideal state, which we have discussed. You have to have a vision of True North that you defined, but True North for a company – for example, in Toyota's case, being the best producer in the world of mobility solutions for customers, is the company ideal state.

You also need an ideal state for your particular process. Maybe it is a workstation, and the ideal state is perfect quality every time with zero waste. Again, True North is not achievable. You would never be able to achieve that level of perfection 100% of the time, but at least you can begin to define the direction of your improvement.

 STEP 2: Grasp the Present Situation and See the Gaps
[Ground problem in reality to further clarify]

Figure 2-5. Plan Step 2

In step two (see Figure 2-5), you need to grasp the present situation and see the gaps. Now we are going to ground the problem in reality. We have the lofty ideal state. We are going to get grounded, and the gap between where we are and the ideal state is like a canyon. This is not a small little crevice that we can jump over successfully. This is also true for Toyota. When they define perfection, seriously, with a very clear mind, being brutally honest, the gap to the ideal state is always huge. It keeps them humble and driven to improve.

 STEP 3: Breakdown Problem and Set Targets
[Breakdown problem to manageable focus and set targets and metrics]

Figure 2-6. Plan Step 3

When looking at the gap to perfection we cannot possibly even know where to start unless we go to step three (see Figure 2-6) and break down the huge canyon into smaller, actionable areas for improvement with defined targets. They may be modest compared to the ideal, but they are still aggressive and challenging targets. This is where you might be asked, "Why did you pick this problem? I understand your ideal state. You did a good job of understanding your current state, but with all of the gaps that separate you from the ideal state why did you pick this one? How did you prioritize it?" In Toyota, you need to have a rationale when you are asked a question like this.

 STEP 4: Analyze Underlying Causes
[Ascertain root causes]

Figure 2-7. Plan Step 4

In step four (see Figure 2-7), now that we know the focus areas and targets we are trying to achieve – for example, cutting defects in half as a group leader for the jobs I am responsible for – then we can start to ask what the underlying causes are. We do not have to find all the possible causes for all of the gaps. We find the cause for the one area we are going to work on improving next. We are going to do that by using metrics and asking why - five times. It does not have to be exactly five, but we recognize that our first impression about the cause, e.g., a person is making errors, is on the surface, and there is often a deeper reason, e.g., the parts have not been designed to easily fit together.

 STEP 5: Develop Countermeasures
[Identify what, when, and who]

Figure 2-8. Plan Step 5

Step five (see Figure 2-8) is the development of countermeasures. You will come up with a set of countermeasures, selecting those that you prioritize—those that have the greatest chance of succeeding and perhaps ones that are relatively inexpensive and easy to try out so you can experiment. If possible, you would like to avoid major capital expenditures and long lead times to get new equipment or software. You might go back to other countermeasures later or generate new ideas if these do not get you to the target. Then we have to develop a plan and determine who is going to do what, when, and how they are going to do it. You could argue that the what, when, and who are part of the doing, or you could say it is part of the planning. There are planning activities embedded in every aspect of Toyota Business Practices.

Toyota Business Practices: Experimentation and Learning

Do, Check, Act

Now you are set to "Do." This is when we hear the statement, "Just do it!" Often we think, "Just do it" means skip the plan and just start randomly doing things. There are occasions where you may want to do that. If you see that the team is stuck and they are afraid to change anything, perhaps analyzing the data to the hundredth decimal place, you want to get them *unstuck*. You might organize a short *kaizen* activity with the coach issuing a challenge as a direction and "Just do it."

When Toyota works with other companies, a big challenge from the sensei to take action fast is common. For example, this happened at Grand Haven Stamped Products, an auto supplier in Michigan. On the very first visit, the sensei walked the production floor and saw that they had disconnected processes. He decided to give them an immediate and dramatic assignment. He asked them to put together a cell, which included moving a welding robot from one side of the plant to the other. He said he would come back at the end of the following day to see how the cell was operating. This was a "Just do it." It was really big. The entire management team, including the president, was in the plant manually pushing this robot, sliding it across the floor to get it in position. This is not the way the sensei wanted the company to improve in the future, but it was a way of getting them unstuck.

The Doing stage is both following the plan and deviating from the plan when required, then noting the deviations as part of the learning process. At every one of these steps is a Plan-Do-Check-Act cycle, and these steps are contained within the larger Plan-Do-Check-Act cycle. In the Doing stage you are going to plan something, you are going to do it, check what happens, make adjustments, and continue PDCA until you achieve the target.

In the case of Grand Haven Stamped Products, the cell did *not* work at first. The robot, for example, was not operating enough of the time and it kept on stopping the cell. The work was not balanced. They could not deal with the variety of products with different cycle times. There was no standard work. It took a lot of PDCA after that initial day to actually get the cell functioning at a high level. The sensei had asked them to build up some inventory in advance of actually setting up this cell because he knew they were going to have problems, but he created a challenge to force them to solve those problems in order to get production out. And it led to an operation that was far more productive with higher quality. They learned the value of learning by doing and involving the executive and management team.

In the Check phase, we have to understand what we have accomplished and not accomplished. In *The Toyota Way,* I refer to hansei, or reflection, and hansei will be happening throughout this process. One big hansei will be in this check phase where we reflect on what happened, in terms of both the results and the processes. We may have achieved results and been a bit lucky with one big idea that worked, but it was one person's idea. That person was the manager. Nobody else was engaged. Nobody else was developed. The process failed even though the results looked good.

In the Act phase, we are going to do another reflection on the entire process. Then we are going to standardize what works and we are going to spread what we think should be spread. The "spread" is something that Toyota calls *yokoten. Yokoten* (in Japan) would give an image of transplanting a precious plant from one environment to another. You have to prepare the new environment and understand the conditions that allowed that plant to prosper originally and how to make your conditions suitable for that exotic plant. The details of the landscaping will be different even though you are bringing over some nice plants you saw in another environment.

You do not simply, mindlessly, implement the best practices. You have to think deeply about your condition. If the "best practice" seems like a useful countermeasure for your problem, you should learn from the best practice; however, what may have worked in some other place may not work for you without adjustment and even further improvement. You may actually come up with some ideas that the original party can learn from, and it can go back and forth like that.

George: "Jeff the word *yokoten* has that meaning where you want to prepare the environment and the word "spread" does not have that meaning. Is this one really good reason to understand some of the Japanese terms, because there is more than one meaning to it?"

Jeff: *Yokoten* literally means, "spread everywhere," and yet that is not the way it is interpreted within Toyota. It may well be interpreted that way in some other Japanese companies. Therefore, the question is whether you have to understand the Japanese language enough to dig deep into it and be able to literally translate? If you talk to a linguist they may say, "Spread everywhere." It does not mean what Toyota is saying it means. It is more important is to understand the underlying thinking and principle than the word itself. I would not suggest memorizing a bunch of Japanese words for that reason.

Toyota Business Practices for Warranty Reduction

As mentioned earlier, Gary faced the challenge of major warranty reduction in North America. The problem came to him from a board member. At that time, Gary was a managing officer representing North American manufacturing in Japan. He was also the head of North American Operations. The global head of Quality suggested to Gary that it might be a good idea if he reduced warranty by 60%. When a member of the board of directors makes that suggestion you take action. It is not simply a good idea, but something that you have to take very seriously, and Gary's response was to take it as an expectation rather than a friendly suggestion.

On the way, back home on the plane from Japan, Gary was struggling. He had a good deal of angst.

"How could I possibly achieve 60%? We are the best in the industry already. We have been reducing warranty for decades. How can I possibly get a further 60%?"

Well, the good news is that he did not have to do it in one year. He could spread it out over six or seven years. Therefore, 10% a year seemed more manageable than 60%. He did not need to worry about 60%. He needed to worry about getting the first 10% (the first year) and he could even divide that into months, which is more manageable. Often we will hear in sports, "We are not concerned about winning the championship, we are concerned about the next game." Gary had to worry about the next game.

What would you do if you were Gary as the head of manufacturing? What you might do is assign this to some of your best engineers, but you **do not** do that if you are in Toyota. Gary was personally responsible. He said yes. He was personally going to lead this activity, and it was big enough that it deserved to be handled at the executive vice president level, at the head of North American manufacturing level. Gary knew he could not do it only within manufacturing. There was no way he could do it without moving into product engineering, which automatically means you are moving into Purchasing, because a lot of the design comes from suppliers. This also means you are moving into Sales because they are the ones that have the data on the warranty problems and they run Warranty. He was now leading horizontally which, within Toyota, is considered the highest level of leadership. This is when you are leading without using your formal authority to reward and punish.

Figure 2-9. Grasp the Situation at the Center of PDCA

So, what was the first step for Gary? Obviously, he had to define the problem in Toyota Business Practice terms. Before he did that, there was a prior step, Grasping the Situation (see Figure 2-9). You have to learn enough to understand what is going on. This way, you at least know you are in the ballpark when you define the problem. Grasping the situation meant visiting with the leaders of all the major departments that influence warranty. He met with the head of Toyota Motor Sales, with the head of the Toyota Technical Center in Michigan, with some of the heads of different parts of manufacturing – for example, the Quality Group. He went to Japan, and he met with the head of Quality for Japan. He met with the head of Engineering in Japan.

He was not only meeting and getting information; he was doing what we will talk about later as *nemawashi*. He was starting to build up a coalition of support, and those people he visited ended up being on his task force, on his team. They were all either at his level or higher. He could not boss anybody around, but he was able to get them all to agree this was important, serious, they were on board, and they would do everything they could to contribute to the target.

The team then met, and started working through Toyota Business Practices. The ideal state is that customers are completely happy, and never have to bring in their vehicles for a warranty repair – and by the way, if they bring it in for a recall, that is another type of warranty. It is a warranty that happens to have safety implications, but it is also another warranty problem. Bringing your car in is a nuisance (see Figure 2-10). Even if it is free of charge, it takes time. It means you might not be with your car for a day or you sit there and wait. It also means that you have lowered your impression of your Toyota vehicle and you now are a little bit concerned. If there are three or four warranty repairs required in a short period, you ask, "Can I trust this car? Can I trust this company?"

> Ideal is customers who are completely satisfied. Currently some customers are inconvenienced by automotive problems.

Figure 2-10. Plan Step 1: Clarifying the Problem as compared to the Ideal State

The present situation (see Figure 2-11) was that, even with Toyota being better than others in the industry, they were not good enough. There were still too many customers who were bringing in their cars for warranty work, and that led to high costs for Toyota.

> Too many customers are bringing in Toyota vehicles for warranty work which costs them time and satisfaction and costs Toyota money.

Figure 2-11. Plan Step 2: Grasping the Situation and Seeing the Gaps

The breakdown of the problem (see Figure 2-12) was to confine it to two areas the team identified as sources of warranty issues—one was in manufacturing and one in product development. In product development, they might have been designing the product in a way that could not be easily manufactured. For example, they needed to do things like error proofing the product to avoid confusing a left and a right side-view mirror.

> Warranty problems originate in product development (e.g. poor error proofing), are contributed to in manufacturing (e.g. errors) and discovered in the field. Immediate focus will be on manufacturing through to customer feedback and response. Target=60% reduction.

Figure 2-12. Plan Step 3: Breaking down Problems and Setting Targets

If they were not doing that well you may see problems in manufacturing caused by design, but there are also mistakes that are made in manufacturing and there is also a final inspection in manufacturing that may be letting some defects slip through.

The immediate focus, as they decided to put boundaries on the problem, was **not** going to start with a brand new vehicle design. This would take years before you would get any results. Instead, they looked at vehicles currently manufactured. They looked from the point of manufacturing to the point when there is customer feedback about problems and how that feedback works its way to the right place, whether it is quality, manufacturing, or engineering, and then, what actions are taken because of that. The target already had been set at 60%. They broke that down to 10% per year.

Toyota needed to identify the largest warranty issues, easy, and then analyze the underlying causes, not so easy. As they added middle managers and engineers to do the detailed work, the team grew to several hundred people. They were measuring and finding out where the problems occurred and they found the biggest problems were by far in engineering, not manufacturing. Engineering was part of the team. Nonetheless, within manufacturing, there were defects that slipped through and each factory needed to continue work on understanding the root causes (see Figure 2-13). For example, one interesting problem was that in the final testing station, which all vehicles go through in the plant, there was a lot of ambient noise. Sometimes the inspector would not hear a shake or rattle. The solution to that was relatively straightforward. They could put in soundproof booths to do these shake and rattle tests. They tested this at the Georgetown, Kentucky plant and saw an immediate reduction in defects slipping through inspection.

For engineering, it was not as easy as that. There were many problems, and even finding the root cause of a given problem was difficult. The standard process, which you are all familiar with, is you have a problem with your vehicle, or maybe there is a recall, and now you need to bring your vehicle into the shop. They keep it for some amount of time. The car comes back to you, usually properly repaired. You may see the bad part that they return to you.

> Manufacturing-poor understanding of potential errors throughout manufacturing process and miss defects in inspection.
> Feedback and response-Problems in field not well diagnosed and communicated and requests for changes are diffuse and ineffective.

Figure 2-13. Plan Step 4: Analyzing the Underlying Causes

The dealer enters the information into Toyota's computer system and their job is done. Unfortunately, their description of the problem is usually very vague. There are many categories on the computer, they can simply select one, and it gives you an idea that there was a failure in the electronic system and where the failure occurred. There was a short circuit in the sound system, but you do not actually know why the short circuit happened. You do not know the root cause. You just know that some part failed.

What was happening was that this kind of information was not very useful to engineering. When a common problem occurred, time permitting, they would investigate the concern. In addition to that, the team observed that every part of Toyota in North America was generating requests for engineering changes. This represented every plant, sales organization, field people, field warranty groups, and quality from all over North America. They were not prioritized and they were overwhelming engineering. The problem was now further clarified: how can we get a root cause diagnosis of some of the more common warranty problems and how do we prioritize the defects so engineering knows the highest priorities?

The countermeasure in manufacturing was what Toyota calls, "Built-in Quality with Ownership," in which they want to go back to the original principle of Sakichi Toyoda to never let a problem pass beyond the original place that the problem occurred (see Figure 2-14). Never pass on a defect and let it get out of your station. Ownership means once I detect a problem I own it. I am responsible for it. I cannot just let it slip through and let inspection worry about it. And I need to consider the inputs to my process, characteristics of my process, and the method used for any manual work. The idea of "Built-in Quality" has been there for decades, since the beginning of the company, but this was a new, higher-level initiative. Again, to raise awareness you have to go **back to the basics** because people slip backward and it was time to come up with some new tools for analyzing the causes of quality problems.

The countermeasure of the noise isolation booth was one of tens of thousands of improvements made in various manufacturing plants over that six-year period to prevent defects from escaping the plants.

Manufacturing-Built-in Quality with Ownership at every work process + improved inspection process.

Feedback and response-System for finding root causes of warranty returns and streamlining feedback to appropriate engineering design function.

Figure 2-14. Plan Step 5: Developing Countermeasures

In engineering, what could they possibly do to get to the root cause of the warranty problems? They could do things like go to the dealers and ask if they could see the customers' parts, then ship these back to Toyota Motor Sales to develop a more refined checklist for the maintenance person to check something close to the root cause. They came up with a better idea. They realized that they had a captive group of customers right in the company. The employees of Toyota get good deals on leases, they work for Toyota, and they could be asked to bring their cars in and, in this way, get defective parts returned so that the root cause of the problem could be diagnosed.

How did they do that? They picked Toyota Motor Sales where there are several thousand employees. They asked the employees to participate in this program. The employees were bringing their cars right to Toyota Motor Sales where they could do the repairs while they were at work. They set up a customer satisfaction center within Toyota Motor Sales, and one by one, they diagnosed the actual root cause of each problem.

> Deployed through global network of leaders who take responsibility.

Figure 2-15. Do Step 6: Seeing the Countermeasures Through

They also talked to other parts of Toyota. They had leaders from all parts of Toyota on the team, and they said that any request for an engineering change was going to go through this customer satisfaction center (see Figure 2-15). There were going to filter the changes and prioritize them before they get back to either the Toyota Technical Center or engineering in Japan or its suppliers. As much as possible a root cause analysis would be done in America and the problems prioritized before being sent to engineering.

> Monitored closely over seven years with continual adjustment.

Figure 2-16. Check Step 7: Monitoring both Results and Processes

This was an ongoing process, refining and improving (see Figure 2-16). That is why it took, as it turned out, seven years to finally get the 60% they wanted. They saw it through. They continually adjusted the process. Gary, by year four, retired from the company. Toyota by then had made progress in standardizing these new processes within manufacturing, engineering, and sales. They made further progress on the root causes. Again, this was an ongoing process, but this new process needed to become the new routine, the new way of doing business within North America (see Figure 2-17).

> Many new processes were standardized in manufacturing, engineering and sales. Work progressed further on root cause: better training and development of engineers and standardization in engineering, built-in quality with ownership in manufacturing, and an improved warranty reporting system in sales.

Figure 2-17. Act Step 8: Standardizing and Spreading the Learnings

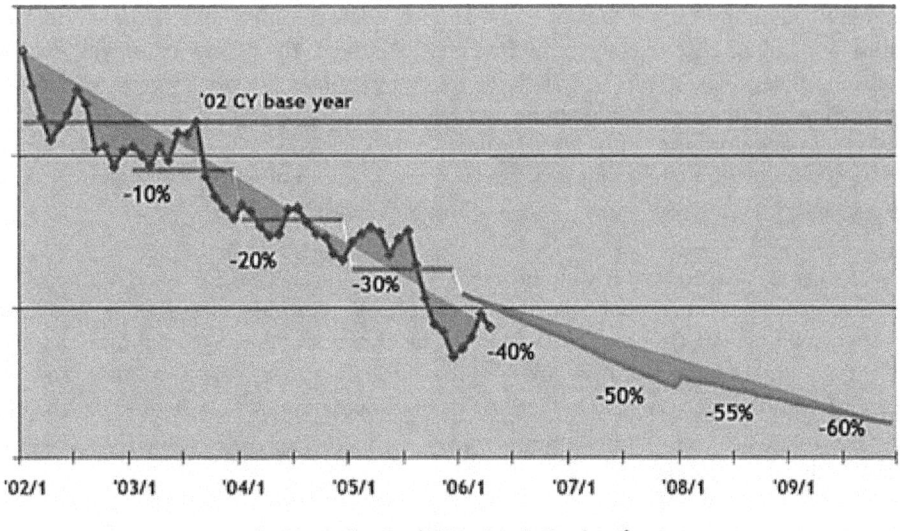

Percent Annual Warranty Reductions

Source: Toyota Engineering and Manufacturing of America, Inc.

Figure 2-18. North American Plants Warranty at 3 Months in Service

Now, you might be wondering how it went. The answer is that it went very well as illustrated above (see Figure 2-18). The individual horizontal lines were the targets. As you can see, it was 10% a year from the base year of 2002. The dotted trend line represents what actually happened during Gary's reign. They achieved 40% after four years, and after he left, we checked up on the process and they did get to the 60% by year seven.

Of course, the actual warranty repairs did not decline in straight lines that perfectly matched the 10% a year. You can see sometimes that they were below the target and sometimes they were above the target. It is best to think about this as all the PDCA cycles that were going on – trying things, some work, some seem to work and now we are ahead of schedule, then we slip back and have a big problem with some part of the car, and then we have to solve that problem.

This process was not a matter of Gary ordering everybody to reduce warranty by 10% as would sometimes happen in companies. It was Gary, as an executive, actively leading a team of executives. They had several hundred people working for that team, and through PDCA, they achieved this remarkable objective. I would call this continuously improving your way to a breakthrough objective. It is *kaikaku* done through much *kaizen*.

Driving to the root cause through 5 Whys

Driving to the root cause is probably the most misunderstood part of problem solving and certainly important. The root cause sounds very scientific – like there is one root cause and you have to use every method possible to find the precise underlying reason for the problem. The reality is that if you are doing problem solving everywhere, all the time and every day, you could spend all of your time trying to find the root cause and never do anything else. You need to take some shortcuts. You need to accept that sometimes you are going to hit the bull's eye and sometimes you are not. Ultimately, it is your best guess that you will then test through experimentation.

Taiichi Ohno taught root cause problem solving through the 5-Why method. He believed your best chance of success is to deeply observe the process, think, and keep challenging yourself. Do I really know that this is the root cause? Why did that happen? – And generally doing this five times seemed to be about the right number. You are looking at data, but you may not be using the most sophisticated regression analysis methods or design of experiments. The goal is to come up with a plausible chain of explanation so you can test it.

The more common problem is not lack of rigor in getting to the root cause. The more common problem is we do not even try. We immediately think we know what the problem is, we think we know what the cause is, and we jump immediately from the problem into the solution.

Figure 2-19: Man Jumping into a Pool with Water (left) and without Water (right)

We show a man jumping into a pool with water (see Figure 2-19). Imagine if that pool had no water, the man simply leaped without looking, and that is what does happen. When you look at the problem, you start brainstorming ideas, and then you implement those ideas, it is like flying blind. Sometimes you need to do that for little problems. For example, you might have an hour-by-hour board, and every hour you ask the people doing the work to write down if they met the target. If they do not meet the target, ask them, why, and then you might have a countermeasure column. What they are doing is jumping from problems to solutions, but they are doing it for small problems that are occurring hour by hour and sometimes the cause is obvious (a part was out of specification and was stuck in the machine). When you collect those problems and find the biggest ones, you should do a root cause analysis – not jump to conclusions.

The 5 Whys, not the 5 Whos

Taiichi Ohno said, "Observe the production floor without preconceptions and with a blank mind. Repeat "Why" five times to every matter." He was very famous for his Ohno circle. Stand in the circle, watch what is actually happening, and keep on asking why? Try to understand the problems and the root cause – start now. Two hours later, he would show up and ask you what you saw. Two hours later he would show up again, do the same thing, and normally he would make you stand in that circle all day. You could take breaks, but otherwise you stayed in the circle. You were observing the same things repeatedly. Each time he came back, you were expected to have a deeper analysis. You would address more issues and have thought more deeply about why. Notice that he did *not* ask you to find the guilty parties. He did *not* ask you to answer the five who's. Often when you ask why, the first why is a person who made a mistake, but when you ask why that person made a mistake it usually will drive down to a system cause.

The Narrowing and Focusing Process

What should be happening is that you are starting with a large problem that may be very vague or even symptoms of the problem (see Figure 2-20). We have quality problems. We want to solve these quality problems. There are many things that cause quality problems. We do not even know where to start. You need to more clearly focus your problem statement. For example, you might end up with: we want to be number one on specific customer satisfaction measures in two years. Or at the level of a production line you are focused on, you may want to reduce defects by 80 percent by the end of the year. Once you get to actually working on a piece of this broad problem statement, like working on quality at the work process causing the most defects, you begin to drill down beginning with the most likely cause. Then you go beyond this to ask where the problem really originated. Then you can find the direct cause. Before you even start asking the 5 whys, you must identify the point of cause—where the problem originated- and the direct cause at that point in the process.

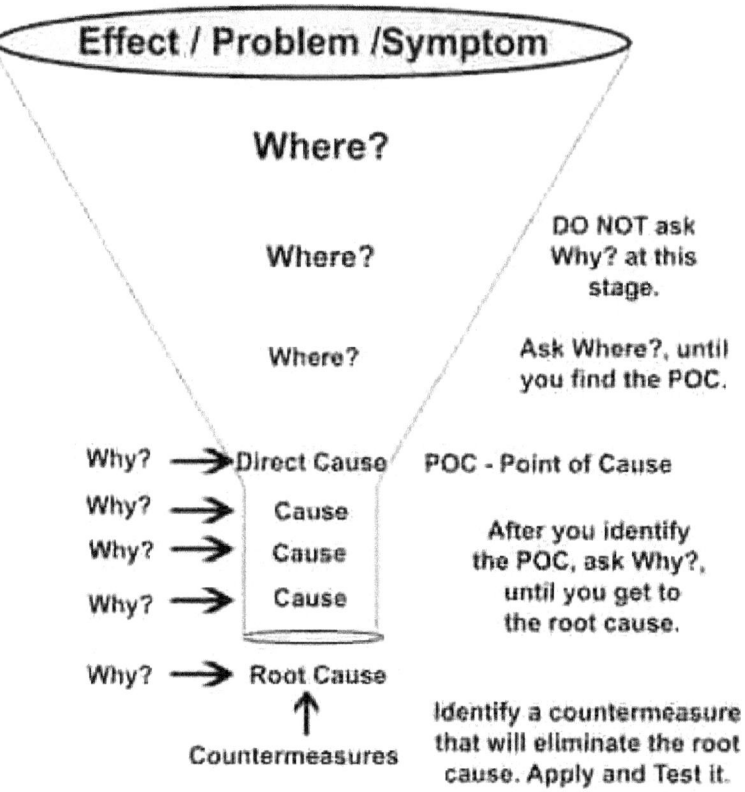

Figure 2-20. Narrowing the Focus

There is a famous Taiichi Ohno story where he told Nampachi Hayashi, one of his best students, to observe the assembly line until he saw a problem. Hayashi identified a serious quality problem and was all pumped up to start solving it. Then Ohno demanded, "Where did that problem occur?" The problem was a part that did not fit right, and when he thought about it, Hayashi realized it might have occurred in how the part was manufactured in an earlier stage. Ohno demanded to know why he was here if the problem was there.

Hayashi started running to the upstream process and Ohno stopped him in his tracks asking harshly where he was going. "Back to the manufacturing process where the problem probably originated to go and see," Hayashi replied. Ohno then asked "What about the problem in assembling the part. Will you let bad assemblies be made?" He was pointing out that Hayashi must think deeply about the problem, but first must contain the problem in assembly before getting to the root cause in manufacturing. Ohno was not a fun guy to learn from, though extremely effective.

Common 5 Why Mistakes: Blaming Others

I said you need to find the point of cause – where it occurs – but there is one caveat to that, which is, you need to focus on what you can control. Here is a reasonable 5 why analysis David Meier and I described in *The Toyota Way Fieldbook*. The problem is that the defect rate is too high – it is not meeting our goal – and the reason is that we have too many defective parts. Why? Because parts are *not* being assembled correctly in the assembly process. Often we stop here and blame the operator. Why? Because the operators are making mistakes. Why are operators making mistakes? Because the parts *do not* align properly. Why don't the parts align properly? Because the part is poorly designed, which means we now need to go to the engineers who may be in a different location or a different country. We need to tell them that they have to design the parts correctly.

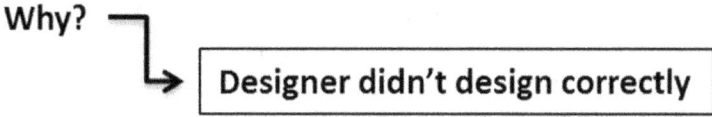

Figure 2-21. First Answer to the Question: Why are the parts *not* aligned correctly?

Once you start pointing the finger at another party (see Figure 2-21) that you cannot directly influence there is likely to be a very long lead-time to address the problem – you may not see that new design for months or even years. You have to ask yourself, is there a different answer to the whys that *will* lead us to something we can control?

Effective Root Cause Analysis

Problem Statement: The defect rate is over goal

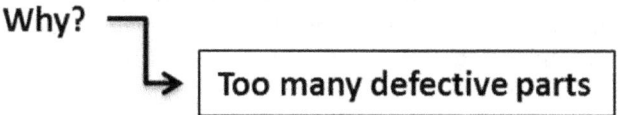

Figure 2-22. Answer to the Question: Why is the defect rate too high?

This is what we call effective root cause analysis. That is what we have done here. We still have the operator error (see Figure 2-22) and we still know that the parts do not align properly, but now we ask ourselves, "Can we do something to align the parts correctly within assembly?" So, why are the parts not aligning correctly?

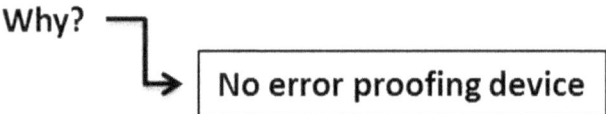

Figure 2-23. Second Answer to the Question: Why are the parts *not* aligned correctly?

We do not have an error-proofing device that will prevent the part from passing to the next station (see Figure 2-23). The error-proofing device you come up with might be as simple as a fixture, but we need some way to assemble the parts that currently do not fit perfectly, and where the end result is going to satisfy the customer. That still means you are going to communicate this to engineering so that they can error proof the design at some point and make it easier to assemble - without the use of a fixture. But to contain the problem we are going to do something right now that will stop quality problems from occurring in assembly. Pointing fingers at another party can be an excuse to throw up our hands and do nothing.

Once we have the root cause, what *we* think is the root cause, *we* need to come up with ideas to eliminate the cause or eliminate the problem of the cause. As mentioned earlier, Toyota calls these countermeasures because we do not know if they will work or are the best we can do. A great solution today may be replaced by an even better solution tomorrow. What we think is a good countermeasure needs to be proven scientifically by running an experiment. Now it becomes a hypothesis. If I implement this countermeasure, I believe it may reduce the gap.

A common mistake is that we think we know more than we actually do. I have the answer. Then we push through that answer. Maybe it works for a short period of time or maybe it helps a little bit, but is that really the best answer? Perhaps somebody in the group might have had a better answer, a better countermeasure. The disease of overconfidence is one of the biggest barriers to problem solving. If you already think you know how to solve the problem then you will only superficially follow the problem solving process, if at all.

Countermeasures and Problem Solving to Develop People

"Nemawashi"

One of the other Japanese words that comes up a lot in every step of the problem solving process is *nemawashi*. You may have read about *nemawashi* decades ago in books about Japanese management. This is not peculiar to Toyota. One way of translating it, based on nature, is preparing the soil before planting a tree. In this case, preparing the soil means that all those parties who will be affected, all those parties who will have to sign off on the decision, have been prepared prior to you actually, formally making a proposal. What you are doing is circulating a document face to face. Skype might be okay but face to face is better. Often you communicate one by one with different members, you discuss with them, you get their ideas, and you listen actively. As you listen, as you discuss and give them some reasons why some of the ideas were considered, and perhaps incorporate their ideas, you are using all your social skills to build consensus. When you finally make a formal proposal, everybody has already agreed to it.

Identify and select improvement options (Plan)

When we identify and select our improvement options – again, our countermeasures are still part of the planning process – we are going to use *nemawashi* to generate many ideas. Then we are going to narrow down those ideas by using different measures of effectiveness, cost, simplicity, and the ability to implement quickly. You could use a whole set of criteria and rate those on a three point scale. You can come up with a quick number. Also, use your judgment to find the smaller number of items that you are actually going to test. In the process, even as you are testing them, you report the results back, you are continuing to build consensus, and the *nemawashi* process is generating more ideas. Again, you are going to keep on doing *nemawashi* in every step of the process. One of the things we will talk about later in this chapter is that A3 is a powerful tool for *nemawashi*. It can be part of the consensus building process, but only if used appropriately for that purpose which means we cannot fill it all out ourselves and get committed to all our own ideas.

Plan and implement improvements (Do)

In doing, you do not want to wait and allow defects to occur or waste to persist until you can find the root cause and then go through the very systematic eight-step process. As mentioned earlier, you first need to contain the problem. For example, in a Toyota plant, when someone pulls the cord – the andon – a light goes on, perhaps a team leader comes running. The team leader's first job is to contain the problem so they can continue to produce cars. Then, if the problem warrants, the team can step back and start to look for longer-term countermeasures. The first Do might actually be the containment before the Plan-Do-Check-Act, and then you go through Plan-Do-Check-Act for the biggest problems that you are going to focus on.

I was at Zingerman's Mail Order warehouse where they were creating a new rack to contain different sized boxes that are used for shipping different products. Selecting the right sized box is one of the most challenging skills for operators. They kept on tinkering with this one rack and letting the operator use it for a while, getting feedback, letting a few operators use it, relocating some of the boxes, and adding on to the rack. They went through the do-check-adjust process for weeks and finally they were satisfied, and then they went live in all the workstations. Doing is a continual process of experimenting, reflecting, and adjusting.

Problem Solving is the Way to Develop People

The Toyota Way is Continuous Improvement and Respect for People, and those two pillars are considered to be completely intertwined. The intertwining is that as people are solving problems they are learning many skills. Those skills include *nemawashi*, coming up with creative ideas, stretching their minds, deeply observing, thinking and asking why. People are developing a whole repertoire of skills and habits. At the same time, they are solving real problems, and they are getting better and better. The result of the problem solving is people development.

When Gary led that effort to get 60% warranty reduction, with some of the best people in Toyota, nobody questioned whether they could achieve 60% or whether it was acceptable to achieve 57%. The goal was 60%. They were going to achieve it. They knew they were going to achieve it. They knew how, through the problem solving process, but they did not know the specific solutions that would work. As they worked through the process, they were all developing higher-level improvement skills, especially Gary.

Toyota Business Practices: Developing People through Problem Solving

What Toyota has done in Toyota Business Practices is two sets of things in parallel. One addresses the question: What are the concrete actions and processes we will take – the steps – to solve the problem? The second answers the question of what values, what skills, we are going to reinforce in people as they are going through this process. They call these drive and dedication (see Figure 2-24). They build drive, dedication, and real skills by going through the eight steps. For example, when you are clarifying the problem you should always be putting the customer first, which starts with asking, who is the customer? What is it that they need from me to satisfy their needs, to solve their problems? When you are developing countermeasures, you are trying to fine-tune your judgment based on facts of how, for example, you prioritize the problems. You are involving stakeholders, and you are learning how to talk to those stakeholders, how to draw out their ideas, how to in a way persuade them, but persuade them by listening to them and taking their ideas seriously.

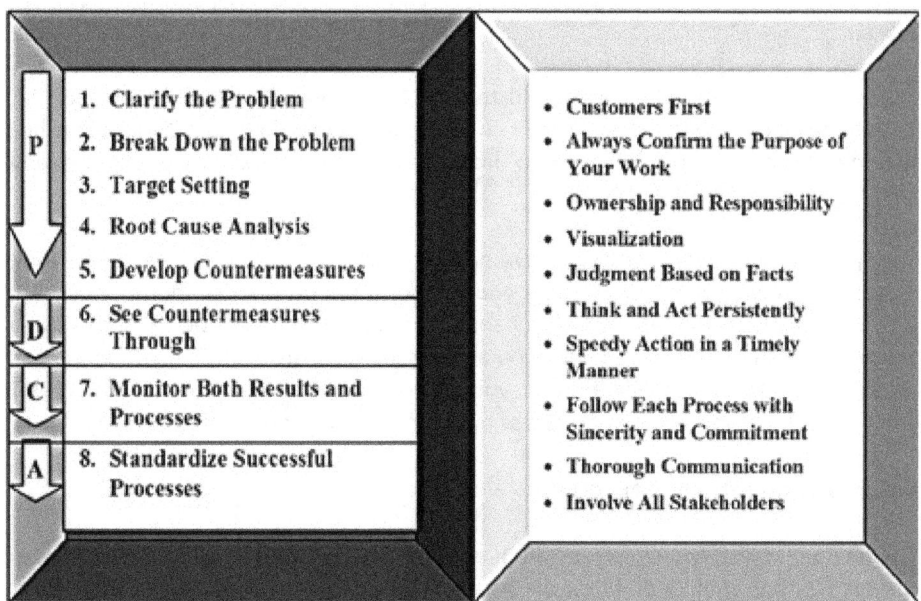

Source: Toyota
Figure 2-24. Toyota Business Practices - centered on a problem solving process.

An Action Plan is about Accountability

When you come to the action plan for testing the countermeasure, we are going to have a visual schedule that will be posted somewhere very visible. Typically, you will have some sort of board at the *gemba* that is tracking the problem solving process including what, who and by when.

You should always have individuals' names written down- not teams, not what is done by the group - in each step, there is a person who is accountable for that step. Part of the checking process involves that person reporting out at meetings. When they are supposed to have something done, it is immediately obvious if they do not or if they have not thought it through carefully. Every single time you meet with a person, every time that person reports out, that is an opportunity for that person to get feedback and to improve their problem solving skills. Therefore, an action plan is really about accountability, and it is another tool for developing people.

Checking is Learning

We can continue with the Check stage of Plan-Do-Check-Act, which is another opportunity for people development. As you observe the situation, you are going to be coached. If you come and say, "Look at my great results," and show just numbers the sensei is going to ask you, "Did you go and observe the process? How long did you observe the process? Did you talk to the people?" They will send you back to the *gemba*.

You need to be prepared to make adjustments. Often we declare victory too early and you are going to view the checking as a checking-and-acting stage. So, these stages blur together because you should learn from observation, which will generate new countermeasures to test.

You have made progress but you have not gotten there. Then you have to do some more. Then you have to check again and you have to adjust some more. This whole process is really designed to develop people and for the organization to learn. That is why you spread out over time what you are learning. You are really not spreading best practices, as some mistakenly believe, you are spreading learning, and your input then becomes the input to a thinking process by whomever you communicate this too.

Future Action is Deep Reflection

The final Act in PDCA is deep reflection, and this goes on until you are convinced that the process has stabilized. Often we hear that the solution is not sustained. You go back a few months later and it is not working the way you had set it up. People are not following the standard method you designed, and the problem usually is that you did not stick around long enough to continue checking and continue coaching and continue supporting until the new process became a routine – the new way we do things. You are responsible, as the owner of the problem, for sustaining the solution and for continuing the improvement.

We often see that a company will do a model area in Lean (sometimes called a "lighthouse" project). Once they do that one area and they have great success their management might order them to spread this everywhere in a cookie cutter way and they stop going back to that model area. The value of the model is that it is a learning line. You can continue to learn and continue to advance beyond other parts of the business, but usually the learning stops prematurely because you are busy spreading whatever you learned and then that area slips backward. In the meantime, the copies are probably not as good as the original because. First, the precise solutions will not fit as well in a different context. Second, the people in the areas in which you spread the "best practice" did not go through the process of learning by doing and do not understand the model well enough to accept all the underlying routines needed to keep on improving it.

Why is PDCA so rarely followed?

Source: *Toyota Way to Continuous Improvement*
Figure 2-25. PDCA (Plan – Do – Check – Act or Adjust) Wheel or Deming Wheel

Does PDCA, as I have described it, happen frequently? Is this just the way people typically carry out improvement? After all, most established companies went through the quality revolution in the 1980s and 1990s. We should all, by now, be quality experts. We learned somewhere in one of those quality courses about Plan-Do-Check-Act (see Figure 2-25) and the basic problem solving tools, and we learned how to make a cause and effect diagram. So, is this just old hat? The answer is, in theory, it is old hat. I am not telling anybody who has been around for a while something they never heard, but in reality, what happens on a daily basis is illustrated in Figure 2-26.

Source: *Toyota Way to Continuous Improvement*
Figure 2-26. PDCA Wheel with only Do – Make it Happen!

We get into a firefighting mode where we are doing and doing and doing - planning, checking, and further acting or adjusting go out the window. Why does that happen? We learned it in a course. We know the right thing to do is PDCA, but when you actually check the process and observe people at work, they are spending almost all of their time "doing." Why does that happen?

The firefighting mode, it turns out, is a vicious cycle, and you can even put that in systems theory terms. It is a closed loop system spiraling down. You adjust the system because it is broken. Then another problem comes up and you are fixing that problem. In the meantime, the last problem you never really solved will come back. Then the problems keep snowballing and you are constantly in the mode of fighting whatever problem pops up today. The system is actually getting worse instead of getting better. Once you are in that vicious cycle you feel trapped because you do not have time to plan, check, or adjust. You only have time to fight the fires of the day.

Once you shift gears into a virtuous cycle of PDCA things start to run better. They are more stable. That then gives you the time to spend planning and checking and adjusting, especially if you have the luxury of an offline team leader instead of everybody working in production. You have extra resources for problem solving. As you solve problems the right way, things start getting better instead of worse. That gives you more luxury to do *kaizen*. We could have a self-improving vicious cycle or a self-destructive vicious cycle. Many companies are caught up in self-destructive vicious cycles.

George: "Now, what is your countermeasure, Jeff, for the many companies that are trapped in this cycle – how do you get them thinking back to the Deming wheel and how do you start them off as a consultant?"

Jeff: The simplest answer is **Leadership**. Somebody has to stop the firefighting and start proactive problem solving. Somebody has to take a leading role. It could be a manager or supervisor in their area who says, "I have just had it. I am going home at night, and I am madder and madder and more frustrated and treating my family badly. I am miserable, and I have just had enough. I have to do something different. I will take any opportunity to learn about Lean and change the way I lead."

I have had people write me emails – "I read your book, and I started following the principles in my area, and we would stop and we would ask what the problem is and ask why five times. We started to solve problems and we used some of the tools of Lean, and things got better and that gave us more time to solve the real problems. Now my management is asking what is different. Why are you outperforming the rest of the organization? My peer supervisors are snickering and badmouthing me because they think I am sucking up to the senior management. What do I do? My management does not understand what I am doing, and my peers are mad and jealous; they do not want to learn from me."

It is a real problem, but I suggest they hang in there and do what they know is right and eventually the others may well come around. A better situation is that someone more senior really has had enough. "I am not going to take it anymore. I am going to change." In *The Toyota Way to Continuous Improvement*, Dr. Richard Zarbo who ran the test labs for the Henry Ford Health System wrote a chapter. He had gone through training by Deming decades earlier and finally looked in the mirror and said to himself: "We are not following anything Dr. Deming tried to teach us. In am going to change that in the labs." And they changed dramatically and it started with Richard Zarbo changing himself. As we will see in the leadership model, the first step of becoming a Lean Leader is self-development. You have to want to change. In one part of the organization, you can change only what you can control.

Many people ask me the question, "What should I do? I do not have the support of management and I do not have the support of my peers." My answer is keep on doing what you are doing because you are probably going home happier, and you are probably a better father or husband or wife and community member, and your life is better. Why would you want to go back?

In the meantime, the longer you do this and the more you get the results, the more likely it is that someone up top will figure out that they should learn something from you. That often happens. You need to start somewhere and it could be at the bottom. It could be at the middle. It could be at the top. What is most effective is when the top has a passion to change. Often that occurs as the result of an outside force. For example, we had the patent. We were charging 100% profit margin. Our patent has run out. We have competitors. They are charging 15% profit margin. We have to change or we are going to die. A crisis, as we will see in the Dana case in Chapter Seven, can open up top leaders to learning.

Why do so many companies miss the PCA from the PDCA cycle?

Let's ask again: Why is it that people will skip over the Plan and the Check and the Act and jump to the Do? Why will they look at a problem and – particularly if you are a high-level manager – think I need to come up with the solution right now. I get the problem. I am now challenged to come up with a solution. Then I have to make sure that mine is the best solution so everybody can point to me and say, "You are the hero. You solved the problem." Why do people do that?

There is actually a lot of new research that helps us to understand that. There is research down to the level of brain chemistry, and then there is a bestselling book called *Thinking, Fast and Slow* by Daniel Kahneman, a cognitive psychologist, who spent his career studying the way people reason and make decisions. He and his collaborator won a Nobel Prize for their work.

In this new book, at the simplest level, he says, "Think of your brain as having two parts that are independent." It is not really what happens, but it is a simplified view. You have these two computer processors in your brain. One of them loves to jump from problem to solution. It wants to think fast, wants to react. Stereotyping comes from fast thinking. I see you, and I immediately make assumptions. This person looks intelligent. This person looks lazy. This person is a low paid worker. This person is a highly successful manager. I quickly generate many attributes I associate from past experience with the first thing I learned about you – your job title perhaps or just your appearance. That is the fast thinking part of your brain that wants to draw conclusions as fast as possible. Slowing down that part of the brain is painful and frustrating.

There is another part of the brain that says, "Wait a second, Jeff. How do you know that? You just saw the guy. How do you know anything about him until you start asking questions and finding out things about him? Slow down a little bit." Now these two parts of the brain are fighting with each other because the fast part wants to be correct immediately and move on, and the slow part wants to stop and reflect and check and collect data. The fast part is saying, "You jerk. We do not have time for this. We have to solve the problem. Get your head out of the clouds." The slow part is saying, "Slow down, slow down, before you get us in trouble before we think this through."

One of the things that Kahneman shows through his experiments is that when you have a scarcity of information then system one – the fast thinking part – operates as a machine for jumping to conclusions. The fast part is going to win when there is an absence of information. The fast part says, "We do not know much for certain so I am just going to do what I think is right." The more information that is available, accessible, visible, the more the slow part can win the argument, jump in there sometimes, and slow down the fast part.

One of the things we do with Lean is Visual Management, where at a glance, you can see if this process is in control or is out of control. That is absolutely critical information that the fast part cannot easily dispute. We know this is broken. We stopped the line, the fast part contained the problem, and now the fast part has to defer to the slow part to start thinking a little bit. Why did this happen?

George: "That is quite interesting. So, is this book merely a good read or did we just learn about everything we need to know from what you said?"

Jeff: "I think you learned a lot of it, but it is a long read. It is hundreds of pages. An academic wrote it, but the academic happens to be a brilliant communicator, so brilliant that he took a 400 to 500—page book that you can use as a paperweight and made it into one of the top 10 bestsellers on the *New York Times* list for a year or more running. People bought this book by the millions, and presumably, bunches of them read it. Personally, I think that many people do not read the whole book. I have not read the whole book, but it is very engaging reading because he writes in a colorful way about fascinating experiments."

George: "What you point out about Visual Systems – I never thought of it that way. I never thought to explain it that way, but that is such a good way to explain how they are critical because we are fighting against the human side of wanting to jump to conclusions without information."

Jeff: "Right. It helps also if the manager comes down, looks at what you are doing and slows you down a bit, and slows himself down a bit by asking questions. It is a great tool. That is another conclusion of Kahneman – and it is a conclusion from brain scientists – that we are naturally visual creatures. If the data is buried three levels down in the computer, it is worthless, and if there is too much of it, it is worthless."

You have to have very crystal clear, focused information that telegraphs there is a gap. There is a problem. Then you have to take the time to solve the problem. We will cover much more about visual management in Chapter Three.

The other implication is that – also shown in brain science – most people naturally prefer fast thinking. It feels good. It generates endorphins. It is like a high. You feel good. I solved the problem, and it happened right now. When you slow down and start asking specific questions such as, was that the right problem? – Peoples' eyes glaze over. Their working memory is activated which is painful. Learning something new is painful. Deep thinking is painful. Kahneman refers to "The law of least mental effort" and fast thinking is the least mental effort.

The positive thing that Kahneman demonstrates, and the brain scientists have learned, is that the more you use the slow thinking part of the brain, the more powerful it becomes, just as exercising your body makes you stronger. It is really hard to do five pushups. You keep on doing it, and suddenly you are doing 25 pushups. The slow part of the brain can be exercised and can learn, and then you get even more pleasure from really finding the root cause of the problem and really solving it than you got from all those little fast wins that you had gotten in the past. The good news is there is some benefit at the end of the tunnel if you go through this tough process of learning to train your brain to think more slowly, deeply, and systematically.

Source: Toyota Georgetown Plant
Figure 2-27. Visual Management Board

It is important to capitalize on visual management as a tool to encourage slow thinking. This was the visual meeting area (see Figure 2-27) for a group leader at Toyota's Kentucky plant. This looks elaborate enough that it could be for a whole plant, but it is just for one group leader. As Toyota group leaders typically have about 25 team members and in Georgetown, Kentucky, they have 6,000 people… there are many boards. They still print out the paper, even though it comes off a computer, and they post it. They have a simple visual that may be hard to see, but you will notice the red Xs, and that is where your eye should be drawn because that is where the problems are. A problem means we are not on track. This is what we should be doing this week. This is what we should have accomplished in quality improvement and safety improvement and cost reduction, and we did not make it in safety on the first shift and we have a problem. That is where they need coaching support. The top levels of management come down and see that and they discuss it. They walk through the factory, meet with the team in front of the board, and they try to help them mostly by asking them challenging questions. We will return to this board in Chapter Six when discussing effective work groups.

A3 Thinking to Slow Down Problem Solving

A3 Reports have become a standard part of the lean tool kit though they are rarely used as intended. One thing the A3 process can do is help the slow thinking part of our brain. The report itself is one side of one sheet of A3-sized paper and you fill in boxes representing the process you are using, such as the problem solving process. The right way to do this is with a coach and you are filling it out box by box, as you go through the process. For example, in problem solving you can spend weeks on defining the problem—the first box—before the coach will let you move on.

The history of A3 is, in a sense, disappointing because you would like to think that there was some huge breakthrough where suddenly somebody said, "Eureka! I have discovered the A3, and this is an essential tool for the Toyota Way." It did not happen like that. What did happen was that there were a series of recognitions.

One recognition that we need to document the process as the process goes on, and that is part of *nemawashi*. You have to have something to show people, and when you show something to somebody and it is your responsibility, not theirs, you want to show it in an as clear and simple way as possible. Short is better. Sending a big report with tables and reams of text is almost certainly going to be a loser. You are expecting that they will read the 40-page report and maybe just before the meeting they will glance through it, but they will not necessarily see the most critical points. That is why we have executive summaries.

A3 was a way to get the most critical ideas on one piece of paper where the people we are going to be showing and talking to, and our coach, can at a glance, understand the key points, follow our thinking process, and give us feedback. Why A3? A3 is roughly 11 by 17 inches, which at the time was the largest size paper that you could fit through a fax machine. Sending a fax was the main method for communicating to others outside your building. Nobody came up with a model to optimize paper size; it was just the biggest they could fit through the machine.

The A3 in Toyota is referred to as a story, because a story is something that unfolds. A report is something you do usually at the end when the story is over. By then it is too late because the story might have been poorly conceived and a failure.

Four Types of A3 Stories

Much of what you will hear formally coming out of Toyota on A3 reports was actually developed by Americans. For example, in the 1990s at the Toyota Technical Center in Ann Arbor they realized that the American managers had not been formally trained in problem solving. This was rather assumed. The original employees had one-on-one Japanese coaches, and they would show them things like, "Please make a report on one side of one piece of paper. Make it look like this, and I will help you do it." The Americans were learning A3 even thought they might not call it that.

As the R&D center grew and many new people were hired they had not learned it from the small remaining Japanese staff. So a training group developed courses to formalize the knowledge, something they had not done in Japan. They developed courses on nemawashi. They developed courses on the problem solving process, and they also developed an A3 course where problem solving and nemawashi were prerequisites. They formally defined the different types of A3 stories that they saw from the Japanese. Figure 2-28 is showing four different types of A3 stories in a logical sequence from your original consciousness that there is a problem to your current situation.

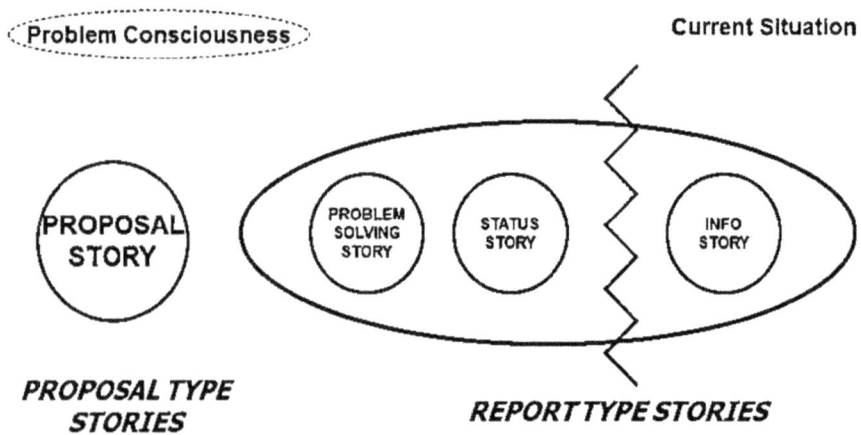

Source: Toyota Technical Center
Figure 2-28. Four types of A3 Stories

The proposal story is when you are conscious that there is a problem and need to get approval to proceed working on the problem. Once it is approved, you can begin the problem-solving story and you are going through, for example, Toyota Business Practices. At various points in the problem solving process, or in your daily work, you may have to report on the status of production, quality, of safety, or whatever, and you might want to communicate that based on an A3 that shows the key data. That shows the status of where I am compared to where I should be using a Status A3.

On the other hand, you might want to share information. For example, you may learn something technically in body engineering that you want to share with all of the other body engineers and you use an A3 Information Story. Again, this will be on one side of one piece of paper that states the problem that you had and what your countermeasure was and then shows the data.

These are different A3s. What we are most familiar with is the problem-solving story. I will talk briefly about the others, and then I will focus mostly on the problem-solving story.

A3 Report: Planning Vital Points

There are some general vital points – key points – in any A3 story regardless of the type. You should take some time to grasp the entire situation before you even start the A3. That means considering a wide range of information sources, getting others involved like Gary did going to key leaders and doing *nemawashi*, and that is a way of forming your team that is going to be executing, leading, the process. Try to find facts, not just opinions. So, when you get an opinion you want to be like a detective to find out if it is true or not and also consider some of the long-term effects on what you are working on or whether this is just a short-term fix.

What kind of story do you need to tell? Which of the four? Who is the audience? What information would be useful for them to have? Then what are those company values and philosophies to which this particular story relates? You should tell the story in the context of those values, like customers first.

I will give you one quick example of a report based on values. There was a famous announcement some years ago. It was actually after NUMMI, Toyota's joint venture with GM was closed, and this humongous plant was available and then Toyota arranged with Tesla to move into the plant. Tesla is a relatively small manufacturer of electric cars, a very innovative company, and then Toyota invested in Tesla and Akio Toyota made an announcement that, "We are partnering with Tesla, because we want to learn from them." What they wanted was some of the excitement, drive, dedication to innovation, to rub off on Toyota engineers who had been around for a long time in a bureaucracy.

I saw a project report-out for the RAV4, which involved putting the Tesla powertrain into a RAV4, and it had to work with the transmission of the RAV4. Many problems needed to be solved. One of the challenges was that there was proprietary technology in Toyota's computer modules and in Tesla's computer modules; they could not actually share the code. They had to view it as a black box and understand the inputs and outputs and what happened when we try this. They had a very tight deadline – about half the time it would normally take to do something like this. The team defined in their A3 their goal as to learn a new level of innovation and a new level of teamwork by working with Tesla. Obviously, they needed to get the RAV4 out into the market. That was the business purpose, but the people purpose, the values, were really to be among the best innovators in the world. Those are the values they were really tapping into, the ones stated by Akio Toyoda in collaborating with Tesla. They reported out how they met the challenging targets on time, but also how well they did in learning about innovation and what they would share with others.

A3 Report: Execution Vital Points

Let us consider a few more vital points. Like any good story, there should be a flow. In this particular case, you are not going to elaborate like a novelist might, and you only want key points, bullet points, for example, not paragraphs, and graphs and visuals are preferred over words. Every word should count. It should be specific. You should avoid jargon that others who might see the report will not understand. You might avoid some acronyms that you are used to and others are not. You should consider, like an artist, how each box on the report would visually come through to the intended audience. What impression are they going to get by looking at that box? Will the information leap off the page to them?

A3 Proposal Story Purpose

Going through the various A3 types the starting point is a proposal story , and we are going to use that when there is, at that point, no plan or goal but there is a company value that needs to be addressed or we have some idea that there is something that we can improve upon. It could be some idea for how we are going to make the customer experience at the dealer much more fun and pleasant and customer first is a value.

A plan or goal may exist, but the company, value, or policy might have changed, or the environment might have changed. You need a plan to address that change. It may be a completely new direction or a completely new policy that you are going to make and you need a goal or plan to do that.

As an example, you might need to propose a budget. One time I visited the Toyota Technical Center, and I was interviewing a vice president and he was huffing and puffing and worn out.

He explained, "I just finished this big report I have been working on for the last four weeks."

"What was the report?"

"It was the entire budget for the Toyota Technical Center – thousands of people."

It just occurred to me to ask, "Was this an A3?"

He said, "Yes, of course."

Imagine the entire budget for the Toyota Technical Center, including the rationale for the budget, on one side of one sheet of paper. At that point, the budget was a proposal saying here is collectively, with all the *nemawashi* and all the work I did, what I am proposing as the budget. No decisions will be made until after that report is reviewed. Of course, there is a lot of backup documentation, but the gist of the logic will be clear in the A3 and it was developed through *Nemawashi* involving many people.

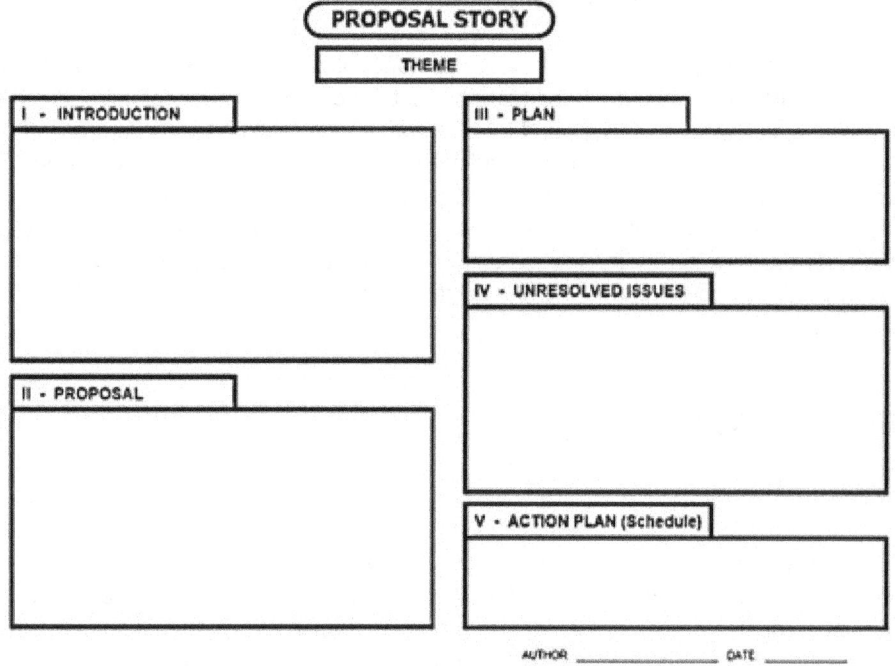

Source: Toyota Technical Center
Figure 2-29. The Proposal Type A3 Story

The format can look like this (see Figure 2-29), and I personally am not a real stickler for having a standardized reporting method where every box is exactly the same size or shape. You need to modify it, particularly in something like a proposal story or a status report, for the particular situation you face. In this case, like any good book, you start with an introduction. You have a proposal that you are making. There is a flow. There is then the plan. There are issues that you have not been able to resolve at the point of the reporting, and there is then a detailed schedule of how you would put this into practice.

If you consider the budget story I talked about, it would not look exactly like this. The introduction does not have to be very long. It is an annual, routine budget planning cycle and simply stating in the title this is the proposal for the annual budget for this period of time for the Toyota Technical Center is probably enough of an introduction. The proposal itself is going to be the budget along with some rationale. The plan might be the process of getting the budget approved. If there are unresolved issues, they should be stated. Maybe there are, maybe there are not. There may be some items where he had to guesstimate and this should be made clear. Then there would actually be a schedule, and the final endpoint might be the budget is approved. Most of this paper – and it is not a lot for a complex budget – is going to be the budget itself.

The steps for the proposal story really start before you develop the Plan – before PDCA – and it starts with grasping the situation. That is going to lead to naming what this proposal is, giving some background information, and describing the current situation. The plan would then be the recommendations. If it is a proposal that involves buying something, you should have cost and benefits. Then you provide the details of how you are going to implement and also perhaps some statements about how you are going to follow up to know if you are successful. You are not actually going all the way to act because this, if approved, is going to lead to the actual PDCA cycle for executing what you have gotten approved.

The other A3 Stories

A3 Status Story Purpose

The third type of story – we are skipping over problem solving for now – is reporting on status. In the case of *Hoshin Kanri* (Chapter Seven), there is always a major review halfway through the year and a major end of year review, and that would be reported in the form of A3 status reports by each group.

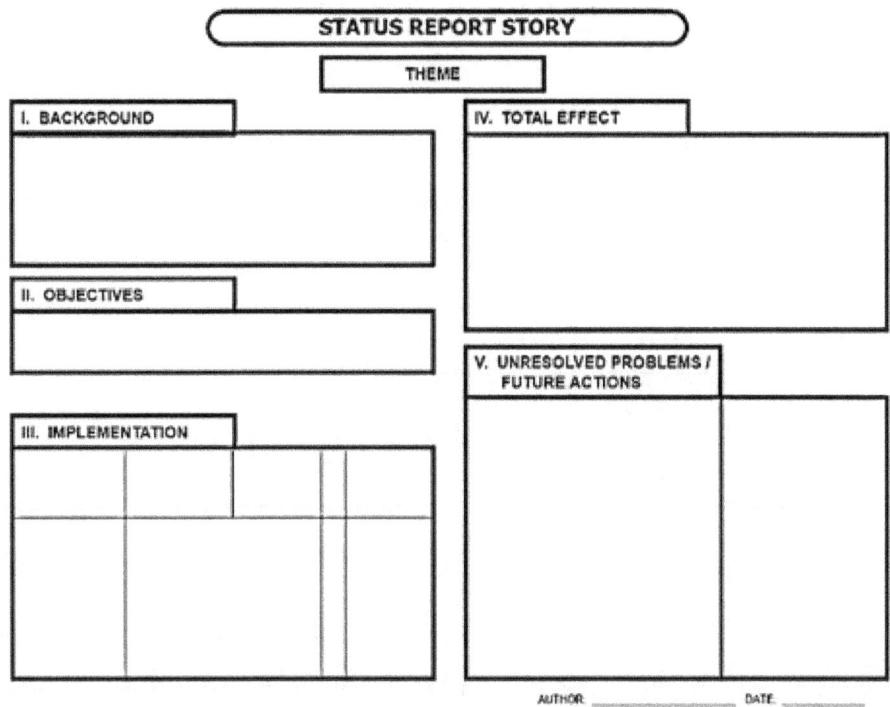

Source: Toyota Technical Center
Figure 2-30. The Status Type A3 Story

What it looks like might be something like this (see Figure 2-30). What is the theme of your status report? You need to give some background and what your objectives were and then how you are doing compared to those objectives. What is your status of implementation – or sometimes it can be as simple as either green on target, yellow I am not on target but I have plan to be on target, or red meaning we still have to find a countermeasure to get back on track. There may then be a bigger summary with graphs and charts of the total effect of what has been done up to this point and also unresolved problems, obstacles, that still have to be faced and where you are going next.

A3 Information Story Purpose

The information story is usually summarizing the current situation or some new information. You do not need to evaluate. You are trying to be conscious of the problem and make others conscious and share something that they might find useful in their work. For a technical information story, you might include something that looks like a problem solving process – what problem you are starting with and data that shows that it works and what are the conditions and boundaries – in that case, you are actually showing some analysis. Again, you have to ask yourself who is the audience. What is it I want to convey to this audience? How can I do it in the simplest way possible?

A3 Problem Solving Story

The problem-solving story is the most common (see Figure 2-31), and if we define problem solving as the core of Continuous Improvement and Respect for People, then the problem solving A3 supports that core.

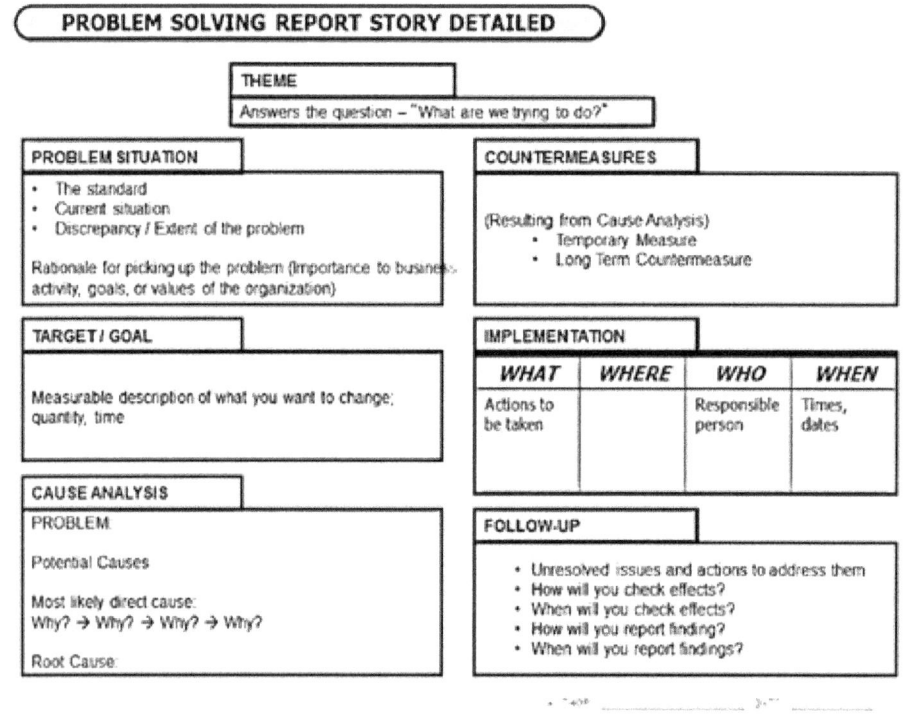

Source: Toyota Technical Center
Figure 2-31. The Problem Solving Report Story - Detailed

A3 Problem Solving Story Purpose

The purpose of an A3 problem-solving story is the purpose of problem solving itself. There is a plan, a goal, or standard, and we are not currently meeting it. On the other hand, we may be meeting the current standard, but we have been asked to set a new standard like the 60% reduction in warranty.

This is an example format – and I really want to emphasize this – for the problem solving case. It is pretty high level and you could probably fit almost any good PDCA process into these boxes. For example, you could fit the Toyota Business Practice eight steps into these six boxes.

As you go through your problem solving approach, we are going to be very flexible. If you have a standard approach in your company use it unless there is some inherent weakness because it is missing something in this process. You need to have a definition of the problem and you need to have a target or goal that you are trying to reach. You have to do a cause analysis. You have to come up with countermeasures and it should be more than one countermeasure. If there is some way that you use to prioritize, you should have that prioritization in the report. Why is it that you picked the countermeasures, or countermeasure, you picked to trial? You need an implementation plan and you need to follow up. You see that the plan goes all the way through the countermeasures. Then the doing is the implementation, and the follow up is the checking and acting. This particular report format assumes you have not yet done the check, but the report could include the results from the check. It is also fine to make eight boxes following Toyota Business Practices. The number of boxes is not as important as the acid test; am I really following the entire Plan-Do-Check-Act process?

In each of the boxes there is some detail provided. Once again, this is not the be all and end all to what every single report should look like, but it gives you some guidelines. By looking at the theme, the problem statement, the top description of the problem, I should understand what you are trying to do. For the problem situation, I should know what the standard is that you want to achieve and I should know the current situation. I should know the discrepancy, the gap, and I should know the rationale for why you picked this particular problem.

When you state the target I should know what is going to change, the quantity, and by when. In the root cause analysis, I should understand the point of cause – where you found the cause to occur – and how you drilled down, what methods you used. If it is 5 why, it is 5 why. I should see the 5 why analysis and what you believe may be the root cause. Then for the countermeasures, I should understand if there was a temporary containment measure that should be reported. Then what are the longer-term countermeasures going to be that you will be testing? The action plan, schedule, of who, what, where, when and then the follow up of this – the checks and the actions. Again, I am not pushing this in saying that you need to follow this format, but if you go through these questions and you say, "You know our current method really does not do a great job of stating the gap, or identifying the root cause," then you can add that to your A3 reporting method. You do not have to throw it out, but you can add whatever you are missing.

A3 Problem Solving Manufacturing Story

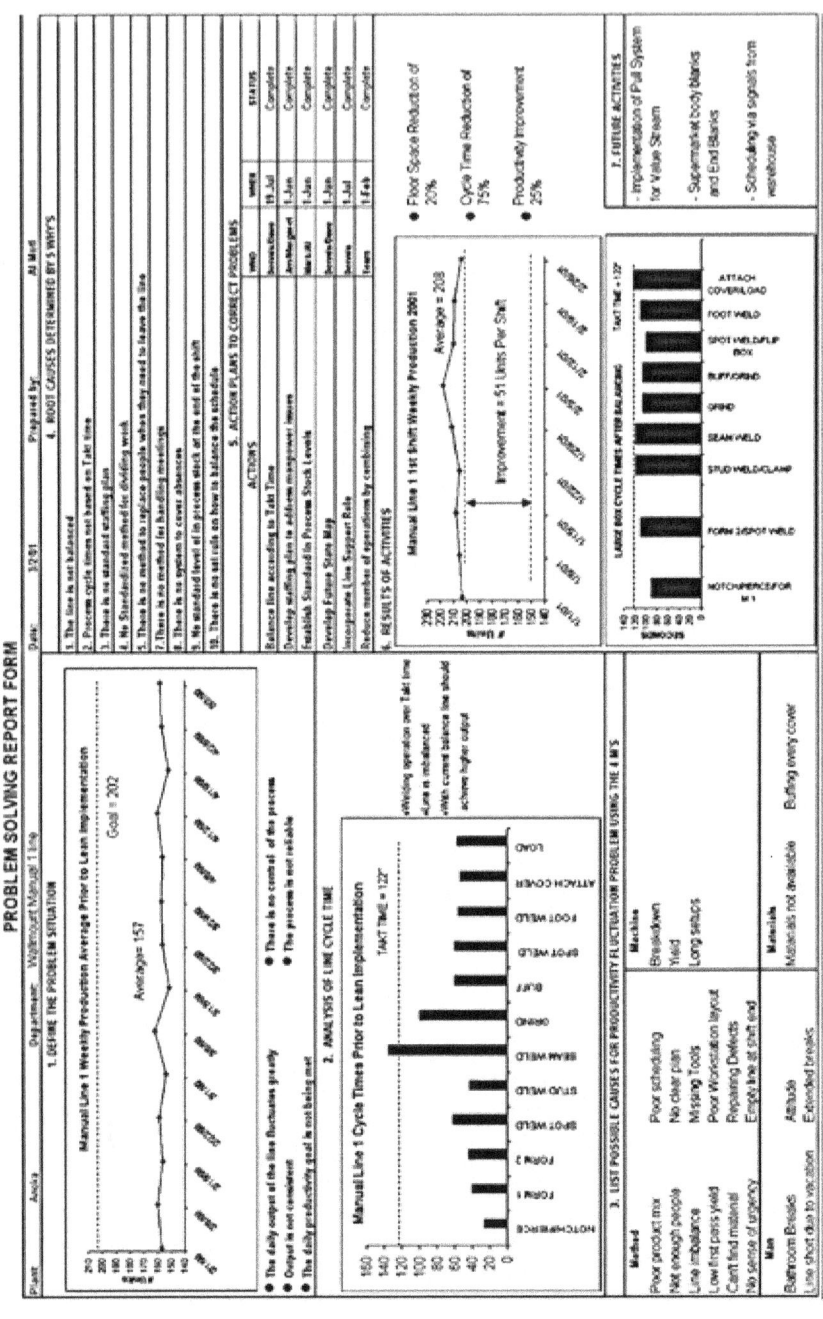

Source: David Meier
Figure 2-32. A3 Problem Solving Story – A Manufacturing Story

This is one example from a manufacturing plant that we discuss in great detail in *The Toyota Way Fieldbook* (see Figure 2-32). It is something my coauthor, David Meier, worked on at an auto parts supplier. The problem was that they were not making the schedule. They were under-producing consistently. To understand the cause, one tool they used was a work balance chart. They looked across the different processes and measured how long they actually took for a cycle and immediately it became apparent that compared to the Takt, compared to the desired output, they had bottlenecks and they also had some processes that were under loaded.

In this case, they went further in the analysis of root causes and looked at the methods, man, machine, and materials. They used the 4Ms. Some have 5Ms. The point of this is to broaden your look. You might only focus on the machines and forget that there are people involved or forget that there are materials, and if the materials are out of spec, then that is going to stop production. They wanted to get a broader look of a wide variety of possible causes before they zoomed in on the causes they would focus on. The countermeasures are in the action plan which shows who is going to experiment with each and by when.

Then you see the results. There is a direct correspondence between the problem statement-analysis of causes and the way the results are presented. We were not meeting production. Now we are regularly meeting production. There was an imbalance in the workload, and now the work has been rebalanced. There are no bottlenecks, and all the people are fully loaded.

We have eliminated a lot of waste and there are fewer people needed for this process. Then, there is also a set of future activities. This is a nice problem solving A3. In manufacturing, you can often be more precise about your measurement than in an engineering process where the work is less routine.

One thing you might notice is that this particular A3 was done on a computer. It was done in Power Point™, and you might have heard you should use paper and pencil. Why use pencil? This is so you can erase. This is a story that is unfolding and you are actually writing the story as you are living it. The early stage of this was done by paper and pencil and, for purposes of sharing it; they decided to put it in PowerPoint™. If you look at the A3s in Toyota they are often in Power Point™ or Excel™, but they all started with writing things down on paper. Maybe some use a pen and cross things out, but the story is documented live as it is occurring box-by-box. This might be done on a blown up version on the wall and later shrunk down to A3 size.

What is happening is that we first define the problem we are going to work on, and you might show the data demonstrating that we are missing production. In this case, it is obvious that something has to be done. In other cases, it may be a proposal to improve efficiency through a new technology, and you have to get permission to even go ahead and do any analysis and check vendors. Your initial box is going to be challenged. Is this actually a problem today? Is it a problem that requires IT? What is the problem? If the problem is that we want to improve productivity, then state it that way and that leads to lots of different ways of improving productivity, not simply IT. If you are getting push back box by box, it is a good process. If you sit in front of a computer or you sit at home with paper and pencil and you write out the whole A3 then you are not living the story. You are not doing real problem solving. You are just report writing.

Example A3 Report to Create a Purchasing Card for Toyota Technical Center Personnel

This purchasing example (see Figure 2-33) illustrates it applies beyond manufacturing problems. This was an actual report later used for training purposes in the Toyota Technical Center and, in this case, they were trying to get approval for a purchasing credit card that employees could use for buying items that cost less than $500. You can imagine some of the proposals when you are dealing with the launch of a new product that might even involve major equipment costing hundreds of millions of dollars in scope, and then you have every employee asking if they can buy a stapler for a few dollars. That went through the same approval process as the several hundred million dollar piece of equipment.

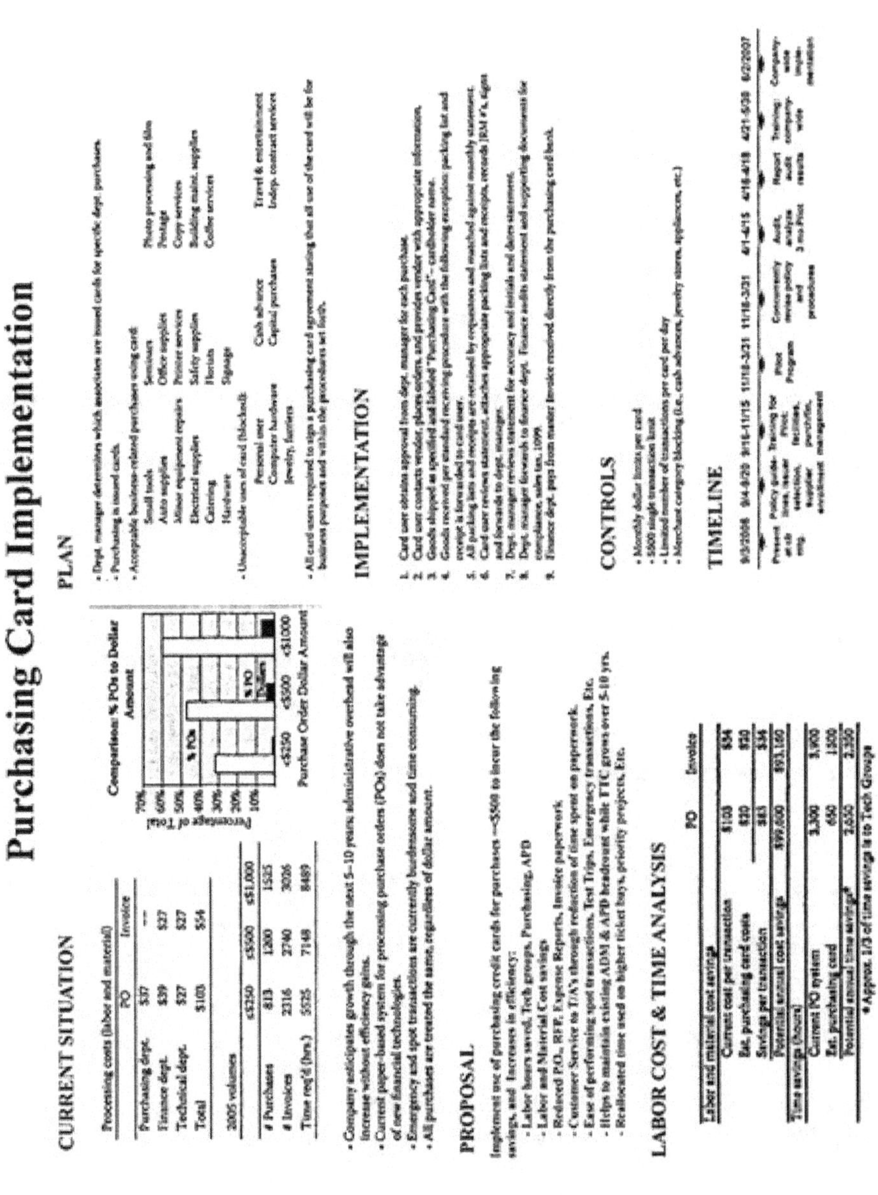

NORTHEAST GEORGIA HEALTH SYSTEM

Source: Toyota Technical Center

Figure 2-33. A3 Problem Solving Story – A Purchasing Card Implementation

Even though it seems overdone, the Toyota leaders at the time wanted to very tightly control costs. They stuck to their budgets very carefully unless there was a good reason to deviate, and they wanted a well thought through plan starting with the problem definition. The description of the problem uses a graph to show that the majority of purchases were actually very small, and they took most of the time for processing these small requests. They were tying up staff time. They were tying up purchasing time. It was waste. I should be able to just go out and buy that stapler if I need to. Then they go through how they are going to do that. They actually get to the point where they have the specific way the credit card will be implemented - the specific controls put in place where you cannot use the card to go out and have lunch or go to a bar. Then they have a timeline for implementation, and they did implement this purchasing card. It was well received, and it satisfied the people watching the budget, managers, and the employees.

A3 Problem Solving Story: Hand Injury Reduction

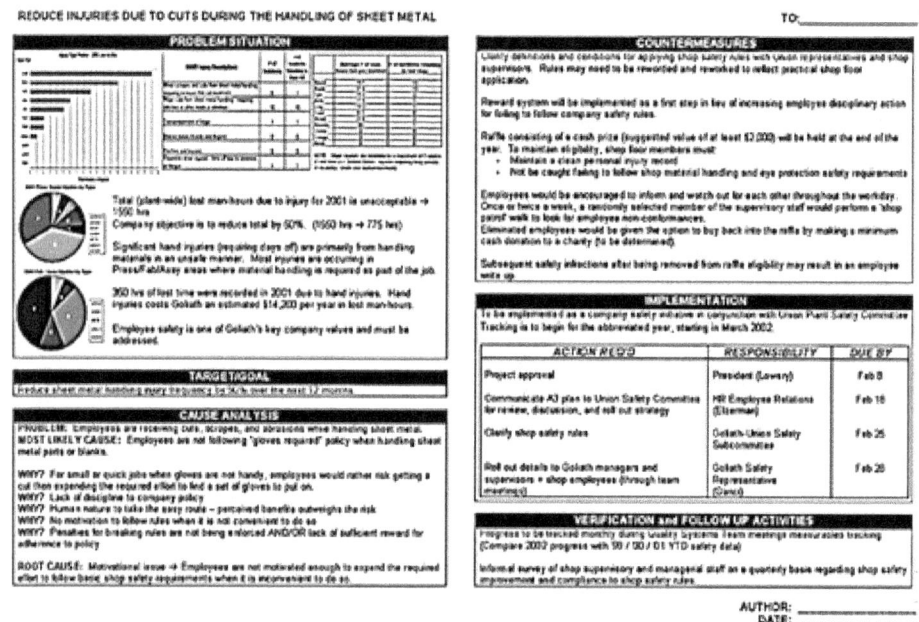

Figure 2-34. A3 Problem Solving Story – Another Manufacturing Story

Another type of A3 problem is a safety issue and the problem is how can we reduce injuries? (see Figure 2-34) This was another manufacturing example.

This manufacturing plant was stamping steel parts. There were many hand injuries – mainly cuts – when you are handling sharp sheet metal, and they document the kinds of problems they had and they show in a chart how many hours of production were lost due to injury (see Figure 2-35).

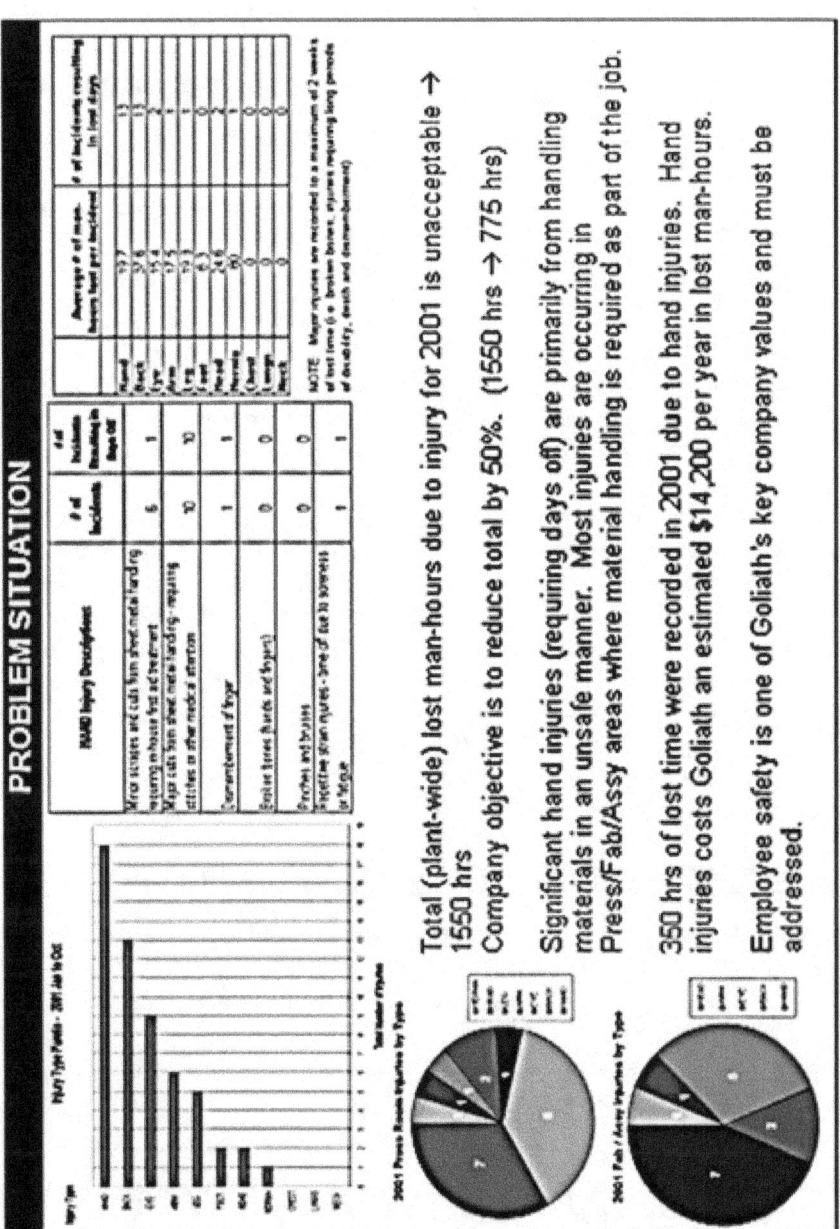

Figure 2-35. Reduced Hand Injury Report – Problem Situation

They then go into the target, which is to reduce the hand injury frequency by 90% over the next 12 months, which is pretty ambitious (see Figure 2-36).

TARGET/GOAL
Reduce sheet metal handling injury frequency by 90% over the next 12 months.

CAUSE ANALYSIS
PROBLEM: Employees are receiving cuts, scrapes, and abrasions while handling sheet metal. **MOST LIKELY CAUSE:** Employees are not following "gloves required" policy when handling sheet metal parts or blanks. **WHY?** For small or quick jobs when gloves are not handy, employees would rather risk getting a cut then expending the required effort to find a set of gloves to put on. **WHY?** Lack of discipline to company policy **WHY?** Human nature to take the easy route – perceived benefits outweighs the risk **WHY?** No motivation to follow rules when it is not convenient to do so **WHY?** Penalties for breaking rules are not being enforced AND/OR lack of sufficient reward for adherence to policy **ROOT CAUSE:** Motivational issue → Employees are not motivated enough to expend the required effort to follow basic shop safety requirements when it is inconvenient to do so.

Figure 2-36. Hand Injury Target/Goal and Cause Analysis

When they did their 5 why analysis this was one instance where answer to the final why was motivation of employees. Often we say the final why should not be a who – blaming somebody – but in this case they are not actually blaming an individual or blaming people for being lazy. They are saying there is really no motivation that is reinforced and built into the system for employees to put effort into following basic good safety practices that they already knew about. They really needed to make very clear what the problem was to employees and make very clear what the employees should be doing and why. This is defined in the countermeasures (see Figure 2-37), along with incentives, in this case including a cash prize, and then they have an implementation plan and they have not gone as far as to implement.

COUNTERMEASURES
Clarify definitions and conditions for applying shop safety rules with Union representatives and shop supervisors. Rules may need to be reworded and reworked to reflect practical shop floor application. Reward system will be implemented as a first step in lieu of increasing employee disciplinary action for failing to follow company safety rules. Raffle consisting of a cash prize (suggested value of at least $2,000) will be held at the end of the year. To maintain eligibility, shop floor members must: • Maintain a clean personal injury record • Not be caught failing to follow shop material handling and eye protection safety requirements Employees would be encouraged to inform and watch out for each other throughout the workday. Once or twice a week, a randomly selected member of the supervisory staff would perform a 'shop patrol' walk to look for employee non-conformances. Eliminated employees would be given the option to buy back into the raffle by making a minimum cash donation to a charity (to be determined). Subsequent safety infractions after being removed from raffle eligibility may result in an employee write up.

Figure 2-37. Hand Injury Countermeasures

In this case, we have a hybrid between a proposal story and a problem-solving story in that it proposes countermeasures, but did not go all the way to implementation. This is planning with a proposal, and then they would have to build on this to show perhaps a status story of how they are doing on implementation as they get closer to the 90 percent target (see Figure 2-38). In a sense, the report is not complete. To complete it they should have experimented with various countermeasures which would have allowed them to report on what they learned in the check and act stage. The assumed cause might not have been correct. The countermeasures they propose may or may not get them to the target.

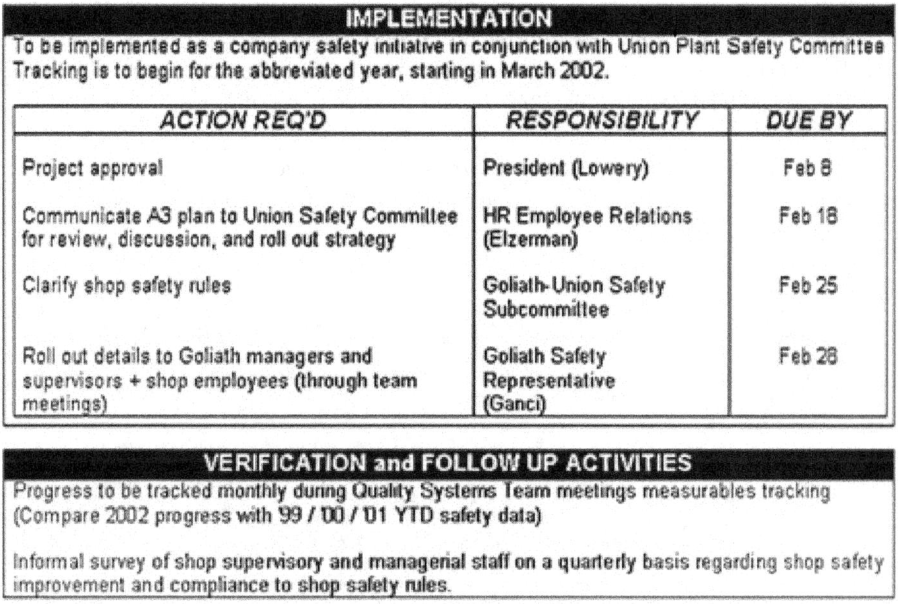

IMPLEMENTATION

To be implemented as a company safety initiative in conjunction with Union Plant Safety Committee Tracking is to begin for the abbreviated year, starting in March 2002.

ACTION REQ'D	RESPONSIBILITY	DUE BY
Project approval	President (Lowery)	Feb 8
Communicate A3 plan to Union Safety Committee for review, discussion, and roll out strategy	HR Employee Relations (Elzerman)	Feb 18
Clarify shop safety rules	Goliath-Union Safety Subcommittee	Feb 25
Roll out details to Goliath managers and supervisors + shop employees (through team meetings)	Goliath Safety Representative (Ganci)	Feb 28

VERIFICATION and FOLLOW UP ACTIVITIES

Progress to be tracked monthly during Quality Systems Team meetings measurables tracking (Compare 2002 progress with '99 / '00 / '01 YTD safety data)

Informal survey of shop supervisory and managerial staff on a quarterly basis regarding shop safety improvement and compliance to shop safety rules.

Figure 2-38. Hand Injury Countermeasure Implementation, Verification and Follow-up

This is a good opportunity to talk about the idea of spread everywhere. In this case, this was done in a manufacturing plant. I happen to know this case and it was in the Detroit area. It was within a culture where employees are used to the idea that if I do something positive that management requests I should get some money for it. Money was the currency for motivation. Within Toyota plants, they usually try to avoid giving out money. They might even give awards for departments that have particularly good safety records and there might be platinum, gold, silver awards and gifts that they bought and you can pick from different tables. They try to avoid developing a culture in which I will not do anything, even if it is the right thing to do for my own safety, unless I am getting money. In this particular Detroit-area culture, they thought of holding a raffle. It was not everybody being paid every time they did something in safety, but there was a raffle and a significant award if you were selected and it made sense to them in their culture. It seemed to help in this Detroit-area example, but that does not mean other companies with different cultures should copy their solutions.

The Improvement *Kata*, Another Approach

We refer at various points to Mike Rother's *Toyota Kata*. The term *kata*, often used in the martial arts, means a routine or habit. We want people to develop good habits for improvement that include full PDCA. We will not go into great detail about this systematic approach to pursuing objectives as it is well detailed in his book and in a handbook being developed. Follow the link to the handbook. (http://www-personal.umich.edu/~mrother/Homepage.html). We do want to summarize some major differences between the Improvement *Kata* and the A3 approach discussed in this chapter. In fact, a group of us developed a slide share to address this very issue (http://www.slideshare.net/mike734/a3-and-the-improvement-*kata*).

The starting point of the Improvement *Kata* is the recognition that there are simply too many problems that can sap our limited time and attention and chasing problems is a loser's battle (see Figure 2-39).

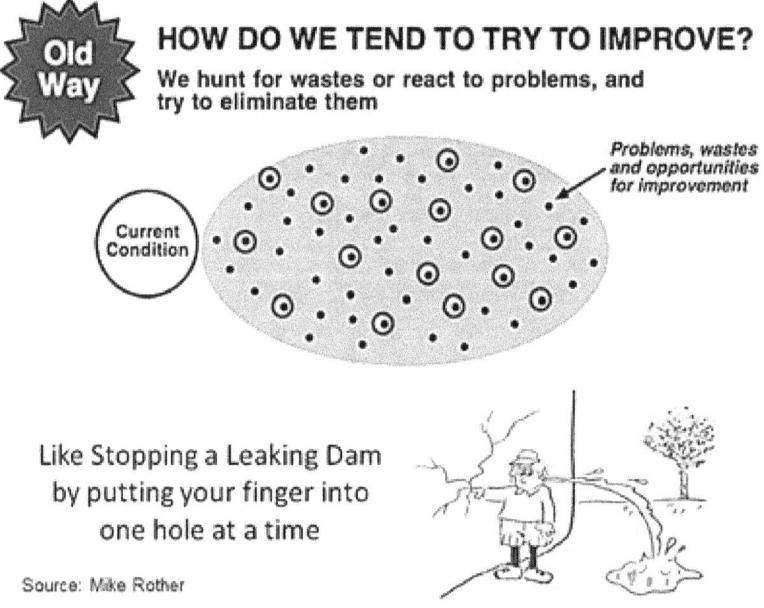

Figure 2-39: Hunting for wastes and reacting to problems is a losing battle

When we study carefully what Toyota sensei teach and how they teach they always start with a challenge that provides direction to the improvement effort (see Figure 2-40). Then they guide the student to try things through PDCA that are always aimed at the target. Notice that many wastes are intentionally ignored to focus attention on reaching the target. It is like putting blinders on a horse so it does not get distracted. Also note, we do not know how to reach the target. There is uncertainty and we must experiment to learn our way to the target. A focused search through experimentation will lead you to achieve the next target condition, which will lead to meeting a defined challenge.

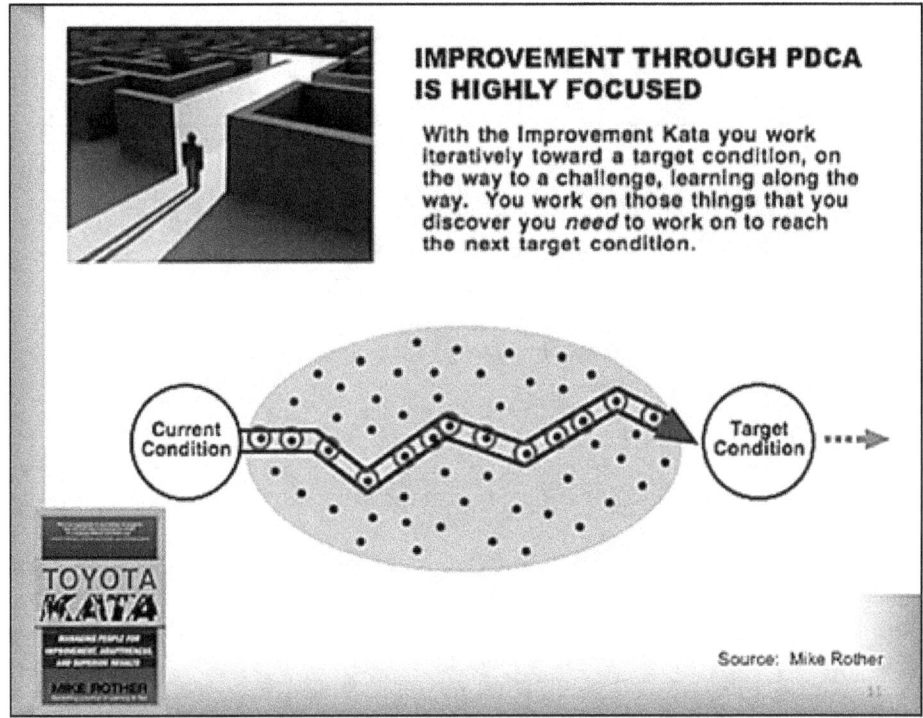

Figure 2-40: The Improvement Kata is focused Experimentation toward a defined target condition

THE STEPS OF THE IMPROVEMENT KATA

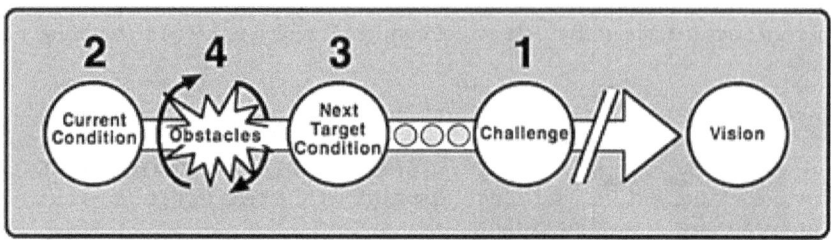

Step 1: In consideration of a direction or <u>challenge</u>...
Step 2: Grasp the <u>current condition</u>.
Step 3: Define the next <u>target condition</u>.
Step 4: Move toward that target condition iteratively, which uncovers <u>obstacles</u> that <u>need</u> to be worked on.

© Mike Rother

Figure 2-41: The Four Steps of the Improvement Kata

The four steps of the improvement *kata* are simplified compared to Toyota Business Practices, though there is clear overlap (see figure 2-41). We start with the challenge that is typically 1-3 years out and is in measureable terms. The challenge should support the business strategy. We break down the challenge into specific process characteristics (target conditions) that we believe will move us in the direction of the challenge, typically these are 2-6 week target conditions. These are process patterns we are trying to achieve that we believe will move the needle on the output indicator. Thus, we are forming a hypothesis that if we work like this or the process works like that we will as a result see improvements on the results indicator.

One controversial part of this process is the choice of the word "obstacles" instead of "root cause analysis." Mike has observed many organizations struggling to find THE root cause and wasting precious time that could be used experimenting at the *gemba* to test our assumptions. Thus, he suggests identifying obstacles to get to our short-term target condition and testing countermeasures we believe may overcome each obstacle. The experimentation will reveal the root cause or causes.

Toyota *Kata* distinguishes between the learner who is leading the improvement project and the coach who is guiding the learner. The learner uses a storyboard that documents the four steps of the process (see Figure 2-42). The Learner leading the improvement project records what is happening in real time on a storyboard in a standard format using the kata exactly under the guidance of a coach.

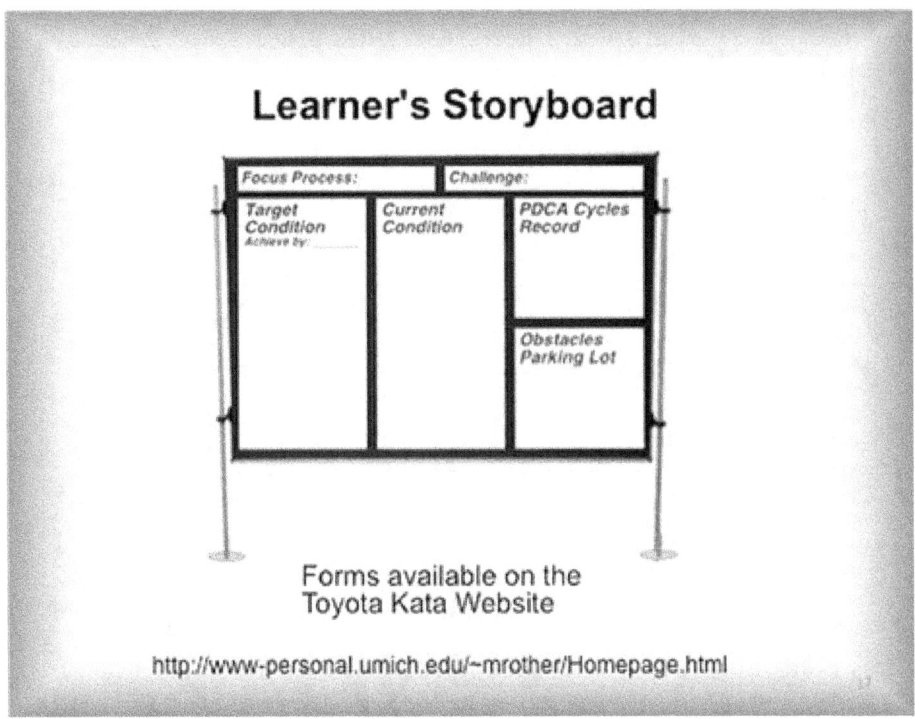

Figure 2-42: The Storyboard for Coaching the Learner of the Improvement Kata

Some organizations committed to A3 story telling have struggled with how to integrate the improvement *kata* with A3. This can be done and it is useful to think of the A3 as a snapshot summary of the more detailed live information generated on the learner's storyboard (see Figure 2-43). The Check and Act steps of the A3 can be at key milestones to reflect on what has happened so far and where we need to go next.

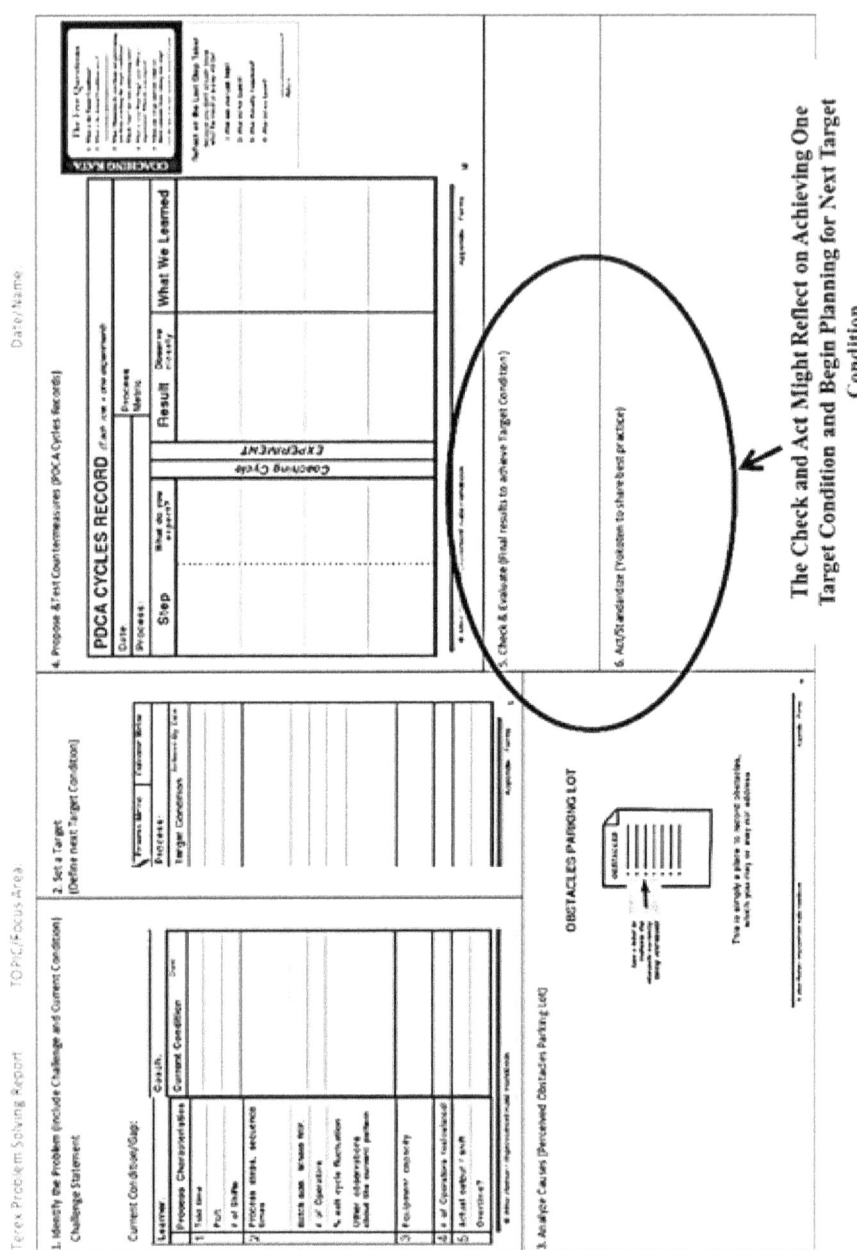

Source: Example by Jenny Snow-Boscolo

Figure 2-43: The A3 and the Improvement *Kata* can work together

Toyota *Kata* is not intended to replace the Toyota Way philosophy but rather to develop a practical methodology to turn what is intended into actual behavior. It is designed to break down the improvement process into smaller steps that can be deliberately practiced like learning any complex skill. You would not study a Mozart concerto in order to begin to learn violin, as a beginner. You would start with learning how to use the bow perhaps. You would have a teacher there guiding you on proper technique. You would take regular lessons and practice every day to develop positive routines for playing the instrument and for practice to get better. As you learn the basics, you do not have to focus on the *kata* of the basics and can focus on higher-level skills like interpreting the music. It may be that jumping into Toyota Business Practices and the high level steps of the A3 are too advanced for beginners who do not have daily coaching in an established improvement culture like that of Toyota. In any case, the philosophy of PDCA, breaking down a big challenge into smaller steps, doing something every day, having guidance from a coach, and learning through successfully difficult challenges is common to Toyota *Kata* and the Toyota Way.

Lean Leaders Strive for Continuous Improvement

In summary, Continuous Improvement means that improvement is continuous. It is not a one shot solution that you implement. When David Meier, my coauthor of *The Toyota Way Fieldbook*, and I were finishing up the field book he sent me this diagram (see Figure 2-44), and he said, "Jeff, we have to include this someplace because this is really the way I learned Continuous Improvement from my sensei in Toyota."

Source: *The Toyota Way Fieldbook*
Figure 2-44. Climbing the Stairs Daily

David was busy firefighting in the plastics department as a group leader and not finding time for *kaizen*. His sensei called him to a white board and drew a stair step, and then he drew a stick figure of a person. He said, "You are now here and you can only see this far into the future. You need to do *kaizen* every day, and as you do that, you will start climbing these stair steps. At each new step, you are going to see a broader horizon. You are going to see more problems that were invisible to you when you were at the bottom. Every day we move a little up. Some days it will be a big up." What he was emphasizing to David was do not wait until you get inspired for the perfect solution or you have solved all today's problems and have time left over. Until you make the time to take the first step, it will not be possible to see the next step.

This encompasses a philosophy of problem solving which says I need to know the direction I want to achieve. I need to have that true north. I need to have an explicit target that I am right now aiming toward and then I need to be comfortable accepting that I do not know how to get to that target. I do not have a map. I have to figure it out, and the way I am going to figure it out is one-step at a time… and the first step will start today.

That gives you a feeling of uncertainty where many people are uncomfortable. They want the plan. They want to know this is going to work before they start the journey, but with real creative problem solving you never know the future. You never know if it is going to work or whether it will be sustained. That is why you need drive and dedication. That is why you need Continuous Improvement and not a one-time improvement where you walk away. *Toyota Kata* by Mike Rother, provides practice routines to learn naturally how to follow PDCA, how to define a challenge, how to break it down into manageable pieces, and take another step every day.

This is the essence of Lean. Unfortunately, we have been duped into thinking the essence of Lean is copying Lean solutions that we see in Toyota plants. Those happen to be their countermeasures today for their problems which they know are going to change. What are your problems that you are going to work on? There are always problems. There are tens of thousands or maybe even millions. You have to prioritize what you will work on, develop a target that is meaningful, get consensus, get a team, but take responsibility for leading the effort and taking a step, then reflecting, and then taking another step. PDCA, PDCA, PDCA – that is the essence of Lean.

One of the most supportive statements David got from his sensei was, "David-san, do your best and just try something, and I will support you."

CHAPTER 3

STANDARDS, STANDARD WORK, AND VISUAL MANAGEMENT

Standard Work and Visual Management

In this chapter, we are going to talk about my favorite topic and also one of the more controversial topics in Lean, which is; the role of standardization and standard work. First, we will review the fundamental principles and the benefits of standards and standard work. We want to understand how it applies not only in manufacturing, but also in service processes. The service processes can be routine – say, a call center – or non-routine – like on-site sales calls. We are going to argue that Lean Leaders are responsible for leading development, checking, and improving standards and standard work. After this, we will define visual management as a key tool for leaders and team members to easily see the gap between the standard and actual condition—critical for continuous improvement.

The Philosophy of Standards and Continuous Improvement

The ideas collectively called The Toyota Way or Lean come from many different places. The Japanese were known as a nation of borrowers, and Toyota was very proud to borrow. They went beyond copying to understand the principle and then very carefully analyze how this principle or method fits within the system that they were building – the Toyota Production System.

Henry Ford was an important teacher and somebody from whom they borrowed a lot. Unfortunately, for decades, Ford Motor Company did not borrow much from Henry Ford. One of the wise observations from Henry Ford was about standardization, which, as you know, can lead to red tape, bureaucracy, endless books of procedures that nobody follows, and if you did follow them, you would never get any work done.

Henry Ford wrote, "Today's standardization is the necessary foundation for tomorrow's improvement." This is a profound statement. He is arguing that standardization is necessary (but not sufficient) for Continuous Improvement. Without standardization, you cannot have Continuous Improvement. He also said, "If you think of standardization as the best you know today, which can be improved tomorrow, then we are going to get some place. If you think of standards as confining, then progress is going to stop."

This comes from his book *Today and Tomorrow,* from 1926, but even today, in most organizations, we see standards being used in a confining way. We have bureaucratic departments with staff experts, and their job is to make up rules, rules, and more rules so other people can obey. They may not even go and check to see whether the rules are being followed, or what happens if somebody follows the rules, which could be disastrous. Departments of black belts who become keepers of rigid standards and then police these standards often run even six sigma, Lean, or lean six-sigma programs as bureaucracies.

So, why do we need standard work or standards at all? There is an old saying that "repetition is the mother of skill," and, by that, we mean that the way you develop any complex skill is through practice. When we practice enough to develop routines, we might not even have to think about it and then we will have consistency. We do not think every morning about how to tie our shoes.

Of course, we can develop consistency of bad habits or consistency of good habits and what we want to come out of standard work is consistency of good habits. That includes consistency of direction, so that whoever is doing the task has a clear understanding of the purpose of that task. We want consistency of performance. Whoever is doing that particular task is performing at a high level of quality and providing the outputs that we want which then gives us consistency of customer outcomes so we will consistently satisfy the customer.

Henry Ford also said, "What we end up with, when we have a standard, and then people follow that standard, and then we look at the standard, and we find that there is a better idea and we change the standard, now we have consistency of a better way, which leads to Continuous Improvement."

As we have argued throughout this book, the better ideas can come from many different places, but if the work group itself is not responsible for filtering, documenting, and instilling the better way into work standards there will be no consistency and there will not be continuous improvement.

Standard Work in Repetitive Tasks or Processes

If you walk into factories that have some experience with Lean, perhaps your own, you will often see posted by each workstation a standard worksheet (see Figure 3-1) that describes the way the person should do the job. This is one common kind of standard worksheet, and what we show is a list of the steps for that particular task. We also show the time it should take to do the work or the value adding tasks, and we show the time that it takes for walking, which in this case would be non-value added time, or waste. If a customer is paying someone to walk their dog, then walking could be value-added, but in most jobs it is waste.

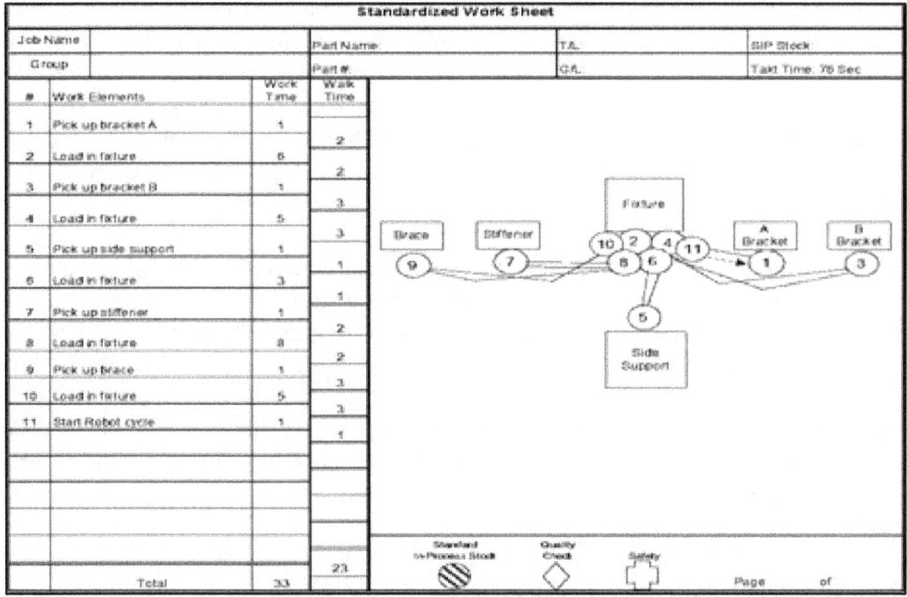

Figure 3-1. The Standard Work Sheet

Within this diagram (see Figure 3-2) is a portion that shows how the person should be moving in the current arrangement. This is also known as a spaghetti diagram. We can zoom in and isolate one person to determine how they move through one cycle of work. We could develop a spaghetti diagram to look at a document and at how it moves throughout your organization. We can map a person's movements through an office building as they are walking to the copy machine and to somebody's office and back to their office, and we could watch their pattern. For any pattern of movement of either a thing or a person, we can track it like this.

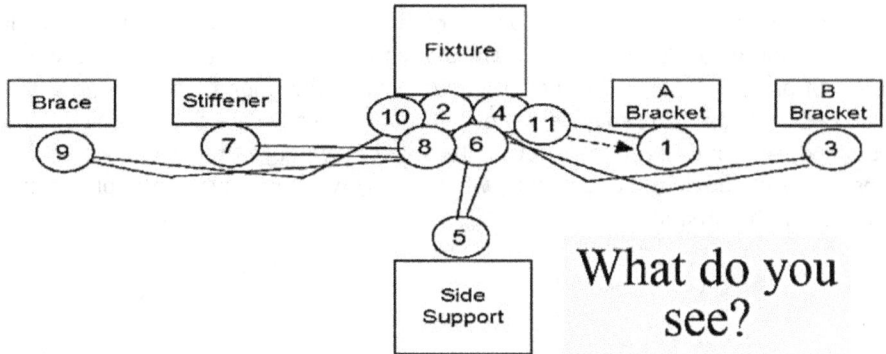

Figure 3-2. Work Flow Steps

In this case, we see this person going from machine to machine, and they tend to come back to that center machine and then they go out to another machine. What you would see in watching this person would be a lot of waste, and as you watched this walking pattern, you should ask yourself why they keep on walking away from the machine and back to that machine. Is there a way to reduce that walking? What this diagram is doing is making the waste visible. Then we can start coming up with ideas for improvement.

The one thing about this kind of standard work, which is for repetitive tasks, is that we can specify, with quite a bit of confidence that these steps have to be done. The best way to do them is in this sequence, and this is a pretty good estimate of how long it is going to take for each of these tasks.

We can add it up, and then we can say the total cycle time is the sum of the work tasks and the walking tasks, and we can compare that to customer demand and see how many people are needed to meet customer demand. This is very nice, but it is only feasible in the case of a repetitive task.

There is another document, that I will discuss a bit further in Chapter Six on work groups, called a job breakdown (or work element sheet), and in it we subdivide these steps into more microscopic sub-steps, and for each step we would ask, "How do we do this particular step in the best known way?" For example, if we are reaching to get a tool, should we use our right hand or our left hand? Is there a particular way of holding the tool so that we do not hurt our wrist? These tips would become key points for the operator and would be used in training. These more detailed steps, the key points, and the reasons why the key points are necessary become the basis for what is called job instruction training. This is summarized in our book *Toyota Culture* and explained in great detail in *Toyota Talent*.

Standard Work Document for non-cyclical Work

What do we do with work that does not have repeating steps within a cycle? Certainly, that would be the case in many of the tasks in the office. Perhaps we staple a bunch of pieces of paper together. Then we answer the phone. Then we go get the mail. Each of those tasks may be somewhat routine, but we are doing many different tasks and each one has its own set of steps and maybe even the sequence of doing those steps is not clear. For example, what we say when we answer the phone often depends on the situation.

Standard Work Instruction

Department	Operation Name		Revision Date:		
			Prepared by:		
No.	Major Steps			Key Points	
1					
2					
3					
4					
5					

Figure 3-3. Standard Work Document for Non-Cyclical Work

In that case, we have a standard work document (see Figure 3-3) for non-cyclical work that does not follow a repeating pattern, and we may not be able to specify the sequence of steps. We might show the steps in no particular sequence along with the key points. If you know the key points and you know the steps, you can now teach somebody and the standard now is; I have to make sure I do all these steps in this way. The order does not matter, but I have to do all these steps correctly or at least check all these items – and it could act as something like an airplane pilot's checklist. It may also be that one particular step does not apply to what I am doing so I can check the box "Does not apply" and the key points are going to be reminders – make sure you pay attention to this. When you use the stapler, for example, hold it at the base with your left hand and put consistent strong pressure pushing down with your right hand.

This is the lowest level of standard work where we just know we have to do these things and here is the best way we know, as of today, to do each of these steps. We could have a standard work document for answering the phone. There may be parts of that task that are repetitive and in a sequence that we ought to follow when a customer calls, like always introduce ourselves, always ask the customers a little bit about themselves, and there may be a few key questions. We still might have some information on paper or the computer to answer common questions they ask, but we do not want to go overboard and try to specify everything anybody might ever want to say or do. Rather, we want to specify the repeating parts and then key points in general for any task like this.

Two Types of Bureaucracy: Coercive and Enabling

There are other types of standards in addition to standard work. For example, a machined metal part might have a quality standard that indicates a hole has to have a certain diameter with a tolerance of plus or minus one millimeter. We might have a performance standard that each salesperson should be making at least 15 cold calls a day. Another standard may be a target for purchasing to reduce cost by 1% per quarter for the year.

There are various kinds of standards and we have organizations whose main job is to create standards. This is a part of what we call bureaucracy. When I talk to groups of people and ask, "Tell me the first words that come to your mind when I say bureaucracy," they answer rigid, red tape, top down, controlling, and waste of time.

Professor Paul Adler, at the University of Southern California, studied NUMMI; the now shuttered joint venture between Toyota and General Motors in California, because he heard about all the employee engagement of the Toyota Production System. He expected a flat organization with little bureaucracy and found the opposite. He was surprised to discover that there were standards for everything. You walk up to any given operator, you walk into the office, you go to engineering – posted all over the walls are various types of standards. The standard might be, for example, this is a good quality part. Here are five different ways that the part can be damaged causing a defect. It could be a standard work sheet. It could be a standard of how often and what steps you take for the preventative maintenance of a specific machine.

One might think, "These are a bunch of bureaucrats, and there are people in the office who are generating all this stuff." However, he found relatively few office staff and the standards were the responsibility of work groups on the shop floor led by two layers—team leaders and group leaders. Group leaders are the equivalent of first-line supervisors. Team leaders are hourly employees, but they have a leadership role. Working with the engineers, they were improving upon the standards as Henry Ford proposed. The standards often were initially developed by engineering or from some staff function as a first draft, and then the workgroups, with the approval of the group leader, had the right to change the standards and then test whether the changes actually improved the process.

He concluded, as Henry Ford proposed, that bureaucracy is not always confining. Bureaucracy can be the basis for improvement. But only if the rules, standards, and procedures *enable* people to better do their jobs and improve how they do their jobs. The problem was that, too often, we experience bad bureaucracy, which he called *coercive*, and bad bureaucracy includes rigid rules created and enforced by staff people who do not understand the work or how to engage the team members. Under coercive bureaucracy, managers monitor workers in order to highlight poor performance. They are looking for people to mess up. When you do not follow the standard, then the standards police come to threaten and even punish you to get you back in line. In the coercive bureaucracy, everyone is expected to follow the standard exactly, and deviations are punished. The assumption is that those credentialed people who came up with the standard sitting in their office know better than the people who are doing the work.

In an enabling bureaucracy, it is just the opposite. The assumption is that the people doing the work, and the people leading those doing the work, have the most detailed understanding of what is going on, and when there is a deviation from the standard, they are at the *gemba* to identify the problem and find the root cause. Why did this deviation occur? Why was this person late in getting their task done? They were late because they took too long. Why did they take too long? They took too long because they were not well trained. Why were they not well trained? They were not well trained because we do not have simple to understand standard work to train them to.

In coercive bureaucracy, specialists plan and monitor the standards so they are doing the thinking, and in enabling bureaucracy the standards are visible for everyone to see and the workgroup owns the standards, and the work group is expected to think about how to improve upon the standards. In Adler's words: "Coercive bureaucracy views standards as instructions to follow and not challenge, and you may want to do exactly the opposite and maybe you want people to be constantly challenging the standards." The standard then becomes what we might think of as a template, but we want people to question, challenge, think, and improve upon the standard.

Standards and Continuous Improvement

In summary, a standard, whether it is a particular target – for example, the number of calls per day or the percent customer satisfaction – or a standard work sheet, gives you your baseline, and then when we can regularly achieve that standard we should establish a new target that is more difficult. We had 80% customer satisfaction. Now we want 95% customer satisfaction. That is our new standard. The bar is now set higher (see Figure 3-4).

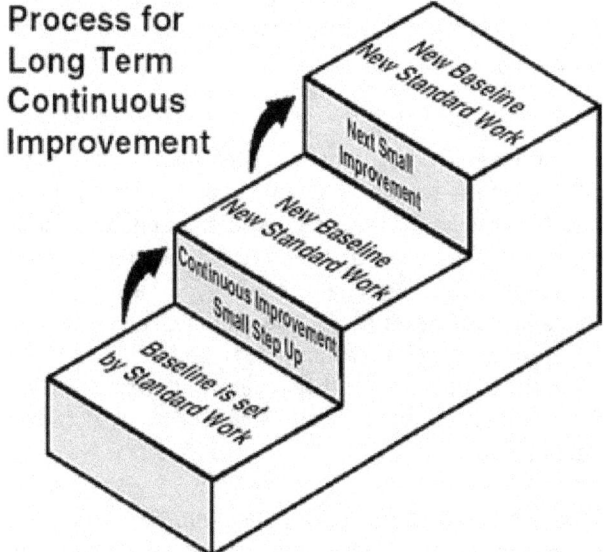

Figure 3-4. The Process for Long Term Continuous Improvement

To get to that new standard we have to make improvements, and we normally suggest not jumping say from 80% to 95% but take a smaller target like going from 80% to 81%

first. Then we take a step, and we check. Now we are at 81%. What did we learn and what are we going to do next to get to 82%? Through these steps toward a next target, which then becomes the new baseline, we will move toward the ultimate target of 95%.

This is what we mean by Continuous Improvement. It is everybody, every place, all the time looking at where they are compared to what the standard is calling for, and then that gap provides the aspiration to move forward in steps by trying things – experimenting with a countermeasure, checking if it worked, and then standardizing what works and moving on to the next experiment—repeated cycles of PDCA.

One of the problems we sometimes see in companies is they will set a standard – for example, an executive will tell the managers, "We want to get to 95%. Currently we are at 80%." It is announced, and then the managers will tell the supervisors, "Here is our target. This is what you need to get to." Then they go away, and the workgroups are just struggling. Even if they improve to 90%, they are going to be disappointed. They are going to be discouraged because they are not at 95%.

In enabling bureaucracy, we want active leadership. The Leader is actually there with the people. Their message is, "We need, by the end of the year, to get to 95%. We do not have to get there all at once. We do not even have to think about 95% right away. What we need to think about is a first step. What is the first thing we can do? Let us look at the data. Let us understand the deviations from the standard. Let's pick the biggest one, and let's understand why that problem occurs and come up with ideas for improvement, pick one, try it." This is the essence of the Improvement *Kata* (see Chapter Two).

They are leading a problem solving process systematically, and if they are effective leaders, they will engage the team. The team will always have good ideas, and some not so good ideas, but through persistent experimentation, iterating toward a target, you will see progress. Then you need to celebrate that progress as you are making it. It could be a big jump in a given week, and maybe you have a party to celebrate or maybe you get small gifts for everybody. The ultimate target of 95% should be out there, and the team knows, "we have a long way to go." You might even show how we are doing relative to the 95%. We are halfway there, and it is halfway through the year. Sometimes a thermometer or some other visual can be used to illustrate progress toward the final target.

By asking the right questions and motivating the team, they will take a step at a time and begin to make steady progress. When they try something that does not work that is as useful as trying something that does work. What did not work? As Thomas Edison would say when working to develop a functioning light bulb: "I have not failed. I've just found 10,000 ways that won't work." That learning philosophy needs to be nurtured.

Look for Gaps

What we are really saying is that standards provide a point of comparison. We can compare what we believe should be happening to what is actually happening. The difference is a Gap to be closed. The way a person should be doing work in many cases is unclear, and that is why people all use different approaches and we do not really see improvement except maybe at the individual level and individuals may not share what they learn.

Standard work becomes our theory about work – our theory about the best way we know today to do this particular work. We do not actually know that the standard work is perfect or the best way. In fact we assume there is always a better way. So, when we diverge from the standard work then we either have a problem, which could be that someone is not well trained, that the equipment does not work right, that the person who is providing you with input did not give you accurate information. There are many possible causes, and then we can work on fixing those. Alternatively, it may be that the deviation from the standard is a better way. In either case, what we have is an opportunity for improvement. Standard work is actually the basis for surfacing problems or gaps, which is then the basis for kaizen.

Develop People

Standard work is our theory about the best way to do a job – again, we may not specify every contingency or situation a person might face, but we know some basic things that everybody in that job should do. This is the way an accountant should handle receivables. We have some ideas about that and that encompasses our theory. If we document that theory, then we have a way to train people – training people to our standard work for that job. What we would like ideally is for everybody to follow that theory – that standard work – so that we can then see the problems that occur when you do it that way.

That allows us collectively to improve the process, and then at the same time, as we improve the process, we are becoming better Lean Leaders. We are getting better at spotting deviations. We are getting better at improving on the standard work. We are getting better at problem solving, and we are developing other people who are getting better. In addition to that, we have an obligation to share what we think might be useful to others in the company. We do not have a right to order other people in other work groups to follow what we have done, because what we have done might only fit our situation and they have to look at their situation and may have a better way. Yet, we have an obligation to at least share what we think is general knowledge potentially useful to others. Perhaps management will encourage others doing similar work to test our standards, and then come up with their own improvements.

True North is our Ultimate Standard

We discussed in Chapter One that the Toyota Way is one way to define True North. It gives Toyota values and standards for the right way to treat people and the right way to improve. True north is the direction we want to be heading and we can judge if we are on track toward that ideal, even though we cannot reach that ideal. As an example, we might define one aspect of True North for a customer service department as 100% of customer complaints are investigated at the customer, not by sitting in the office and speculating. We are actually going to determine the real problem, and find the root cause, which will then lead to solving the real problem. Ideally the problem should not come back and the perfect process will lead toward the perfect outcome—100% customer satisfaction.

Again, we will strive towards that ideal. We are not going to investigate 100% of customer complaints in our lifetime, and if we were to identify all customer complaints and go and see in every case, we might not in 100% of the cases get the root cause right, but it is something to which we can aspire.

As you learn from identifying customer complaints, and addressing the problems, you should reflect this in new standards or revisions of existing standards. If you do not create the standard, then whoever did that investigation will solve the problem in the short term, but in the long term when that person moves out of that position the problem will come back to haunt you again.

Lean's Core Leadership Model

Standard work and standards are an integral part of Lean Leadership. We are trying to visualize production in a factory or visualize the process in any other type of process compared to the standard (see Figure 3-5). This is the spirit of *genchi genbutsu*.

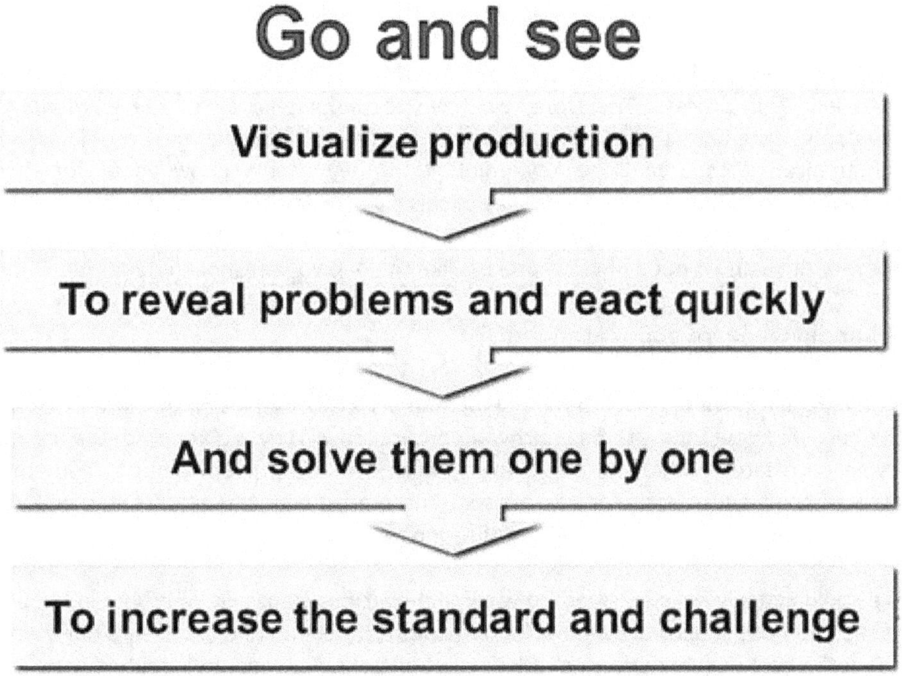

Go and see

- Visualize production
- To reveal problems and react quickly
- And solve them one by one
- To increase the standard and challenge

Source: Michael Balle

Figure 3-5. Visualize Actual vs Standard to solve problems one by one

The reason we want to visualize the current reality versus the standard is to reveal problems and react quickly. When we can quickly see the gap between the standard and the actual, then we can solve problems as they occur one by one instead of letting problems accumulate in problem buffers.

For example, we might look at the last months' data – what happened in the last month? All sorts of things. On the surface, we know that this kind of problem occurred a number of times, but we do not know the situation in each case where that problem occurred. Imagine a detective getting to the scene of a crime one month after the crime. Now if we solve those same problems as they occur, we know in detail that actual situation—the facts. By the end of the month, we have solved the problems, and then perhaps we reflect on that month and ask which of our problems and countermeasures we should share with others.

Doing this will helps us achieve a more consistent repeatable process operating at a new level. We used to have 80% customer satisfaction. That means 20% of the time people were not happy. We have achieved 95%, which still means 5% of your customers are not happy. Now it is time to set a new standard, perhaps 99% customer satisfaction.

The new standard is going to require PDCA cycles all over again. We need to visualize where we are compared to the standard. We need to solve problems. We need to come to a new level of consistent, stable performance, and the Lean Leadership model is to lead this process. Therefore, we have to understand all of the elements of developing standards and visualizing standards, of solving the problems, of communicating to others the key points that they should know about for their improvement efforts. In the second part of this chapter, we are going to talk a lot more about visualization – how we actually visualize the process even when that process is not repetitive and is not a physical process like the one you see in manufacturing.

What did we learn about Standards?

Reflecting back, we began with Henry Ford and his wise observation that standards are the best we know today, to be improved on tomorrow. They are not rigid. We are not trying to create robots. We are trying to create thinking people, but give them a starting point and a basis for comparison. There are many standards. They could be policies, procedures and technical specifications.

We could actually develop standard work that specifies steps and what should happen in each of those steps and even timing of those steps. Standard work itself is our theory about the best way to perform a task or a set of tasks. For repetitive, routine tasks, we can specify in a lot of detail the steps, the sequence, the time that it should take, and the key points. For non-repeating tasks, we have to be more modest. There may be certain aspects of the non-repeating tasks that are highly routine and then we can create standard work sheets for those parts. For non-routine parts, we can still identify the necessary steps and key points, which can be the basis for a checklist and for training people.

Standards can be treated very rigidly and become part of a coercive bureaucracy, or they can be used flexibly, as guidelines, and turned over to the team to improve upon. We call that enabling bureaucracy. There is bad bureaucracy, that which we call coercive, and there is good bureaucracy, which we call enabling. We have to get past the point where we think that bureaucracy is always bad…or that standardization is always good.

It can become meaningless rules, but it does not have to be. What then is the alternative? Is anarchy good and bureaucracy bad? Paul Adler taught that we need bureaucracy, but there is a certain way of using rules and standards and procedures, which leads to learning and Continuous Improvement. Enabling bureaucracy depends heavily on leadership at the *gemba* to maintain discipline to the standards and lead improvement of the standards. In addition, this means you cannot have too large a group reporting to one leader, hence the addition of the team leader role at Toyota discussed in detail in Chapter Six.

Standards for a team that is trying to improve their process will be most effective when they are visual – when we can see whether we are in standard or out of standard. That will be the subject of the remainder of this chapter. If we see something that is out of standard, it is not necessarily a reason to panic, but it is an opportunity to close another gap and improve the process.

Finally, there is a set of procedures that you can use so that even your own work as a leader can have some degree of standardization. That is, there are certain things you as a leader do that are routine, and your whole day does not have to be set just by the meetings you have. You can have certain routines, and the routines that really should be focused on are the things that you might naturally not do in favor of firefighting.

For example, we know that you should go and see and check how people are doing, whether the standards are being followed, and where there are deviations you should be a coach. That is something that is easy to forget about as the day goes on so if we actually standardize that part of going and seeing and coaching – what is now called Leadership Standard Work – then we can actually schedule it and make sure it happens. This is a topic in Chapter Six on supporting daily improvement.

In summary, standards can be confining, red tape, cause inefficiencies, and make work unpleasant. On the other hand, standards can be useful, enabling, and actually improve the pleasure of doing your work. Now that may sound odd that we have rules and procedures that make it more pleasurable. We are going to discuss in the second part of this chapter a case called, Menlo Innovations, that develops software, and their mission statement is to create joy in the world and joy in their workplace and they do it through a great deal of enabling bureaucracy—clear and visible processes for defining requirements and developing software.

Visual Management to See the Gaps: Standard vs Actual

Visual management builds on what we talked about as standard work, standards, standard processes, targets, target conditions, by bringing to life otherwise lifeless information that is stuck around the office – posters, files, boards with information, and even computer displays. Workplaces are full are visuals, and sometimes people stop and read them and then they go back to work.

Visual management – as compared to visuals – is what you actually use to help guide your work. To clearly show what you should be doing now and the gap, if any, between what you should be doing and what you are doing. Imagine somebody standing in front of a job board and then tearing off the slip of paper with the phone number to store away in a pocket for later. Then it is back to work and that transaction had nothing to do with performing their work.

Figure 3-6. The Traffic Light

Visual management is live and is a part of your work. A traffic light is a great example. The traffic light (see Figure 3-6) is something that we have all learned to use as part of the work of driving. When we see a light we do not have to pull out a manual to understand what green, yellow, and red mean, and we know exactly what we are supposed to do. Whether or not we follow the rules, we know that red means you stop and green means you can go and yellow means go quick before it turns red (just kidding!). At a glance, we know what we should be doing.

Look at something like a well-designed machine gauge color coded with green, yellow, and red, and you can probably guess that trending toward the red is bad. It is right on the borderline of being red and that means the machine is on the verge of having a problem—perhaps the fluid level is low. Again, you look at it at a glance and you know the status of the machine.

You look at a graph and let us say that green is the target for something - it could be sales, it could be profit – and red is the actual. You could very clearly see whether actual is running ahead of the plan or running behind the plan.

These are all good examples of visual management. They become visual management when you are using them to pace your work, using them to know when action is needed, using them as targets for improvement. As a Lean Leader, your job is to be sure that there are useful visuals that are being used on a daily basis to help you pace the work. They help you know whether the work is high quality, whether you are in control, whether you are giving your customer what they want in the amount they want when they want it.

There are very simple components of good visual management. Can you by looking at the visual tell whether you are in a normal or abnormal situation at a glance? We have to define normal, and normal is what we talked about as the standard. Abnormal means there is a gap between the standard and the actual. If I can see that gap, then I can take action. The faster I see that gap, the quicker I take action.

Figure 3-7. The Office Workplace without 5S

Consider the office workplace in the photo (see Figure 3-7). What is standard and what is out of standard? Can we tell at a glance? Actually, this is not a bad office environment. The desk seems reasonably organized. A visual board shows something about what we are working on with color-coded post its. Perhaps that is clear to the person who works in the office, but there is a lot of other information on the bulletin board. There are many items on the desk. Certainly, a leader walking through the office would have a hard time telling what is in standard or out of standard.

Figure 3-8. The Office Workplace with 5S

Now what about the same office (see Figure 3.8) above? A 5S workshop was done and there is a place for everything and everything in its place. When we say there is a place for everything, this means we have standards. We know where the phone goes. We know where the folders go. There may be a set of folders for what is coming in and a set of folders for what is going out, and we may even have a certain number of spaces for the folders so we know that if we get more than five folders coming in, we are on overload and we need some extra help. That can be a visual that sets a cap on the amount of work-in-process inventory.

Michael Ballé in *The Lean Manager* defines this well– "Visual management is about *seeing* together, so we *know* together, so we can *act* together, from the operator to the CEO." We have highlighted seeing, knowing, and acting, but the word that keeps popping up is together.

This becomes a collaborative process in which it is clear to all team members and leaders what is in standard, what is out of standard – are we ahead? Are we behind? – And then we can find a course of action if we are out of standard. The course of action should be solving the problem at the root cause so this directly connects to the Continuous Improvement process.

A Non-traditional Lean Case: Menlo Innovations

Visual management is most useful when we break down the work – for example, in an office process – into small pieces, and then it can be an aid to creating flow to the work, even in non-repetitive work outside a factory. Menlo Innovations develops custom-software—knowledge work—which would seem impossible to pace with any rigor (as described in the book *Joy, Inc.* by CEO Richard Sheridan). This is a creative design process, yet they have created a way to use collaboration and teamwork so that the programmers – the people who create the code – know whether they are ahead or behind every hour of the day, sometimes two hours, sometimes three or four hours. They have defined small chunks of work, which immediately makes you think of a regimented process, and we begin to imagine software developers as demoralized slaves to a clock.

The goal of the company is exactly the opposite. The goal is to make software design and development a joyful experience, for all team members and for the customer. This is right in the mission statement. To achieve this joy, the leaders of the company fundamentally changed the way software design is being done.

Menlo Innovations is a small company in the town I live in – Ann Arbor, Michigan. They were created in 2001 and the mission is "returning joy to one of the most unique endeavors in our history and that is inventing software." They also state what they are trying to avoid, "ending human suffering in the world as it relates to technology." You can see that their evaluation of normal practice in software development is pretty dire.

The CEO and one of the founders, Richard Sheridan, talks about his past experiences in software companies. Every day he was losing a little bit more enthusiasm and energy and he wanted the experience of his new company Menlo Innovations to actually bring something positive to people, to enrich their lives, to develop them to build energy.

His inspirations included the Edison Invention Factory, originally in Menlo, New Jersey, hence the name Menlo Innovations. There is a book called *Extreme Programming, which* is a manifesto for a radical approach to software development, consistent with many Lean principles. He learned a lot from the author of that book and also from Peter Senge's *The Learning Organization* about systems thinking. Systems thinking allowed him to look at the bigger picture and then zoom in and see the details and for everybody in the organization to learn together.

In Menlo's case, they learn *with* the customer. They have roughly 40 employees and subcontractors. They have been expanding year after year. They are very selective about the people they hire and even about the customers they will accept. They want to hire people who will fit the culture, who will be capable of collaboration, and who are excited about learning. Customers are required to be heavily involved in the development process.

Collaboration at Menlo

Let us tour Menlo. The first image is a big picture view of a day at work in their original building they grew out of (see Figure 3-9). What do you see when you look at this office environment? Does it look like what you might expect from a software development factory? Do you see isolated individuals or do you see collaboration?

Figure 3-9. The Menlo Environment

Typically, when I have walked through software development environments I see individuals sitting in front of their computers in dark cubicles. You want to leave them alone to work and not distract them. They have their faces focused on the computer and they are doing something or other, but as long as they are busy, it seems as though they are productive. Different people are working on different parts of the software, and those pieces may or may not work together. Richard understands why collaboration is so critical, not only in software development, but in general in the world we are living in that is increasingly based on knowledge, knowledge sharing, and learning at a faster pace than your competitors.

Does collaboration look like chaos or does it look like structured teamwork? If you did not know anything about what Menlo is doing and their Lean processes, you may think their office looks like chaos. You have people standing around. You have two people looking at a computer screen. Why do you need two people? Why not just one person? They look contemplative. Does that mean that they are thinking about their programming or are they thinking about some problem they have at home? This may look like a disorderly environment because there are no cubicles, because people are in groups. What you are actually seeing are pairs of people intensely focused on creating computer code based on very clear instructions. The instructions specify what the customer needs and there is constant self-checking of the quality of the code as it is being developed. Richard explains:

> "It is a requirement now of our industry that teams of people work together to a common purpose. We know of no better way to do that than to create an entire culture of collaboration. Everything you see here – the way the space is organized, the way the individuals are organized, the way the teams are put together, the way the tables are all pushed together – everything about the way we work is to encourage collaboration and the most effective kind of communication – not meetings, not emails, not status reports – but rather face-to-face communication. We like to refer to this as high-speed voice technology."

Richard is talking about a culture of collaboration that he and his partners intentionally built at Menlo Innovations. By intentionally I mean they thought a lot about what kind of culture they wanted and very deliberately worked to evolve that culture. They had both experienced cultures they did not want, and Richard had an earlier opportunity to try out and experiment with changing the culture in a larger software development organization as vice president. So, with that experience, and with some really smart partners, they started to develop their image of what a joyful, collaborative work experience would look like that gives the customers what they need every time.

The Overall Menlo Process

Let us start with a simplified overview of the process that Menlo uses (see Figure 3-10), and then I will talk about each step of this process. The process starts with the customer, as any Lean process should. What does the customer want? What does the customer need? What they want is not necessarily, what they need. As Henry Ford once quipped: "If I asked customers what they wanted they would have said a faster horse." Menlo Innovations created a new role they call "technical anthropologists."

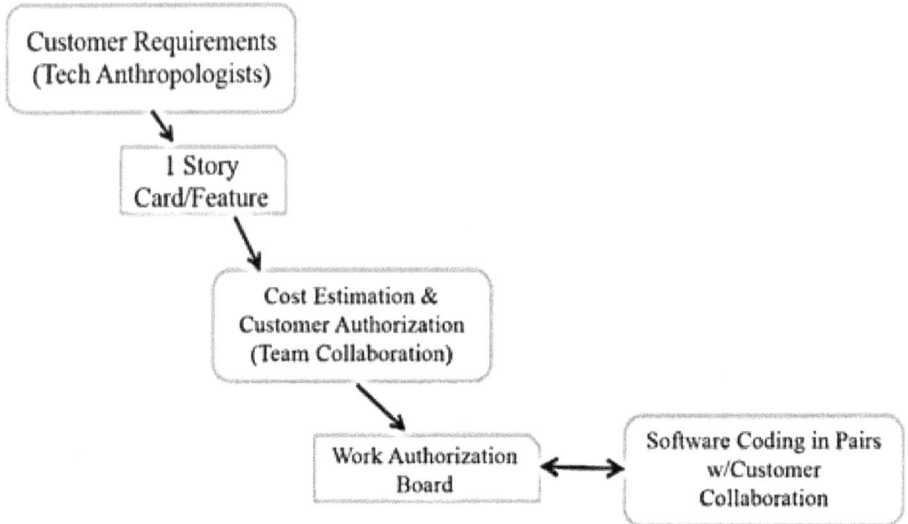

Figure 3-10. The Overall Process

The technical anthropologist lives with the customer "like a fly on the wall" and defines what they believe the customer needs to have a joyful experience with their software, and then they sketch what the computer screens should look like to provide that experience. The features on the various screens are then described in the form of story cards. They use physical cards, and on each card, there is one feature, which could be described with a picture or words. These cards that describe the features are then turned over to a team of software developers and a project manager. As a team, they estimate how long it should take to program each of the features card by card. The estimates are not precise to the minute but rather can be 1 hour, 2 hours, 4 hours, 8 hours, 16 hours or 32 hours.

What the customer should understand

Richard describes what is then done with these features and estimated times:

"What we do is what we call project management by origami. I take a piece of paper, and this particular size is worth 16 hours. If we divide 16 hours in half, how many hours do we obtain? Eight. If I fold eight in half, how many am I going to get? Four and on and on... Now some people say, "What the heck do you do for a 32 hour card?" We tape two 16-hour cards to a sheet of paper, and that indicates that it is 32 hours.

You are probably wondering why we only go to 32. We can go higher than that, but this is what our client buys. Our client buys a sheet of paper. This sheet of paper is worth two people for 40 hours (32 programming hours and eight hours of standard activities) and that is turned into dollars per sheet. Those are the three things that we want to know as project managers. In the very beginning of every week, we have project communication, stand-up, iteration kick-off estimation and show and tell.

This is a really simple project management tool. It is very easy to understand. I have two 9-year-old boys, and they can both come in here and do this because there is no reason for them to count higher than 40. If you can count to 40 and you can fit 32 in the box, you got our system. You can start tomorrow. Right? The other 8 hours of tasks, our client is still paying for, but we recognize that they are repeatable ones. They have to happen every week, like estimation, and a project review meeting with the customer, and so we actually make them just part of our permanent plan. Every week those things are going to happen. You are allowed to pick 32 hours' worth of other tasks for us to work on."

Let us consider the overall process from the customer's viewpoint. To estimate the overall scope of work the customer comes, meets with the team, and they will decide what they are willing to spend and whether they want all these features or they want to leave out some of the features because it is too costly. Maybe in the first stage of the software they will cut out some of the features with the thought of adding some later. These cards then, once the customer has agreed to play them, actually are authorizing work, and these are visually displayed on the wall on a "work authorization board." This visual display of the cards is the programmer's only schedule laying out one week's worth of work day by day. The software programmers then select a card. It tells them what the outcome should be – what feature they should be programming – and they code it and then they meet weekly with the customer to show what they have done for the week. They are getting customer feedback every week. Let me break this down still further.

Visual Management and Teamwork at Menlo

The customer requirements are defined by the technical anthropologists who do not have software development backgrounds. They could be salespeople or school counselors or journalists and they have used software, but they are selected because they have a good intuitive feel for what people need to help them do their work. They are able to observe people in their native environment, which means people at work. They are able to understand what the pain points are – what is a person struggling with when they try to use the software they currently have?

They need empathy to put themselves in the shoes of the customer, look through their eyes, and understand what they are experiencing. The customers may take some things for granted. Therefore, it is not enough to say, "We give the customer what they want." As Henry Ford observed, what the customer wants is not necessarily what they need. The customer thinks it is normal to go through three extra steps in the software to do a common task because they manage to get the work done and it has become a habit, but better software would not make them go through three steps when they can easily push one button.

The technical anthropologists create initial mockups – actual drawings – of individual computer screens, which are going to be turned into story cards – individual features – which the programmers will turn into code. The story card is a written description of what the feature is, what it does for the customer – why we need it – and tips on how to make it user friendly. This is from the point of view of the anthropologist who is then going to share it with the customer and the programmers and they are likely to make modifications.

Simply writing a card does not mean anybody is authorized to do anything, but when the cards are together, they make up the potential project scope. Notice this is not paperless. I have been on many tours through Menlo, and someone always asks, "Why do you have all of this on paper? Shouldn't it be in the computer? After all, this is a software factory." The answer is that by making it visual, by making it tactile, by actually placing it on this board showing a week's worth of work one day at a time, it facilitates efficient collaboration. It is much more difficult to collaborate in front of a computer screen and spend the time calling up different documents and there is something magical about taking a piece of paper, picking it up, and saying, "No, no. I think it should look like this" and you sketch right on the paper. At some point perhaps computers will be so user friendly that it will be as easy to do that with a computer as it is with paper and pencil. We are not there yet in practice.

Figure 3-11. Estimating the time needed for each story card

Now we have all the story cards, though not yet authorized, and we have to estimate how long it should take to program that feature. We see a group of people who are estimating the time per card, and it looks like they are having fun (see Figure 3-11). The Viking helmet is a symbol that came about by chance when Richard and his wife had gone to Norway and they brought it home as a souvenir. It is used for different purposes. In this case, they are wearing it just to look silly and have fun.

There are three pairs here and that is another part of the culture of Menlo—they always work in pairs. The pairs are looking at the feature and together they are estimating how long they think it will take and then they will take the average of the three teams or they will discuss it if there is a big difference in estimates. At this point, they are not trying to get the estimates perfect. They know that they are always off by some amount, but at least they have an initial idea of how long it should take. Each of these tasks is unique, and they have not done it before, so it is their best guess. On average, they find across cards that they are very accurate. Any given card might be high or low. There is an opportunity to improve these errors and reduce the variation in estimates, but they choose not to. The customer ultimately pays for the time it actually takes to do the work and the customers seem content with the estimates, which provide enough information to prioritize the features by cost.

The customers come first at Menlo Innovations. The company exists to serve the customers, but the customers must conform to Menlo's process. In early meetings, they are doing the difficult task of identifying the scope of work for the project. They are looking at the sheets that show eight-hour workdays, and they are asking questions about the content of the cards – the features. They are giving feedback, and they are asking themselves, "Is this a feature worth paying for right now?" They will move through the cards and create the initial scope of work in this session with the customer. After the initial scoping, each week, the customer will review what was done the past week and they will authorize the work for the next week. It is dynamic and work authorized at the outset of the project might change as the project progresses. This is PDCA in action week by week.

Let us shift again to Richard and let him describe what happens next after the cards are authorized and they become part of the visual management system on Menlo's walls.

The Work Authorization Board

Richard explains:

> "The physical artifacts we put on the wall are meant to communicate our most important notions about what are we working on right now. What are our goals? What is the information we need to communicate? Too often technical firms are tempted to put all of that stuff on a shared drive somewhere where everybody can get to from the corporate intranet. We believe the most important thing we can do is put those things on the wall where everyone can see them all day long."

The work authorization board (see Figure 3-12) is the daily visual work schedule. This is what is actually used by the programmers and by the project managers to pace the work by the day, by the hour. You see that the cards are up there by the day and across the top, there are names, and the names are referring to a pair of coders. The project manager sets up the boards each week. On Monday morning, the programmers find out who they are paired with and what project they are on. They go to the board and get a story card so they can program that feature.

They use colored dots to indicate the status of the card. Red is something not yet started, yellow is work in progress, and orange means that we as programmers believe we finished the task. It is green when a "quality advocate" verifies that the feature does what the customer wants. Originally, these were either green, yellow, or red, but the team added the orange dot as a kaizen improvement. It happened when Richard was off somewhere and he came back and he thought it was a mistake that there was this orange dot but, in reality, it was an improvement. What the programmers realized is that just because they think they are done coding that feature does not really mean that they are done until "quality advocates" check to ensure that the feature works as the customer expects. Orange means we think we are done as programmers.

The programmers build into every line of code a check of whether that code does what it is supposed to. This is called "unit testing." They also compile it to make sure it runs with the rest of the program. In addition, they time how long it actually takes to do the task, necessary for billing the customer, but also as a check against the time estimates. The story card only turns to green when the quality advocates say, "Yes we checked it. We understand from the technical anthropologists what the customer needs and we believe this fills that need. You are good to go." Interestingly the quality advocates do not have to know how to program.

There is also a piece of thread stretching across. Richard takes credit for inventing this visual device. The thread indicates which day we are on. Cards above the thread should be complete. They should at least be orange, meaning the software programmers have done their work. If what is above the line is still red, then the project manager can see at a glance they are behind, an abnormality.

Figure 3-12. The Visual Work Task Board

Now what do you do if you are a program manager and you see an abnormality? In a traditional system you might find the guilty party, and in a Lean system what you do is notice, "Hey look, there is an abnormality." That means I am a leader and I need to understand what is happening, and I need to understand the reason for the abnormality. The program manager is able to, at a glance, see if this process is in control or out of control – in standard or out of standard – and then they will check with the team. The team may have already taken corrective action. It may be a local peculiar problem. For example, maybe the computer went down. On the other hand, it may warrant a PDCA cycle.

They may need to create a new standard or to communicate to other people or there may not be a need. The leader is going to make sure that the right decisions are made and the right people are informed. The leader is both checking the process, checking with the people to be sure that they are reacting in the right way, and they are responsible for any needed improvement of the process.

Visual Management Supports a Collaborative Culture

I mentioned that Menlo has a culture of coding in pairs. They do everything in pairs. There are pairs that do interviews. There are pairs that estimate cost. There are pairs of technical anthropologists who go out to the customer site. Programmers code in pairs. What they have become convinced of internally is that two people working together will be more productive per person than one person working alone, and the creativity and quality will be higher. It does not really make a lot of sense on the surface that two people working together are more productive than one person working alone until you think about what happens when you have a pair.

Figure 3-13. Teamwork – Coding in Pairs

We see that one person has the mouse and is doing the coding while the other person is pointing (see Figure 3-13) and might be saying, "Hey look. There is a problem here." By catching that problem, they are avoiding rework, which actually in some companies gets through to the customer and dissatisfies the customer. Then they have to do even more rework later or live with an unhappy customer – that downstream waste is far greater than the cost of having two people. Again, this is something Menlo has proven to themselves internally. It does not necessarily have to be part of your culture, but it is worth keeping in mind that often pairs can be more productive than individuals can.

We now hear from Richard one of their greatest success stories – the Accuri cytometer that was a new invention – and Menlo worked hand in hand with and received equity in this company as part of the deal of developing the software. Everybody is making a lot of money and customers have been incredibly satisfied with the product. Richard proudly explains that it may have been a higher price to do the programming (although it seems it was much less expensive then what competitors would charge) but the overall cost to the customer in ease of use and lack of rework was far lower:

"My favorite one thus far is a software analysis module for a device called the flow cytometer that we built for Accuri Cytometers, and this is a device that (is) revolutionizing the market for cancer research, immunology, and so on. It was cool. The very first commercial shipment they ever sent out at Accuri – Leo – Accuri's customer service guy - was packing it in the box very carefully."

He called the customer and said, "It is going Fed Ex. It will be there tomorrow. Why don't you call me when you get it unpacked, you know, maybe around nine o'clock or so."
They were like, "Okay, Leo."

He was just really excited, and he watched the Fed Ex site the next morning. Then, "Oh it is signed for. At 8:45 it got signed for."

He camps by the telephone. Nine o'clock goes by and no phone call. Noon goes by and no phone call. Then Accuri's CEO comes over – Jen Baird – and she is like, "Leo, have they called?"

"No they have not called."

The whole day goes by and no phone call. The entire second day goes by and no phone call. Leo is going out of his mind. He is despondent. He is on suicide watch in Accuri. Finally, he picks up the phone, calls them up, and says, "Hey guys. It's Leo from Accuri."

They were like, "Hey Leo. How's it going?"

He is like, "Fine."

He says, "How's it going with you?"

They were like, "Great."

He says, "You got the box, right?"

"Oh yeah, two days ago in the morning, right around 8:45."

He goes, "Well, you were going to call me. Remember? Get you set up; I get you started on it."

To his surprise they answered, "Oh yeah. Hey, Leo, we just unpacked and started using it. We have been doing science with it for two days. It is great. Thank you."

"That is lower cost at a higher price. It is very cool."

What did we learn about Visual Management?

What have we learned about visual management from looking at Menlo and the earlier discussion we had? By definition, visual management should be showing the people doing the work and the leaders where they are compared to the standard. It should be easy to understand. A traffic light is a great example. It is red, yellow or green. We know what we should be doing based on just a glance, and the police would also notice at a glance and might pull you over if you go through a red light. It is a tool for collaboration, used for identifying issues that need to be addressed.

In a positive environment, like Menlo Innovations, there is a lot of collaboration with the customer. There is a lot of collaboration in the upfront stage of defining what the customer wants by the technical anthropologists, with the people who are going to manage the project and the people who are doing the actual coding. There is a lot of collaboration in the pairs of programmers. There is collaboration with quality advocates. When you have people collaborating and we can go to one visual display and see the status of the project – whether we are ahead or behind, whether some things passed quality control or not, what we are supposed to be doing this hour, and how long it actually takes – then everybody has the same picture of the reality compared to what is planned.

That difference between what is planned and what happens then becomes a problem and the term problem is used as an objective fact within Lean. In other words, when we have a gap because it says that it should take 60 minutes and it takes 70 minutes, that gap is defined as a problem. A problem does not mean a particular person is to blame or even that we need to take corrective action immediately. It means that there is a gap.

We have to ask ourselves why is this gap there. We might improve the estimation process. We might realize there is something peculiar that happened out of the control of the parties. We might realize somebody needs to be trained better. Alternatively, we may just mentally log it and do nothing. There can be all sorts of reasons for the gap, and we need to pick our battles and decide what gaps warrant intensive PDCA.

Fear is a killer of a Continuous Improvement culture because everything is so visible and people so vulnerable. Dr. Deming preached "driving out fear" decades ago, and the reason he was preaching it is that in an environment of fear people are going to do whatever is necessary to stay out of trouble. One way of staying out of trouble is to hide your problems, and that is why they say within Toyota, "No problem is a problem!" If you do not regularly identify problems, that is a problem because there are always problems. We rarely do anything perfectly according to plan and hiding problems means we are avoiding improvement.

The system also depends upon leaders doing something all too rare in organizations, which is going to where the work is done, seeing how the team is doing compared to the standard, and leading Continuous Improvement. The leader is on hand. They are noticing the problems as they occur, and they are taking action. The action should lead and encourage Continuous Improvement. That is why you need the skills of a Lean Leader, so you know how to act in a specific situation, so you can model good problem solving instead of pointing the finger at somebody and blaming them, and so you can create a culture that encourages surfacing and solving problems.

CHAPTER 4

COMMIT TO SELF DEVELOPMENT

What are you trying to Self-Develop?

By now it should be clear that there is a method for Continuous Improvement, and there is a method for respecting people. They go hand in hand. You cannot be effective in Continuous Improvement in Toyota unless you are respecting people – your customers, your partners, and your team members. True North in Toyota is defined by The Toyota Way, which defines how leaders should think, feel, and behave. Toyota develops leaders over long time horizons and we have summarized a process for companies wishing to learn from Toyota in a four-step Lean Leadership Model. This chapter provides an overview of the model (see Figure 4-1) and then focuses on the first of four steps, self-development through challenge and reflection.

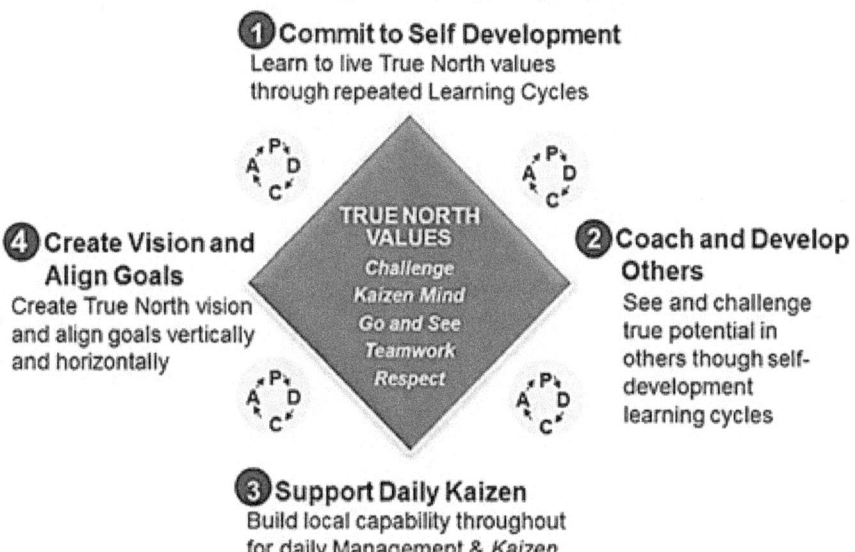

Source: *The Toyota Way to Lean Leadership*
Figure 4-1. The Lean Leadership Development Model (The Diamond Model)

The guiding principles for developing yourself as a leader are the True North values core to your organization. We put Toyota's at the center of the leadership development model. These must be thoroughly understood, but beyond that, you must develop yourself to live the True North Values through repeated learning cycles. You must plan-do-check-act your way over and over until the values are in your DNA—the way you think and act. Toyota's values do not have to be yours, but they provide useful guidance in thinking through your organization's values. It is worth reviewing them one more time.

Challenge: We welcome competition.

The environment is always going to challenge any organization, and there will always be internal challenges. The key is whether "challenge" is viewed as a hardship inflicted on us or the natural order of a complex universe in which challenges push us to adapt and grow stronger. As an example, *The Toyota Way 2001* says, "We welcome competition." You won't hear Toyota complain about competition from American, Korean or German companies, which are all getting stronger. They welcome this competition because it forces them to become even better. Without the challenge of this competition, they might weaken and customers will suffer. They want the spirit of competition in every individual within Toyota.

Facing challenge with a positive outlook is a value, because without that challenge there is no pressure to improve. Studies show that learning and performance will degrade if people are under more stress than they can handle. However, there is an equally important finding that if people are not challenged enough and under-stressed they will stagnate, also decreasing performance and learning. This has been called the Goldilocks principle of stress.

This suggests there is an optimum level of challenge. Think of a bell-shaped curve of performance (see Figure 4-2). Maximum performance is when there is the right level of stress, neither too little nor too much.

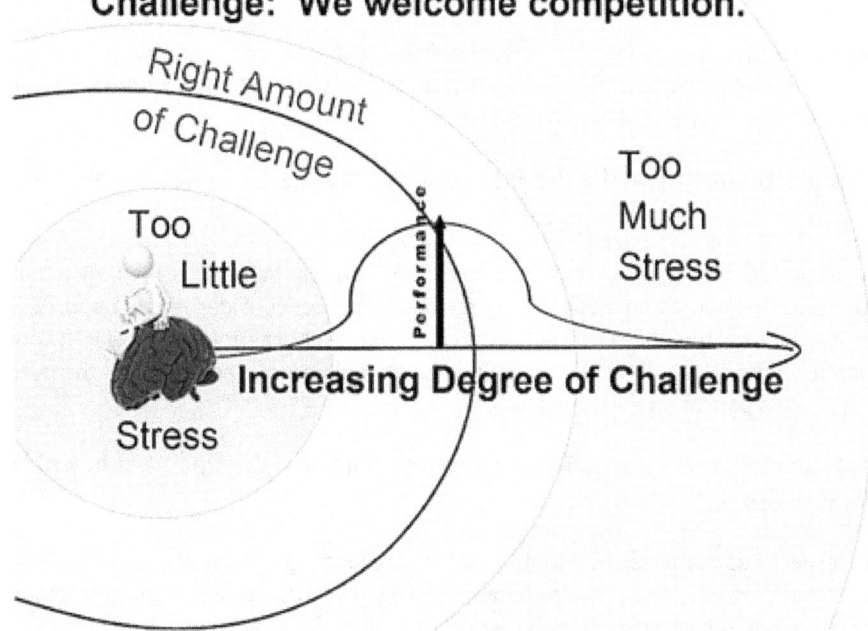

Figure 4-2. Finding the balance in Degree of Challenge

Kaizen Mind - I will achieve the challenge by following the right process.

How you meet the challenge is through a Kaizen mind. By Kaizen mind, we mean that you are confident that with dedication and a systematic process of improvement through PDCA you can meet the next challenge. You might be challenged to cut in half the time to do your task. It seems impossible, you have never done it before, but you know that if you break down that 50% into smaller pieces, take steps one by one, and follow a good process of problem solving you will move closer and closer to that target and eventually achieve it.

You need both the confidence and a good process to work through step-by-step to meet the challenge. Some attempts will be backwards steps. You will fail, but that's okay. You will pick yourself up, learn, and try again.

Go and See - You can learn the most at the *Gemba*.

There is also a value in Toyota of going and seeing, which sounds odd as a value because you are simply going and seeing something.

However, the value is that you can really learn the most from the *gemba*, the place where it is actually happening. There is huge value to going and seeing and learning first hand, not relying on indirect reports, not relying on averages, nor statistical databases from months past, but seeing the actual place as it is today.

Gemba means the place where "IT" is happening. It can be where you make the part, provide the service, the customer is using your product, a supplier is preparing your materials, or wherever else value is being added.

Teamwork - Teamwork and individual performance are two sides of the same coin.

Teamwork is highly valued as it is in many organizations. What is a bit unusual in Toyota is that teamwork and individual performance are not considered two opposites. They're considered two sides of the same coin. You really cannot have great teams without highly developed individuals and individuals will improve and perform the best when they are a part of an effective team.

Respect - Customers, Society, Team Members, Partners, Communities in which you do business.

Finally, respect has many aspects to it. It includes respecting customers, society, team members and partners, and the communities in which you do business. Shutting down a location where you employ people, while expedient from a business perspective, violates this value. You are putting people out of work and damaging the economic welfare of the community. This does not mean your company should go down with the ship if you are near bankruptcy, but doing damage to team members, community and society because of a business decision is to be avoided if at all feasible.

These are Toyota's values, and you probably have your values for your company written down somewhere. Critically evaluate them. If you think they need adding to or changing, fine. If they are already strong and comprehensive enough then start thinking about how to engrain them more deeply in your leadership culture.

Ensuring Your Values are Engrained

Can you as a leader actually get to a point where those values are so engrained in you that you wouldn't think of violating them? They just come naturally; it's the way you are.

There is a funny story an American Toyota executive told me. When he joined Toyota, they gave him a card with Toyota core values on them like a cheat sheet. He carried this card in his wallet with him all the time. He would refer to it just to remind himself of the values. One day he went into the plant and realized he forgot his wallet in the glove compartment of his car. He panicked and started to rush back to his car to get his wallet with the card in it. Suddenly, he stopped himself and realized he did need the card. These values were so engrained in him that he didn't need the cheat sheet anymore. That was a very liberating moment for him, a turning point in his career.

Western Leadership vs. Toyota Leadership

What type of leadership is necessary to drive this thinking vision of the Toyota Production System and how is it different from the western style of leadership with which we are most familiar?

Considering first the western, tool-based approach to Lean, we use the same style of leadership we are most comfortable with and have learned from business school or perhaps our mentors (see Figure 4-3). At the root, a financial plan drives this behavior. If our shareholders want money (and we view our product as money), then money should drive every decision - that is in the financial plan. We should aim for quick results in order to increase the money. We can control sales to some degree by paying salespeople on commission, but the rest of the organization has one lever for profitability, cost reduction.

The traditional Western top executive is the face of the company. What the stakeholders want is confidence that the senior leaders, particularly the people they talk to, are the heroes. I am entrusting you as the CEO to make me money. If you appear fallible then I am going to get nervous. As long as you appear like a superhero who never fails, I am happy. The traditional Western leader has to be strong, proud, and act like a superhero. To get to that point you have to demonstrate that you can get results repeatedly. The way you do that is by achieving financial objectives at every step on the ladder. The person who becomes the CEO has climbed the ladder the most quickly. If you want to be a CEO – if that is your goal entering a company – then you had better learn to climb fast. If there are a few people in the way, you climb over them. If you have to push a few off the ladder, that is okay too.

What you are really doing is getting results, but they are very specific results. They are financial results that are easily understood by shareholders, and the damage you do along the way does not really matter as long as you are not bringing the company into the courtroom.

People, on the other hand, are a bit of a nuisance, because as you are trying to climb the ladder they have emotional needs. They do not show up to work, and they do not always follow or even understand your instructions. People are imperfect machines. If you program a computer correctly, it does what you tell it to do, but people are machines that can be stubborn and resist. What we need to do is to use people properly and learn which levers to pull to get people to behave as we want.

Traditional Western Leader	Toyota Leader
Work to a financial Plan	Reach for True North Vision
Quick Results	Patient
Proud	Humble
Climb Ladder Rapidly	Learn Deeply and gradually Earn Way up Ladder
Results at all Costs	Need the Right Process to consistently get the Right Results
Achieve Objectives through People	Develop People through process improvement

Figure 4-3. Traditional Western Leader versus a Toyota Leader

Let's contrast that with Toyota's ideal leader who is part of the Thinking Production System. They are trying to achieve the unattainable goal of perfection. In order to do that, they realize that there are many steps. They also realize that they do not exactly know how to achieve True North so they have to try many things. The more quickly they can run experiments, the more quickly they can move in the direction of True North. They need to be patient. As a senior leader, they cannot make the improvements. They cannot do the work. They are dependent on the people who report to them. Understanding this leads to humbleness. "My job is to serve the people who can actually do the work; help them in any way I can." This is often referred to as servant leadership.

There is tremendous premium placed in Toyota on what you know - not financially, but in terms of the processes and the business. For example, Sakichi Toyoda learned from the ground up to work with his hands, make wooden things, and eventually invented new, more automatic looms. Kiichiro Toyoda learned from the ground up how to make a car. People generally do not advance in Toyota unless they learn deeply from the ground up. Learning deeply and then eventually moving horizontally and learning deeply again is the right way you get up the ladder. This takes patience. You are spending a lot of time at one level learning. Finally, someone will suggest you are ready for another challenge and will give you a promotion. You wait patiently until that happens.

You need the right processes to get the right results. There is a strong belief that kaizen, which includes respect for people, and a very methodical approach of going through PDCA over and over again, will get you closer to the True North. It will get you to a target you set on the way to True North. We do not know exactly how to get there. If somebody asks us to cut the time it takes to change over a machine by 80%, we say, "Yes I will do it." We have no defined solutions for how. We know that we are going to need a team of people - lots of brains. We know we are going to have to try a lot of things, but if we are an experienced leader, we have repeatedly met our objectives. We have the confidence that if we follow the right process to work with a motivated team of people we will get the right results.

In the process of getting those right results, Respect for People says to get the best out of my people I must train and develop them. So, we have on one hand the results we are trying to achieve – we are trying to conquer the challenge – and on the other hand, we have people we are trying to bring along with us so they are strengthened. Through this investment, they will become more skilled at Continuous Improvement.

How do you work to become a Lean Leader?

How do you work toward the ideal of the Toyota leader? Many leaders would say, "Look, we have been raised to follow the Western Leadership Model. We have learned how to make the numbers. We have learned to be impatient. The people selected to be leaders are selected because they are impatient, because they want results now. Now you are telling me I have to be nice, patient, humble and good to my people and encourage them. This is the opposite set of behaviors. How can I go from one extreme to another?" Certainly changing any complex behavior is difficult, and we know from neuroscience research, even painful. This means we have to really want it, which is why Toyota works so hard at selecting leaders who are passionate about learning.

Step one – Commit to self-development. Learn to live True North values through repeated learning cycles.

We have learned a few things. We know that when people have established habitual routines and ways of thinking etched in their brains over decades, it is really hard to change. Perhaps we should blow up the company and start over. We could bring in some coaches who are really experienced and then bring in people and raise them from the start in the True North values. In Toyota's experience, it takes about ten years before you can act like a mature Toyota leader. You must have all of the routines etched in your brain for that.

Few companies could afford to shut down and rebuild themselves over ten years, and a great deal of expertise would be lost. Better is to work hard to change the leadership you have. Who is in a position to change the thinking of leadership? I can tell you from decades of experience as a consultant it is not me. I have never been able to talk a CEO into changing his mindset. For one thing, I am just one of those people that they have climbed over all their life, and I am a paid consultant, which makes me even less credible. CEOs have very strong wills. That is why they got where they are.

The good thing is that because they have such strong wills they have been able to accomplish anything they really set their mind to their entire careers. If they set their mind to changing the way they behave, they can often do it. It requires extreme dedication, and it does not happen in one try. You do not take the weekend golf lesson special and become a great golfer if you lack the fundamental skills. If you play golf badly and you have a lot of bad habits, you do not change those habits unless you practice repeatedly over a long period of time with a coach who is watching you, telling you what you are doing wrong, suggesting how you might alter your swing, and assigning you practice routines. My golf instructor informed me not to take a lesson unless I have three days after the lesson to practice what he taught me, not play on the course, but practice at the driving range. Then I am ready for my next lesson.

The challenge of self-development is: (1) it takes a deep commitment; (2) You need a coach; and (3) You need to practice. For CEOs or executives who are running a mile a minute to solve today's problems it is hard for them to carve out their time and it takes even more dedication. What I am assuming now is that you as a leader – and this same process applies whether you are a first line supervisor, a manager, a director, or a CEO –have decided you want to change. The way you have been leading has gotten results, but it has led to people who are not engaged. It has led to you solving most of the problems and doing most of the thinking for people. You are frustrated, and you think there must be a better way. How do you get leaders to be like the Japanese leaders who taught Gary Convis? Gary had to try to become one of these leaders, which was a struggle. He had been with Ford for 20 years and had developed a lot of bad habits.

When Gary was hired to run NUMMI there were a lot of things they liked about him. For one, while at Ford, he was acting like a Toyota leader. He was the quality manager and he would actually stop production, (nobody stopped production in Ford). He would go to the workplace, he would talk to the workers, and he would identify the problem and its root cause. He was acting like a Toyota leader in his mind and in many ways, he was. The NUMMI management said that they were impressed that he had this leadership potential, but they had done an exhaustive search before they settled on Gary and what sealed the deal was that Gary repeatedly asked questions, listened, and wanted to learn.

Anyone who has taught knows that you cannot teach somebody who does not want to learn. You can get them to take notes. You can get them to feedback on a test what they hear and read, but you cannot teach somebody, except at a very superficial level, unless they want to learn. You are always looking for that one student who is passionate about learning, whatever it is – a musical instrument a sport. You are an engineer and you are trying to train the next generation of engineers, and you find that spark in someone who really wants to learn.

The first step is to find people who are willing to commit to self-development. What you want them to learn is the True North values of the company. The only way they can learn it is by taking little steps. At first, they have to learn some basic routine patterns of behavior, and then, as they develop, what they learn is more precise and more elaborate. The Improvement *kata* provides one systematic way to learn through practice one-step at a time.

That is what the Japanese were doing at NUMMI in California. They were trying to teach, particularly Gary, because as plant manager he was in the most critical position, and then everybody in the hierarchy up to the team leader of a small group how to develop themselves – how to learn and how to think in The Toyota Way.

Leadership Self-Development Learning Cycles (PDCA)

The Lean Leader is taking on increasingly difficult challenges, meeting those challenges, learning, and then taking on the next challenge. They are following the PDCA cycle to learn (see Figure 4-4).

Source: *The Toyota Way to Lean Leadership*
Figure 4-4: Leadership Self-Development Learning Cycles (PDCA)

You get a new assignment that your superiors and human resources have concluded will help the organization and further develop your leadership skills. For example, you have been a manager in the assembly department and now you have been selected to be a manager in the shipping department because that will broaden you and prepare you for higher levels of leadership. The first thing you will do on your new job in shipping is to immerse yourself to grasp the current situation. This is the beginning of developing your plan for that department.

The current situation includes people and processes. You are immersing yourself in the *gemba* to develop a vision for that shipping area, getting to know the people and the gaps between where shipping should be and where it is today. One way you can do that is by doing the jobs – driving a forklift truck and loading a truck or getting boxes and piling them up and setting them up for the next delivery. You build rapport. You start to understand the strengths and weaknesses of the people and process. Then you develop an agreement with the people on the vision: "Here is where we are headed and here is our first step."

When you have that plan worked out, you can start to lead others toward the vision. Your goal is not just to get it done, but to develop others. They have to accept pieces of your goal and take them on as their personal challenges for their own development. That is another skill set—to teach and motivate people to want to take on a challenge and self-develop. When you have been doing that for a while and you make progress toward your goal, then you will reflect on how you are doing.

You should have a coach to help you see what you are doing well and what you are not doing well. They can help you see your own blind spots. The coach is going to watch you. They know what should be happening. They know what you are trying to achieve. They know what types of paths are good paths and bad paths. They are going to, in subtle ways, influence you toward the good paths. By subtle, I mean they might ask you questions, they might offer a challenge, but they are not going to do it for you and they are not going to tell you exactly what to do.

Here is a question that I would like you to consider. You might even pause and write down some ideas, perhaps with other people in a group: 1) In order to self-develop to learn these values and to learn Continuous Improvement, what specific skills would you need to work on? Think about this as you would any type of complex skill set that you are trying to learn. If you are going to learn to golf and I am your teacher, I had better understand the skills that I am trying to teach you. Then: 2) How can you learn those skills?

It is just like golf – practice, feedback from a coach, reflection, more practice, and eventually you get closer and closer to developing that skill in a way that it is routine, repeatable, and etched in your brain.

Summary of what Lean Leaders need to learn

I am sure you have a longer list than mine, but Let me provide a short list of Lean Leaders skills. First, they need to learn to manage from the *gemba* – go and see. Unfortunately, that is for many a lost art. I think the original founders of companies were very hands on, and they were at the *gemba*. Often the *gemba* was just a few people. Then, as the company grew, the leaders got farther away. They spent more time in offices and meetings looking at financial results and less time actually watching people work, finding gaps, and finding opportunities to train people. And then they moved on and professional managers were hired who were even farther from the *gemba*.

This is a set of skills that take time at the *gemba* to develop. While you are at the *gemba*, you are developing yourself and you are developing others. You have to understand the core values. "Understand" means more than reading them off a card, rather they become the way you are – the way you think. You are living the values. You have to have it within your DNA, so that it is perfectly natural that when somebody is doing work and you spot a mistake, rather than jump in and criticize and take over, you step back and you ask, "What should be happening? What is happening? What is the problem (gap)? What can I do to help?"

Managing effectively from the *gemba* is being able to see and then responding in a way that moves the team forward instead of stopping the team in their tracks. This requires a lot of discipline – more than it requires of the people that you are trying to coach. The discipline is to keep yourself from firing out orders or solutions or criticisms and follow a disciplined problem solving process. The first step in problem solving is always the same – what is the problem? It may seem obvious to you what the problem is. You still ask what they see the problem to be because often what is obvious is wrong and you want other people to think about the problem.

You must develop the skills to follow a disciplined problem solving process that is natural to you, where you can go through the whole Plan-Do-Check-Act cycle in a disciplined, structured way with patience, not short circuiting steps. Then you can start to teach others. At Toyota that means developing some mastery of "Toyota Business Practices." Then you can learn to teach others through "on the job development." A prerequisite to on the job development of others is learning yourself. You are always learning. You are learning more deeply to be a disciplined problem solver, a leader, and a coach, no matter how many times you have been through it.

As I mentioned, Toyota deeply values knowledge of the actual process at a very detailed, technical level. If you come into Toyota and you are an engineer perhaps you are assigned to body engineering. This is designing the steel metal body, understanding how dies are designed, and understanding how the body is going to be shaped in stamping. This specific process is likely to be your focus for the first ten years or more of your career.

Once you have developed that depth, if your career path leads you to be a general manager in body engineering or a technical specialist in body engineering, you might stay there for the rest of your career. If there is a desire to promote you to become a manager of a more general process like technical planning or possibly to become a chief engineer, you will move to a related specialty. Perhaps you will move to the design of the interior of the car.

Figure 4-5. Developing Deep Rooted Expertise Leadership

Figure 4-6. T-Type

The point is that you are developing deep-rooted expertise (see Figure 4-5). In Toyota, they believe that without deep roots the tree is going to end up very vulnerable. The first storm will knock it over.

Then your next lesson is leading people when you are not really an expert at what they are doing. Since you have learned how to become an expert at something, you can learn more quickly the basics of the next technical process, but you are not going to have the same depth. You have to depend more on other people. Toyota calls this T-type leadership (see Figure 4-6) – first, the deep roots. Then the cross of the T represents the broader learning.

How do Lean Leaders develop and get promoted?

Toyota is known for the Japanese management practice of slow promotion. You are evaluated carefully at the *gemba*, both for how you work and the results you achieve, and as we have discussed in the T-model, you are often promoted laterally before you are moved up. This requires patience by the employee.

In Japan, it works well, because when the person comes from college to Toyota (or from the Toyota technical high school) their expectation is they are going to retire from Toyota. They have almost no attrition. Within Toyota, they bring in people without really knowing for certain what their potential is. They do have a rigorous selection process. Early in the career of an engineer, they have a scale – like an ABC scale – where they evaluate potential. However, they do not know until they have actual experience in the company how well they are going to self-develop, how well they are going to learn to develop others, and what skills they have that will enable them to lead. Think of sports teams that draft new players with extraordinary potential, but do not know how that will translate to professional games.

As you move up in any company, the expectation is that you take responsibility for a broader and broader part of the organization and you lead more and more people and processes. In Toyota, employees need to work their way through the leadership development model. They have to self-develop and then learn to develop others. Then they have to be able to lead several levels down so that they are developing a routine of daily improvement at all the working levels. Finally, they will learn how to lead what is called *Hoshin Kanri*, or policy deployment, setting aggressive goals and testing those goals- so that everybody knows what they should do to align with the company needs.

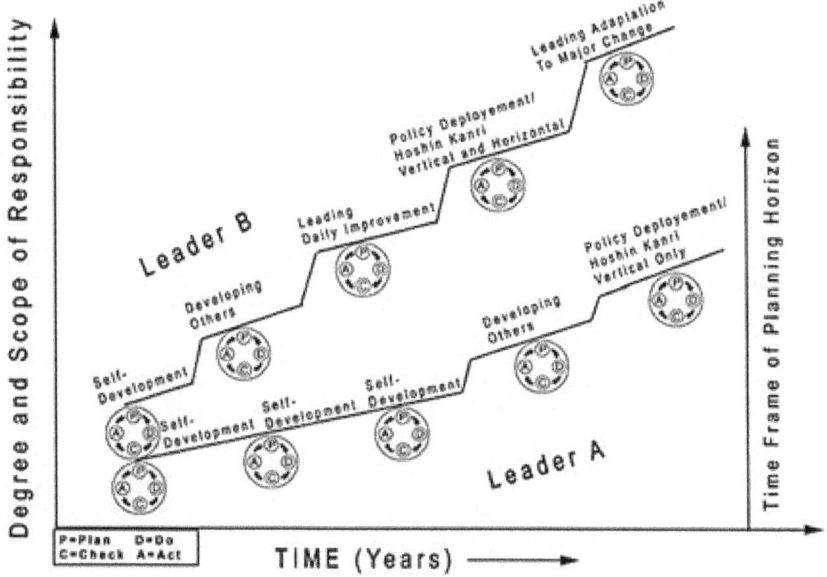

Source: *The Toyota Way to Lean Leadership*
Figure 4-7. Hypothetical Career Paths of two Toyota Leaders

For illustration purposes, we show two different leaders (see Figure 4-7). Leader A spends three cycles – let's say each of these cycles takes two or three years—in the self-development role. For 6-9 years, they do not have any people who report to them. He finally gets some people reporting to him, and then he is only going to be responsible in *Hoshin Kanri* for achieving the goals of his group of people who report to him.

For an engineer that can look much like a technical career ladder. If you are really super technical in your area, and you are not as strong in people skills (or perhaps you are not even that interested in developing people skills), then the best thing you can do is to do your technical work and have a few people reporting to you who have the same technical interests.

Some of these people will get really challenging technical objectives. One Toyota General Manager of die design and production was challenged to cut the amount of time it took to design a die in half. Toyota was already the world leader in the time it took to design a die for stamping. This was very challenging for him even though he had a fairly narrow scope of responsibility.

Perhaps another (Leader B) shows incredible passion for people. She is a great leader. People gravitate toward her. She is working really hard at developing herself, and will move up the ladder more quickly. She may achieve the executive level and be asked to lead horizontally a major change that cuts across a major slice of the company.

The important thing is that you have a population of people who work for you for a long period of time, and you do not have to guess about how they are going to perform when you promote them because you have observed them in their current role over a long period of time. As a *gemba* manager, you are observing them working and you really know how people react.

This takes the guesswork out, and more than one person makes decisions about promotion. At the very least, if you are the manager of the person, you are going to have your boss and human resources involved.

Human resources plays a critical role in Toyota in really understanding how people perform, their skills, how they are leading, how they are respecting others, and how they are achieving their challenging goals. They have responsibility for career progression of people just as the manager does. You have a number of people meeting to talk about you based, not on just rankings, and not just on a single annual review where they ask you questions, but on their close observation of you.

Again, this is something that works for Toyota in Japan because people expect to spend their entire careers in Toyota. It has been more challenging for Toyota as they moved to other countries, for example, America, where if you are a young engineer coming out of school, you have been told if you stay in one company for more than three to five years, you are at a dead end in your career. Companies are steps on a ladder. You come to Toyota and you learn that you are not actually going to get major responsibility for development of a part of the vehicle for three to five years. In that time, you will be learning and proving your skill level. By five years, ambitious new hires believe they should be supervising others and preparing for their next company.

In this case, the Toyota Technical Center in the U.S. realized they were losing young engineers and went through many cycles of PDCA over several decades. They asked, what is the problem? The problem is that young Americans do not expect to stay long enough in the company to be developed over decades as they naturally do in Japan. They worked on countermeasures to speed up the training cycle, but it is very important that you take the time to develop people correctly. That means the person has to stay with you for some period of time. If people are leaving early then you have to ask why they are leaving early. Were the wrong kinds of people hired? Maybe Toyota was selecting the fast track people who look great when they come out of college, but their career goals are to climb the ladder faster than they can at Toyota.

They had to adjust the process of selection to ensure they were not selecting those kinds of people.

You can also ask whether your working conditions are an issue and whether your pay is in proportion to the industry. There are any number of levers you might test, not in one-step, but repeatedly through PDCA to increase retention. The Toyota Technical Center actually had a respectable retention rate, but not by Toyota standards. One key countermeasure that really helped them was to participate actively in cooperative education programs, where undergraduate engineering students work for Toyota part of the year for up to four years, allowing Toyota and them to get to know each other before a long-term job commitment.

The system depends upon having at least a core of dedicated, long-term employees in whom you invest. What Toyota will rarely do is go outside to find the high potential employee from another employer and bring them in at a management level. They would come in at a high level without the Toyota DNA. They could be very disruptive. Toyota instead does everything they can to grow from within.

Toyota also wants to avoid distorting the pay structure. Even if you are a critical person working on a critical project, and let's say you have an outside job offer for a 30% raise with a promotion, they will ask you why you want to leave. They will talk to you about it, but if you really want to leave, they are going to wish you well and they are not going to match that pay raise. If they match that pay raise, it will throw the whole pay structure out of order for everybody else who works there. Leadership and technical development really depend on many cycles of practice by those who view Toyota as a company they are going to commit to and a company that is going to allow them to continue to learn and develop.

Deep Expertise through *Shu-Ha-Ri* Stages

Self-development takes patience. It takes humbleness. You might be an executive. You might be a high-level manager. Unless you grew up being tutored inside a Lean company, you have to go back to school to learn to be a Lean Leader. Just like those who were trained in Toyota, you will have to put your development in a coach's hands.

I played guitar almost every day from the age of 13 to 29 and stopped for 30 years; I then resumed by taking classical guitar lessons. I am a professor at the University of Michigan. I give speeches all over the world. Yet, when it came to my taking guitar lessons, my teacher, a guitar professor who has been doing this all his life, started out teaching me the most basic things that I never learned when I was self-taught, like how to read music and rhythm – how to count. I was doing basic drills and had to humble myself.

Then the hardest thing was that he asked me to become a seminar member with the undergraduate students he teaches at the local university, and to sit there and listen, then play and perform in front of his students. I can tell you one of the scariest things I have ever done in my life was perform a guitar piece for ten kids. My hands were shaking. I could not remember the music. I did that repeatedly until I am more comfortable, but still lose sleep anticipating it.

You really put yourself out there when you have to learn a new skill, one that you have not been working at, at a point in your career where you actually are a master of whatever skills you are using on a day-to-day basis. To do it you need to go through the same process as anybody who learns a complex skill; you start from the beginning. You start with the basics. You have a coach. The coach is giving you seemingly trivial exercises. You practice them as you are told, and you get better and better at those skills. You are not going to learn it in a classroom.

Typically, we send executives or budding executives to class outside the company. They go to Harvard, MIT, or the University of Michigan Business School, and they have extravagant food and dwellings and a fitness center. They are critically evaluating the professors. They come away after the week, and they are supposed to be re-baked and remade into a new leader. It is just not going to happen. They probably performed and exercised the same behaviors they normally perform at work, but now they are doing it in their teams with other executives or with the teacher in a classroom. Do they have a coach when they go back to the company and, if so, is the coach on a daily basis continuing to teach the new behaviors they learned at the university?

Shu-Ha-Ri to advance from novice to mastery

One way to think about developing this expertise is through a model of learning that comes from the martial arts. It is called the *Shu-Ha-Ri* cycle (see Figure 4-8). Many different learning models say the same thing. We learned in Chapter Two about *Toyota Kata*. This is a way of learning improvement and coaching improvement based on a systematic model like *Shu-Ha-Ri*.

Deep Expertise through Shu-Ha-Ri

KATA = A defined routine for thinking and acting

- Shu– Embracing the kata (learn exactly)
- Ha– Diverging from the kata (some improvisation)
- Ri– Discarding the kata (The form is now mastered; focus on deepening skill and understanding)

Figure 4-8. The *Shu-Ha-Ri* Cycle

In the *Shu* stage, if you are a martial arts teacher, what you want is for the student to embrace the *kata*. You are trying to teach them a particular way of standing, a particular posture, a particular way of kicking, of moving their hands. You want them to copy exactly what you tell them to do. There is no deviation accepted.

As a student, you are learning exactly, and you are subjugating yourself to your teacher. The teacher is right. You are wrong. You are going to do exactly what the teacher tells you. You are obeying, and you are practicing diligently all the drills that your teacher gives you.

In the *Ha* stage, once you have learned these routines, the basics have become natural and you do not have to think about them. You can begin to diverge from these rules and do some improvisation within the confines of the *kata*.

Finally, in the *Ri* stage, sometimes called "discarding the *kata*," you are truly free to learn the art of performance. That does not mean that you forget everything you learned of the *kata*. It means that what you have learned is so natural that you do not even have to think about it. Now, when the form is mastered, you can focus on deepening your skill and understanding.

In karate, you are in the *Ri* stage as you attempt to read and react to your opponent. You are building a repertoire of ways to read and react to real situations, and you are trying to continually get a better melding of your mind and body. You want your mind and body to act as one instead of fighting with each other.

Talk to the best violinist in the world or the best guitar player in the world; ask them if they still do basic drills. They will tell you that they start their practice session with scales focusing on technique – the same thing that they were learning in the *Shu* stage. You never really eliminate the stage and then forget it. You are constantly going through these stages, but at a higher level each time.

Apply this now to leadership. I asked you to write down Lean Leadership skills. For each of those skills, ask yourself, "What is the *Shu* stage?" What are the basic patterns of leadership required to develop this particular skill?

Let's say that one of the skills is actively listening to others. That is actually quite vague. What does it mean to actively listen to others? You have to break that down into components of active listening. Then for each of those components you have to have some way of teaching somebody – some practice method – and somebody has to be able to watch them to know if they are doing it exactly right in the *Shu* stage until they eventually master active listening to the point where they are at the *Ha* stage and then continue to move into the *Ri* stage. I would bet that you would be hard pressed to find anybody in your organization that has ever learned even a skill like active listening at the same level of discipline and detail as a dedicated 10-year-old has learned basics of violin playing. A summary of what should be happening for *Shu-Ha-Ri* cycles to develop Lean Leaders (see Figure 4-9) are listed below.

1) Leaders at all levels regularly go and see to observe people and processes to understand gaps to True North.

2) Leaders at all levels are experts at process improvement.

3) There are deliberate programs in place to teach leaders.

4) Leaders are deliberately learning and practicing to self-develop their leadership abilities to fit a continuous improvement culture.

Figure 4-9. Conditions for Effectively Developing Lean Leaders

Do senior executives still need to self-develop?

Here is an extreme example that demonstrates the degree to which Toyota believes in developing people even among seasoned veteran executives. Most companies have the experience of bringing in an executive from the outside, but few would come close to the time and resources Toyota puts into teaching and socializing the new hire into the Toyota Way. This is a case study of Steve St. Angelo who would eventually become the first American CEO of Toyota, Latin America.

Steve St. Angelo was selected as the new president for the Toyota plant in Georgetown, Kentucky some years back. He had worked for General Motors for 30 years. One of his early assignments at General Motors was to be the executive coordinator to NUMMI, Toyota's joint venture with General Motors.

He went to NUMMI as the most senior executive on site from General Motors. At that time, Gary Convis was the plant manager. Steve was treated like every other executive coordinator. He was invited to meetings and he could go anywhere he wanted. He could observe anything, but he was also very constrained as in: "Look, do not touch." Steve was a very "hands on" guy; he wanted to touch.

When he met with Gary Convis he asked, "What can I do to get more involved? I would like to manage something, and really experience the Toyota Production System first hand."

Gary politely said, "Steve, I appreciate that, but your job as an executive coordinator is to coordinate and not to do anything. So, please go any place you want. We will show you anything. We will answer any questions. Just do not get personally involved in trying to manage anything."

Steve was not satisfied with that. Again, he is a very hands on guy. He kept on going back to Gary, pushing, pushing, and saying, "Gary, I want to manage something."

Gary finally, in frustration, gave him an assignment assuming Steve would turn it down. He said, "Steve, if you are going to learn this, you are going to do it the way the rest of us learned which is starting at the bottom. So, you are going to actually have to do production jobs." He was expecting to scare Steve away.

Steve answered, "Fine. I will do production jobs."

Gary then raised the bar, "Oh and by the way you are going to have to learn a different job every day."

Steve replied, "Okay. I will learn a different job every day."

Gary still had not talked him out of it. Now the clincher, "You are also going to have to work both shifts."

Steve agreed, "Fine. No problem."

What Gary did not know was that Steve was hired into General Motors as a production worker, and became a utility person who could do any job in the area. He had also worked multiple shifts when needed.

Gary got him working, thinking he was going to be burned out pretty quickly, and Steve just continued day by day to learn new jobs, perform well, working multiple shifts. By the time Steve met with Gary for his next assignment Gary had gained respect for Steve and decided to make him a group leader, the first salary position. Gary selected one of the worst groups in the plant – the group with the worst quality, the worst attitude. He said, "Steve, your job is to make this one of the best groups in the plant as a group leader."

Steve agreeably said, "No problem."

Within a few months, they were among the best performing groups in the plant, and gradually Steve worked his way up into management, which is the first time an executive coordinator had accomplished that. He then returned to GM in operations, and he practiced what he learned transforming plants to Lean.

Somewhere along the way, Gary was asked to leave NUMMI and join Toyota to become the president at the Georgetown, Kentucky plant, but when Gary was asked to be the president, he was not made the president. The president was Japanese at the time. Gary would be the first American who would become president, but first he was given the job of executive vice-president.

He was told by the president, "Gary, I understand we brought you here with the expectation you will become the president, but first you need to learn the culture and get your hands dirty and prove you can handle it. So I will stay here overlapping with you and act as president. Your job is to go and learn the jobs, understand the people, understand Toyota, and you have up to a year to do it. Assuming that all goes well, you will then take over the presidency." It took about six months for them to crown Gary as the first American president.

Now NUMMI needed a new executive vice president since Gary left and they invited Steve, who was then back at General Motors, to return as interim executive vice-president to run manufacturing. This was unheard of—a GM guy running NUMMI?

Steve went on to do a wonderful job at NUMMI, and Toyota executives continued to gain deep respect for him. When Gary later retired from Toyota, they asked Steve to take over at the Georgetown, Kentucky plant. This was huge, an outsider coming in to take over and an outsider, who worked for General Motors, who had not even worked for Toyota.

Again, what do you do? It was Gary who was influential in getting Steve hired, and Gary made the same deal with Steve. You come in as executive vice-president. I will continue to run the plant with my people, and you can spend your first year learning, or at least some period of time learning.

Steve came to Georgetown, Kentucky and moved his family there. He was an executive vice-president. He was expecting to be president. There were no guarantees. The first thing he was given was his training schedule (see Figure 4-10). It was scheduled from April to September. They were fast tracking him. What you see is that he had to learn a lot of information and he had to go and see – a lot of *gemba* visits all over Toyota.

He was going to the Technical Center, the North American headquarters, and Toyota Motor Sales. He was also getting media training on how to answer questions from journalists, but the deep training was at the *gemba* in the Georgetown, Kentucky plant.

RECOMMENDED EXECUTIVE EDUCATION, Steve St. Angelo, Executive Vice President

COURSE / TOPIC	NEXT SCHEDULED OPPORTUNITY	TIME	STATUS
Functional overview at TMMK	April - June, 2006	3 mos	Completed
Functional overview at TMMNA	Jul-06	2 days	Completed
Toyota Quality Way	2006-05-26	1 Day	Completed
TPS Classroom Training	2006-08-18	1 Hour	Completed 8/18
TPS Floor Training	8/19, 8/22-26, 8/31, 9/7-9, 9/26-30	20 Days	Completed 8/19 to 9/30
Supplier Visits	Scheduled individual basis	1/2 Day each	Completed
Global Problem Solving	May, 2006	1 Day	Completed 5/06
Executive Development Program	4/11-18 & 5/23-27, 2006	2 Weeks	Completed 4/18 and 5/27
Toyota Way Learning Mtg.	Aug. (approx)	2 Hours	Completed 8/11
Health Exam	Scheduled individual basis	1 Hour	Completed
HR Policies (Systems)	2006-10-13	1 Hour	Completed
Succession Planning Process	Scheduled individual basis	1 Hour	Completed 5/7
Labor - History / Current Issues	Scheduled individual basis	2 Hours	Completed
Floor Mgmt Development System	Scheduled individual basis	1 Hour	Completed 8/17
Group Leader 40 Hr. Training	June, 2006 (approx)	2 Hours	Completed 6/8
Work on the Line	Scheduled individual basis	Plastics Body Assembly 1 and 2 Paint 1 and 2 Stamping Powertrain Quality Control Maintenance	Completed Multi
Process Diagnostics	Scheduled individual basis	(2) 4 Hour sessions	Completed 6/3
N.A. Toyota Plant Visits	Scheduled individual basis	10 Days	Completed
Toyota Sales Customer Ex. Groups	November, 2006	3 Days	Completed 11/11
Toyota Technical Center Review	Scheduled individual basis	1 Day	Completed
Cross Dock Visit	Scheduled individual basis	1/2 Day	Completed
Go & See, Exit Counter, Torque Improvement, Traceability	August 3-4, 2006	1 Day	Completed 8/3 to 8/4
Media Training	20-Sep-06	1 Day	Completed

Source: Toyota Motor Manufacturing Kentucky, Inc.

Figure 4-10. Recommended Executive Education for Steve St. Angelo

You can see that he had only one day of TPS classroom training. This was followed by TPS floor training for four weeks. For four weeks, he participated in kaizen activities, not as the leader, but as a member of the team. I have been in companies where we have been trying to get executives to go to the *gemba*, and it is really ambitious to try to get them to participate in one five-day kaizen event and turn their cell phones off. Here just as part of this orientation he would spend four weeks in kaizen, and this was a guy who had been living it for decades and actually ran NUMMI.

He was also given problem solving training, and he was expected to spend several months to solve a problem following Toyota's problem solving method. He went through an executive development program in Japan. In addition, despite his NUMMI training, he was expected to do individual jobs just as he did when he was at NUMMI. In each department in Kentucky, he was expected to do a production job, and these were scheduled individually with the different departments.

So, why would they do that? Why would Steve St. Angelo, who grew up working in production jobs, went through a trial by fire at NUMMI, once again have to go and work production jobs in Georgetown, Kentucky? Arguably, he was at least in the *Ha* stage of development and perhaps at or near the *Ri* stage. In this case, it was not because they wanted to test his ability to do the jobs or for him to learn how to weld or assemble. It was for him to immerse himself in the *gemba*, get to know the people, gain their trust. He was going to be the president of over 6000 people who work in Georgetown, Kentucky. He would be running a small town. He needed to walk in the shoes of the people who he would be representing, doing their jobs, talking to them as a fellow line worker, and starting to understand how they think, the culture, and building relationships.

Now by the end of this he had many ideas about where there were gaps, where there were weaknesses, and what he should be working on when he assumed the presidency position. Even after Gary retired and Steve was running Georgetown, Kentucky, he had a Japanese executive coordinator coaching him. This is probably not something you would see elsewhere.

George: Then when Steve was going through this training did everybody around Steve know that he is being earmarked to be the next president or was it more as he was just another guy?

Jeff: When he came to Kentucky, he was announced as the executive vice-president. Everybody knew this outside guy who worked for General Motors was being groomed to be the president. There was resentment by some: "how can a General Motors guy understand The Toyota Way to Lean Leadership?" There were also people in the plant who were working their way up and thought they were going to become the next president. There was some disappointment and skepticism, and he had to overcome that.

What Steve did in those six months was critical because he had to build bridges with people – some who were just hostile toward him, some who were going to give him a chance. It was a critical period of adjustment and of gaining trust. At first, he was not treated like everybody else. He went into a kaizen workshop where everybody knew who he was.

What I have experienced in kaizen workshops – and I bet others have – is that when an executive becomes a team member and they are wearing blue jeans and they are scrubbing the floor, they quickly become an ordinary person to the team members. If you are working all day next to somebody welding who is a whole lot better than you and you are the executive vice-president, the hourly worker has some superiority. Normally what will happen if you are humble is they will take you under their wing, they will give you tips, and they will help you out if you get behind. I actually experienced that when I worked in production for two days at NUMMI and the team members wondered why a professor was doing hourly work. Steve was putting himself in a subordinate position where he had an opportunity to build trust from that position.

Important Factors for Leader Success in an Exceptional Company

This summary reflection is from a former Toyota veteran who spent decades in Toyota Motor Sales becoming an executive VP. He said, "The most important factors for success are patience, a focus on long-term rather than short-term results, continually reinvesting in people, product, and plant, and an unforgiving commitment to quality."

If this becomes the way you think and behave, then you are becoming a Lean Leader. Self-developing takes patience. It takes a long-term focus. It takes a focus on developing other people even when you cannot tangibly see the results that will come from investing in those people. It takes absolute passion for the customer and quality.

Here is another homework assignment. Think about some part of your organization. It could be your whole company. It could be the department you are in. What I have written down are the key conditions for developing Lean Leaders discussed earlier (see Figure 4-11). Please identify whether there is a critical gap ("one") between this description and what it is like in your organization. You can even apply this to yourself as a leader. A "four" means that there is a minor gap and "five" means you are there, in the *Ri* stage just humming along. I would be surprised if anybody is in the *Ri* stage on any of these things.

> **Current state of leadership in your company?**
>
> 1=Critical Gap, 2=Major Gap, 3=Some Serious Gaps, 4=Minor Gaps, 5=We are there
>
> 1. Leaders regularly go and see at the gemba to observe the gap between the actual situation and True North.
> 2. Leaders at all levels have been coached to lead process improvement at a high level of expertise.
> 3. There are deliberate programs to teach leaders disciplined problem solving through on the job development.
> 4. Leaders deliberately practice process improvement to enhance their skills every day.

Figure 4-11. Current State of Leadership in your company

The first question is whether leaders in your organization are developed to regularly go and see to observe people and processes and really have a picture of the current situation compared to True North. That of course means there is consensus on a clear vision of True North, so this is a multiple part question (not good for a survey question, but this is not a research project).

Two, Are leaders in your organization experts on process improvement? It does not count if they have delegated that to staff people or Lean coaches. In addition, it does not count if they took a course or went through some basic certification, but rarely use what they learned. Remember, process improvement is more than doing the math or filling out the worksheets or using the Lean tools. It means you can actually improve the process, which requires that you influence the people to learn and follow the new process in a disciplined way. You are not done until the process is operating at the new higher level and it becomes standard, routine work for the people running the process – it has stabilized.

Three – there are deliberate programs in place to teach Lean Leaders disciplined problem solving through on-the-job development, and there are coaches. The leaders have coaches like my guitar lesson today. Every week I go to my lesson. I play what I practiced this week. I get feedback. I then receive new drills and new assignments. Is anything like that happening in your organization to teach you how to be a leader who coaches process improvement to achieve difficult targets?

Finally, are leaders deliberately learning and practicing self-development? My guitar teacher cannot do anything if I do not practice any of the drills or assignments he gives me between lessons. Is deliberate practice focused on self-development common in the organization?

If your answers on all four of these are somewhere between one and three – there are some serious gaps or critical gaps – do not panic. It means that you are an average, regular company because very few companies focus intensely on developing Lean Leaders. Even Toyota has many weak spots.

Finally, develop a personal plan. What can you as a leader work on to begin your self-development? Part of that requires a coach. You may not be able to run to your boss right now and say, "Go and hire me a professional Lean coach." You have to go find somebody, and there are many different ways to find somebody. I have a friend who went on the Internet and found somebody and through one of the social network programs asked that person if they would do coaching online. That person was honored and said yes, and she really changed the life of my friend who moved from the bottom of the organization to an executive leading Lean coaches across a region of America.

There are many creative ways to find coaches. The Lean Leadership Institute has a website (www.LeanLeadership.guru), and there is coaching provided as part of the courses. Take advantage of any opportunity you have to find and use a coach. You can always improve yourself and others!

CHAPTER 5

LEARNING TO COACH AND DEVELOP OTHERS

While self-developing begin to learn how to develop others

You need some degree of self-development before you can begin developing others. The Lean Leadership Model (Figure 5-1) makes this look like a purely sequential process, but it is not. In fact, there is overlap across the four stages of the model and you are continually cycling through the stages getting stronger and stronger as an individual and as an organization.

The question for this chapter is how to move from self-development to coaching others to self-develop. In fact, we might ask how those new to Lean are coached to begin with so they might one day coach others. Unfortunately, while there are many excellent examples of coaching in sports, music, the arts, and crafts like plumbing and quilt making, it is difficult to find similar quality examples in work organizations.

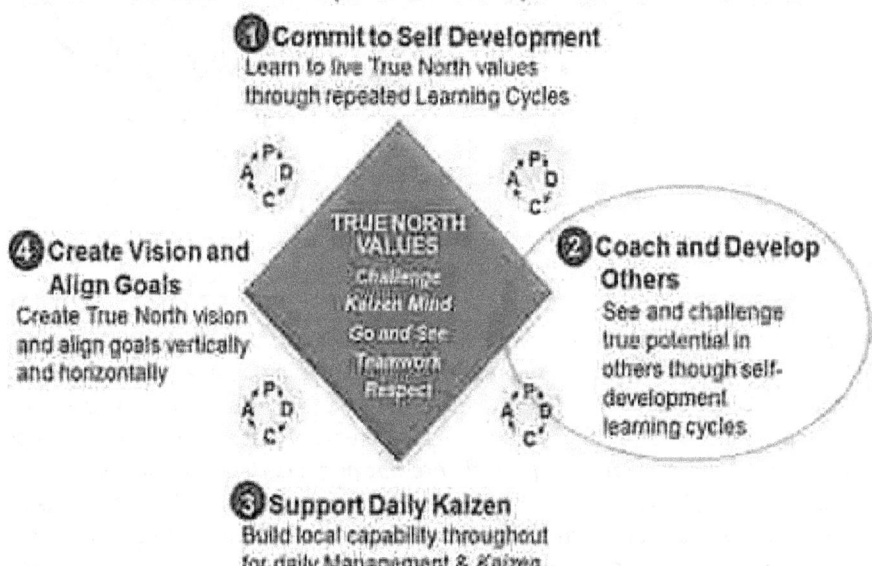

Source: *The Toyota Way to Lean Leadership*
Figure 5-1. The Lean Leadership Development Model

As we used Toyota as a model to develop the leadership model, we could trace a good deal of the concepts back to the master-apprentice relationship (see Figure 5-2). In that relationship, the master was the master, and the apprentice was the student who is humble, who is groveling, and who wants to learn from the master. The master can basically ask him to do anything, and the student is expected to do it. If the first lesson in learning to be a blacksmith is to clean the floor with a toothbrush, you clean the floor with a toothbrush. You assume the master has some reason for wanting you to do it – that there is some lesson that will come out of it.

Figure 5-2. The Master-Apprentice Craft Model

This very much influenced the Toyota culture. That is how Sakichi Toyoda was taught carpentry, and today that is still the method for developing people. Toyota now calls it "on the job development" (OJD), but the method of teaching skills within Toyota is the master-apprentice relationship. It does not happen every place. As I continually repeat, *Toyota is made up of people and people are not perfect.* There are all sorts of things that happen in a global company like Toyota, good and bad, but the model based on the principles is that you learn by doing with someone who is more expert watching you, analyzing what you do, and giving you feedback. They are asking you challenging questions. Toyota defines the most important role of a leader as teaching.

Learning to Develop Others

Up to this point the self-developing leader has been learning to live the values, and practice the process of "Plan, Do, Check, Act" through repeated learning cycles. Each time you take on a problem, you have to deal with teams of people, you have to show respect, take on the challenge. Each time you do that, you have gone through one learning cycle—like learning another musical piece and performing it. The next one should be a little easier to learn and you are getting a little better in your performance. Now you are ready to begin to go to the next step, which is, teach others what you have learned. You do not have to be a bona fide expert to develop others. In fact if you are honest and humble you may never feel ready.

According to Toyota, nobody is an expert. Nobody gets certified in The Toyota Way. You are always learning which should continue through your entire life. At some point, you have to decide either I need to or I am ready to begin to develop other people. As you learn in teaching a course, all you have to do is stay ahead of the students. You are on the next chapter ahead of them.

There is an old adage that the teacher always learns more than the students. As you try to teach others, you find that you start to question the holes in your understanding. You wonder: what if they ask this question and I do not know the answer? Alternatively, you question your judgment in a given situation. As that is happening, you are filling in the holes and you are deepening your understanding. In addition, you are very motivated because you are trying to teach and have responsibility. The students should also be engaged and motivated, but they are often in a more passive situation.

The teacher will usually deepen their understanding and you do not want to wait to start developing others until you are absolutely sure you are ready. When you think you have something to offer others take on the challenge. It still is important to have a coach to help you critically reflect on your own coaching. Now you are the coach, there is a learner, and the second coach is watching you coach and then, only after the coaching session, reflecting with you.

Teaching skills are different from learning skills. As a student: You listen, you try things, and you are tested by challenging questions that help you see your weaknesses and what to work on next. With you as the coach, you have to develop the skills to challenge and guide the student, without thinking for the student.

Coaching and developing others requires a different set of skills

You learned, practiced, reflected and used feedback from the teacher to get better at the improvement process. How do you convey these skills to others?

If you had a good teacher, you have a model. You can look at the model and plan how you are going to coach borrowing the effective methods of your teacher. Nevertheless, your teacher got really good through many PDCA cycles of coaching, and developed her own ways of responding to new situations. You cannot simply imitate your teacher's mature level of teaching even if it looks easy.

One of the first skills you need to learn is to see true potential in others. You are going to have to look at a person objectively, deeply, and kind of get inside their heads to really understand how this person is thinking. How is this person thinking about the problem and the current situation? Do they understand the purpose clearly? Have they picked the right problem? Are they good at root cause analysis? Are they patient in going through all the steps in problem solving or do they leap quickly from what they think is the problem to the solution? Are they good at listening? Are they good at taking coaching?

You have to judge these things because you have to teach at the right level for each particular student. Going back to analogies like music, if you have been playing for five years, you have been going to the summer festivals, and you are a star performer for your age, your teacher should teach you differently than if you are a novice just starting out.

The skill is to gauge where the students are in their maturity, in their problem solving capability, in their interpersonal skills, in their attitude. Are they embracing learning or are they resisting with their arms crossed? You have to treat them differently to get them to open up their arms. That is a key skill-set like seeing what is really going on at the *gemba* is a skill-set. What is the right challenge for this person (see Figure 5-3).

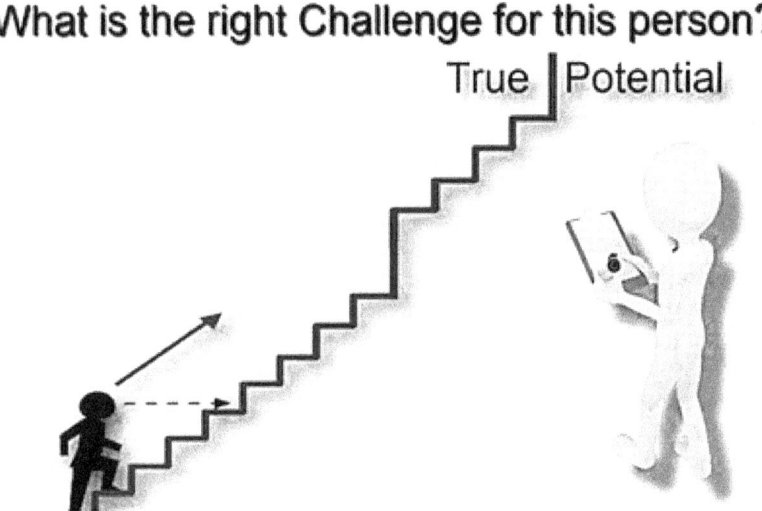

Figure 5-3. Defining the Right Challenge for the Student

This is just good Coaching and Teaching

If you have ever been a coach, perhaps of a young people sports team, one thing that may occur to you is "wait a second, this sounds like good coaching and good teaching, and it does not sound like something Toyota made up." If you feel that way, it is because you are right. Very little of what I am talking about was invented within Toyota. What happened is that Toyota would take the best pieces they found from many places and then put them together into their approach, into their system.

Job-Instruction Training is Learning by Doing with a Coach

One of Toyota's big influences on coaching and developing others is called "job instruction training" which came from a U.S. defense program "Training Within Industry" (TWI). It was one of the modules of TWI developed during World War II to quickly teach civilians to take over the jobs of the men going to war. Then it mostly died in the United States after World War II and it became very much alive within Toyota. (It is making a comeback recently because of Lean). The training method is very focused on learning by doing with a coach.

Unlike many large companies, in the history of Toyota there has never been an interruption in the model of the master-apprentice relationship. Again, is that something Toyota invented? Obviously not, but at least in concept it is something that they use throughout the company, in knowledge work jobs like engineering, as well as in repetitive jobs like production.

Beginning the Steps of Coaching and Developing Others

Leaders must be Developing as Coaches for Sustainable Improvement

I go to many different countries and many different industries and I have worked for the Navy and Air Force and in government, in healthcare, and "Lean" in its many forms has survived for three decades and is spreading. I believe it can legitimately be called a movement. However, the key weakness I still see is failure of leadership to ensure it is a sustainable way of life. Leaders need to be developed... preferably by other leaders in the organization. That is the only path to sustainable advantage.

Here are six steps to being an effective coach:

Step One: Assess in Others Their Current Understanding and Skills

The first step is to assess the current understanding and skills of the people who you will be teaching. If you thought about this on a mass basis, let's say you are in the human resource department, and you get the task of Lean Leadership training for hundreds of managers, it is quite natural to do an assessment, and the assessment will be done on some sort of paper and pencil test or computer test.

That is not what we are talking about. We are talking about the master-apprentice relationship. We are talking about one-on-one coaching. Even if you have a team of five to ten people, you have to have individualized instruction for those people. You are not really interested in statistical averages. You are interested in each person individually, and you cannot easily assess them by giving them a test with a paper and pencil. You can assess them by getting to know them by observing them in the workplace. As you begin to teach them, you will deepen your understanding of their skill levels.

In Toyota, they call this "Immersion at the *Gemba*." You have to immerse yourself where the people are working and they even give time for that in Toyota. As discussed earlier, as in the case of Steve St. Angelo, when a manager is moved to another department they will give them several months, 3 to 6 months is ideal, where the old manager will stay in place and the new manager will simply be grasping the situation. They will be trying to understand what is going on, trying to grasp the strengths and weaknesses of a process, of people. Again, they are developing a lesson plan. What should people work on? Who should work on it?

Step Two: Develop in Others Disciplined Problem Solving

The second step is to develop in others the disciplined problem solving you have been working on for yourself. You have repeatedly gone through all of the steps of PDCA. Now you will select someone to coach who will lead all of these steps and together select an improvement project. The learner, who is leading the improvement effort, will go through all the stages from defining the challenge, understanding the current situation, and defining the target, to PDCA cycles to move toward the target. You can use the Improvement *kata* methods introduced in Chapter Two, A3 thinking, or your own problem solving approach as long as the focus is on reaching for challenging targets and you have broken down the learning process into manageable pieces.

The student needs some sort of orientation to the improvement process you will be using, but do not assume that any type of problem solving training in a classroom will teach real skill. In fact, if you hold a formal class with a group of students you should perhaps post the following: "WARNING: At the end of today you will not have REAL SKILLS! This class is only for awareness to get you started. Skills will be developed at the *gemba*, going through the steps one at a time, and I am going to be there with you."

Step Three: Break Down Tasks & Give Assignments to Increase Skill Level

What is the right assignment for each person? Your student must work with a team to identify the problem, break it into smaller problems assigned to team members, with the goal of increasing their skill levels. Your student is going to have to keep the team together, focused on a common direction, and motivated to spend the time to work on their agreed upon tasks.

Now in the first session of problem solving, whatever it is, a half day or a day, you are doing some talking and you are more active as a traditional teacher. You tell them stuff. You check their understanding. It helps if you ask them questions and get people talking. You can use a case study or simulation to get them actively thinking and to provide opportunities for corrective feedback.

After the initial awareness training, you shift to your OJD mode. Now think of yourself as the master craftsperson and you have a young apprentice who is fumbling around and does not know the basic tools and you are giving them a first assignment. What is it you want to do to teach that person? Remember, that person is not being taught, that person is learning. Learning is coming from within. It is self-development.

It sometimes helps to think of teaching a common skill. You are teaching violin. You start out with scales for that person. They first have to get a good sound out of the bow. They have to hold the instrument correctly. Obviously, you have to show them how to hold the instrument and you have to show them what good bow technique is. You might ask them to use the bow with open strings so they can focus on the quality of the sound without the distraction of changing notes.

You notice that they are getting a terrible sound. What are you going to do? One thing you can do is to say, "Give me that" and pull the violin out of their hands. You can start playing and say, "See, this is what you are supposed to be doing" and hand the violin back to them. But guess what? They are still going to get the same terrible, screechy sound. They did not learn much by seeing you do it, and you put them under stress, which hampers learning.

A better approach is to say, "Try holding the bow like this, at this angle, and try again." Now they get a good sound, and a bunch of bad sounds. They are getting a little closer. Then you are going to let them play again and say "remember, I showed you how to hold the bow, I showed you the angle." Soon they play and they get a few more good sounds. The more you personally are touching the violin the worse you are as a teacher.

The following sayings make this clear:

- Tell me, and I will forget,
- Show me, and I may remember,
- Involve me, and I will understand.

Step Four: Teach by Questioning instead of Telling

Then you might ask them questions, for example using the five-questions of the coaching *kata* described at the end of this chapter. You will shift from some telling and explaining in the awareness course to getting the students launched on a project, then you have to let the students struggle, then you want to test the student's understanding by asking them questions instead of giving the answers. You have to let them struggle a bit and make some mistakes, but not so many mistakes that the wrong way becomes engrained in their neural-pathways. Then you are going to give them homework if you are teaching violin, and they are going to practice without you there, do daily drills, until the next lesson. Similarly, you are going to give assignments to the leader you are coaching on problem solving, they are going to practice, and you will come back and check on them, preferably daily. Without practice, they will not learn deeply.

Teaching by questioning instead of by telling is a kind of art. You can think of it as the Socratic method of teaching. The idea is that you draw out of the person what they know or what they can figure out, what they can reason through. If they can reason through it, and do the mental work, they are deepening their understanding. If they only listen to you, they are simply parroting back what you are expressing. You are the one doing the thinking. The coaching *kata* is quite routine to get started and you ask the questions exactly as written, though some clarifying questions can be added. As you progress in your skill level you can ad lib to a greater degree.

Now teaching by questioning does not mean you do not have to tell them anything. It is just that what you want to tell them are in bite size pieces. "Hold the bow this way; strike the string at this angle. Now try this with open strings." Then you ask them question after question, maybe give them another tip, and then give them exercises to do to practice. You as a coach will get better at it with practice, especially with your own coach looking over your shoulder.

Step Five: Build Trusting Relationships with your Students

Master trainers have many different styles. You have all heard about or experienced the boss, or perhaps a master trainer, who is very punitive. They yell at you until you get things right. In most cases, if somebody is yelling at you your reaction is going to be defensive, or you are going to shut down, or you are going to be nervous. You are going to try to hide your mistakes. It is far better to build a trusting relationship and if I am the student what I have to trust is *not* that you will never criticize me, but that you have my well-being in mind.

This is not about you. This is not for your ego or to demonstrate your control as a leader. This is for you to actually teach me something because you care about my development and me. If I trust you in that way, even if you raise your voice sternly, and if deep down I know you care about my success, I will take the feedback more productively. Taiichi Ohno was a yeller and he got great results with his students in Japan, in part because of the culture, in part because of his high level of credibility, and in large part because they knew he deeply cared about them.

Step Six: Balance Praise with Critical Feedback

Trust is very important. Again, do not confuse trust with always being a nice person and only saying positive things. On the other hand, you need to judge the right balance of praise and critical feedback for that individual. Every good coach knows that they cannot coach everybody the same way. Some people will only value critical feedback while others will fall apart and they need to be lifted up with praise for the good things they did.

When the Japanese from Toyota first came to America to set up shop they discovered that the approach they used for coaching in Japan was creating some problems here. In Japan, Ohno's stern approach was quite acceptable at the time. The subordinate will bow, they will bow more deeply the more guilty they feel, and then they are going to try their best. They are going to reflect and they are going to say "I am going to try better next time," and then the master will say "Ok." You will rarely hear the master praise the student. It is very unusual. If it happens once in a year, you will mark that day on your calendar. "My boss actually said something nice."

In the United States, when Toyota established the Georgetown, Kentucky plant in the 1980s, the critical approach of some Japanese trainers caused Americans to get mad, to go to the human resources department, and to feel insecure. The American leaders had to point this out to the Japanese who, instead of being defensive, took this as the reality from which to learn.

Their initial step of containment was to come up with a standardized rule coaching Americans: for every one thing that you say that is critical, you should say three things that are positive. They found that this ratio seemed to work. First, find three good things to say about how they are learning quickly, the quality they have achieved, how well they are doing at following the standardized work and then say "but, there is this one thing you can work on that I think will help you improve even more."

Larry Miller reviewed literature on this subject and found a research study divided teacher-student interactions into positive (approving, praising, etc.), neutral, and negative (wrong answer, correcting behavior) and found that the highest rates of learning were achieved when the teachers behavior was 3.57 to one, positive to negative (http://www.lmmiller.com/blog/2014/06/28/corporate-culture/coaching-kata-2/). This is remarkably similar to what the Toyota teachers intuited.

Again, a very positive approach will work with some people. Other people will say, "Why are we playing these games? Why are you telling me all these things I know I do well? Let's just get right to what I can do to improve!" Over time, I think more people get that attitude as they come to trust the teacher. "I really want critical feedback because I am interested in developing myself."

How to Coach and Develop Others at the *Gemba*

What does a great coach do to build a winning team?

Figure 5-4. Vince Lombardi and another victory

Vince Lombardi (see Figure 5-4) is certainly looked up to in America as a great coach based on what he did for the Green Bay Packers football team. One of his infamous quotes:

"Winning is not a sometime thing; it's an all-time thing. You do not win once in a while, you do not do things right once in a while, you do them right all the time. Winning is a habit. Unfortunately, so is losing." *–Vince Lombardi*

You can be, or your student can be, in the habit of winning or losing. Now in this case, winning might mean I did the project, we improved, and I met my target so I won. That is one possibility.

Another possibility is I went through the process, tried some things, some failed and others succeeded and we made serious progress, either meeting the final target or not, AND we reflected throughout and **learned** a great deal.

For Lombardi, in practice, and in the regular season, he expected his team to continually learn and get better. He also expected them to win—losing was not a success no matter what. On the other hand, in the game of Continuous Improvement, particularly in the early stages of changing the culture, the game is all about learning. What you want to do is make it a habit of doing the right things in the right way. Then you will win more often than you will lose. Whether you win or lose, you can go back, look at the tape, and figure out how you can do better next time. There is always a next game and you always focus on getting better by the next game.

Great Coach Characteristics Exercise

When I do a live course, we have small groups of people and they have table discussions addressing these questions. I recommend that you pause, address the questions, and even write down some thoughts. Perhaps you have been a coach, you have experienced winning or losing, you could be a fan of a team and you may know when there is a good coach, and might get mad and frustrated by bad coaching decisions. Ask yourself:

- What are the characteristics of a great coach?
- What is it that they are doing that allows them to build a winning team?

Over time, develop routines that come naturally and free yourself up to adapt and innovate.

What any good coach is doing is identifying weak points and asking you to practice repetitively without playing through your mistakes. The natural tendency is to want to jump ahead, and feel like "I got it," or "I did it wrong a couple times, but I did it right 10 times, that is good enough," And move on. The coach is going to be pulling you back. Eventually you are going to develop routines that come so naturally you do not even think about it, moving beyond the *Shu* stage. After you have been playing violin for years, you do not start your practice session by saying "now where do I put my fingers again to properly hold the bow?" You just grab the bow and naturally hold it correctly.

Occasionally you might have to go back and revisit that, but for the most part that has become a routine, a habit. You know where the notes are. You are not thinking, "Where is the C note?" As these things become routine, the right ways are engrained in your mind. Now you have some freedom to begin to think about how to interpret the piece or how to creatively approach this problem. Then, how much time do I really have to spend on root cause analysis before I feel I have it? Maybe I should spend more time on brainstorming alternative solutions or engaging this one person who still is resisting. You can actually read, react, and adapt to the situation creatively instead of wondering, "Am I following problem solving step four correctly?"

10,000 Hours of Practice to Mastery of Complex Skills

It has become a truism that 10,000 hours of practice is necessary to become an expert at a complex skill. Really this is an imprecise rule of thumb demonstrated for some specific skills. It is certainly not a law of physics. However, 10,000 hours is an awful lot of time. If you think about practicing 10 hours a week, that is 1000 weeks, and if you take a couple weeks off per year, you will take 20 years to master the skill.

That does not mean that we need to either practice for 20 years, or decide it is not worth it, and give up trying. It should inspire us to strive for mastery, with the humbleness to realize how far we are from perfection.

The Key to Lean Leadership is Developing Others at the *Gemba*

Figure 5-5. Coaching to develop in others knowledge and skill

I am using the term "Lean Leadership," and a key characteristic of Lean Leadership is that you are learning (see Figure 5-5), and you are developing others at the *gemba*, "where it is happening." I would like to make sure that the concept of *gemba* is broad enough. Some people think the *gemba* is only where core value-added work is happening. In manufacturing, the factory is sometimes thought to be the only *gemba*. A Medtronic factory in Florida, one quite advanced in Lean, had a cafeteria they had to walk through to get to the factory and they made a big sign over the door to the factory that said "welcome to the *gemba*." They wanted to emphasize that the factory is doing the value-added work that is paying the bills.

On the other hand, for the cooks, the kitchen is their *gemba*—where they are preparing and serving the food. The accountants have a *gemba*, and human resources have a *gemba*. For human resources the *gemba* is where the people are, and the people can be in the cafeteria, they can be in the office, they can be on the factory floor. For sales, the *gemba* is where the customers are. There are a lot of *gemba* but it is really where, for the type of work you are doing, value is being added from the customer perspective—internal or external. The value added is happening when you are actually accomplishing your goals. You are serving high quality food efficiently to your customers. Your customers are happy using the product and they are satisfied that it is reliable.

Using *Kata* to Coach One Person at a Time

How do you roll this out in your organization?

There are a lot of ways to roll this out whether it is deeply in a small area, whether it is the top, middle or bottom, whether it is one level of management and you are going across broadly. The one constant in all this is you have to have enough coaches to coach the number of people you want to learn. I would say a reasonable ratio is one coach for about five people and not more than that. If you want to coach 100, you need 20 coaches. That will immediately cause some people to step back and say, "Wait a second, I do not have 20 coaches who have the deep skills."

My advice is scale back your initial plans and focus on what you have the resources to do well. You can get coaches from the outside, but you have to select them carefully because they need to have the teaching ability, not only the doing ability. Then they perform like yeast. You do not start the bread rising until you have the yeast. Moreover, if I have yeast for one loaf of bread I cannot make 15 loafs of bread at the same time. You have to start somewhere. Again, we need to understand the problem, the gaps, the root cause, develop a plan, a countermeasure, and you have to match the resources with what you are trying to accomplish, then you try, then you check, then you adjust and figure out the next step. The problem is a gap between the skills you want your leaders to have and their current skills. You are applying PDCA to the process of developing people. If you follow this process, you are going to make good progress.

Using the Coaching *Kata* to teach the Improvement *Kata*

The recommended approach to roll out improvement and coaching skills in Toyota *Kata* is to start with an "advance group." This is the group of senior leaders who are responsible for deploying the *kata*. Advance means they must go first in learning the improvement *kata*, often with external coaches (see figure 5-6). They then learn to be the first coaches of learners in their organization. Even when they develop coaches they do not disappear, but are still regularly at the *gemba* checking the process and making adjustment as well as decisions about where to go next with the training, how many people will be trained, and the speed of deployment.

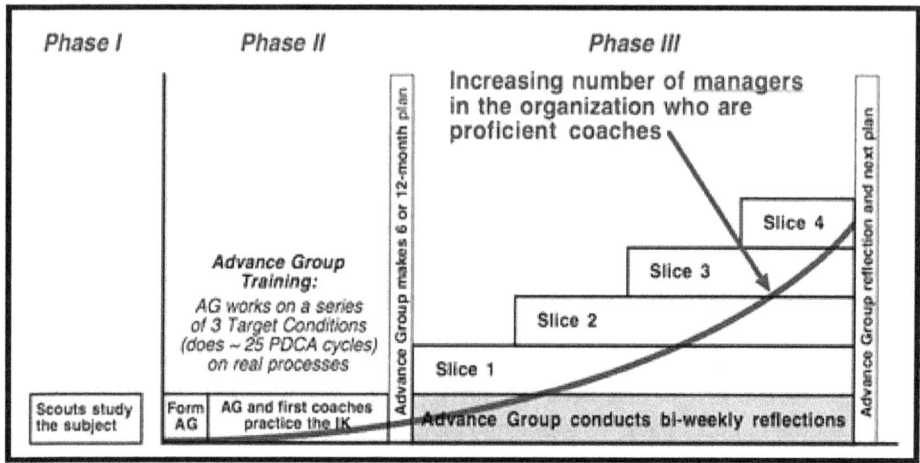

Source: Mike Rother

Figure 5-6. Recommended Approach to deployment of the Improvement *Kata*

The Improvement *Kata* (IK), from Mike Rother's book *Toyota Kata,* was summarized in Chapter Two. He also developed the Coaching *Kata* for deliberate practice of coaching routines. Just as OJD in Toyota is the mirror image of Toyota Business Practices, the Coaching *Kata* is simply a reversal of roles. The learner of the IK becomes the coach and is teaching a new learner of the IK.

There is always one coach who is responsible for developing one learner leading a particular project. The learner will be using the specific pattern of the Improvement *Kata* and the coach has a pattern to follow as well (see figure 5-7). The coach will work closely with the student through the four steps of the IK starting with establishing the direction, which should be linked to broader business goals of the organization.

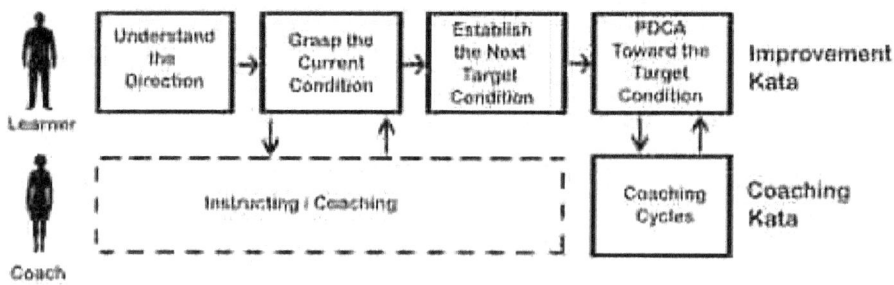

Source: Mike Rother

Figure 5-7: The Improvement *Kata* and Coaching *Kata* are Mirror Images

The documentation method will be the learner's storyboard presented in Chapter Two. That is where the coach and learner will meet. By the fourth step, after the next target condition has been established, the focus will be on PDCA cycles where the doing takes place (see Figure 5-8). In the PDCA cycle the learner is planning the next experiment, conducting the experiment, checking what happened, and reflecting on what was learned which leads to the next experiment. These experiments are focused on the next target condition, which is in the direction of the broader challenge. When the target condition is met (perhaps every 2 weeks) then the next target condition is identified.

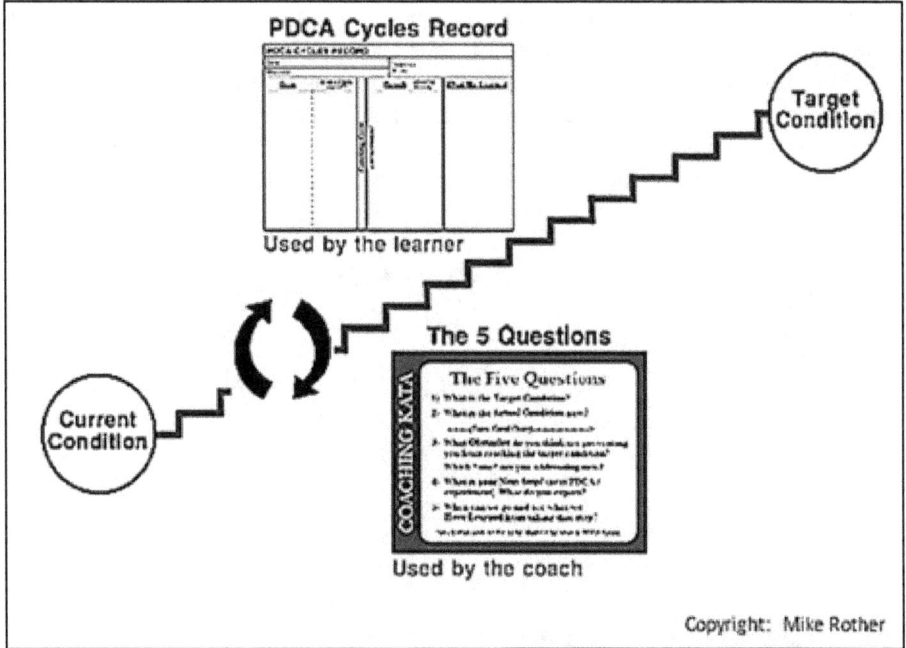

Figure 5-8: The coach has a defined routine of questions during step 4 of PDCA cycles to achieve the next target condition

The standard work for the coach is very clear in the PDCA Cycles stage. It is focused on asking prescribed questions precisely as shown in Figure 5-9. You are standing with the learner in front of the Improvement *Kata* storyboard and the learner is answering questions. All the information needed to answer the questions is summarized on the storyboard. The coach is asking the questions and the learner is answering them while pointing to the board. The coach has some leeway. The coach can ask clarifying questions if an answer is not satisfactory. The coach can suggest we go and see at the *gemba* to clarify the learner's explanations. But for the most part the coach is expected to follow the script—to learn the pattern as the learner is learning the Improvement *Kata* pattern.

Notice that the coach asks general questions about the project causing the learner to think about the gap they are trying to close—target condition versus actual condition now. Then they reflect on only a single step—the last one taken. They take the time to think about what they learned from that step. Then they identify the additional obstacles to the target condition and describe to the coach the next step they plan on taking. They commit to a deadline for completing that step. Then the whole process starts over.

Figure 5-9: The Question Card is the Standard Work for the Coach

Three-Part Recipe for What Lean Leaders Must Learn

Recipe for what Lean Leaders need to Learn

1. Live the core values of the philosophy – *Toyota Way* 2001
2. Become a role model for disciplined problem solving – Toyota Business Practices (or Improvement *Kata*)
3. Become a teacher and coach for disciplined problem solving – On the Job Development (or Coaching *Kata*)

You can look for examples in my book, *The Toyota Way*, as providing principles, step one. Then you look at Mike Rother's book *Toyota Kata* and he is providing what to do, the Improvement *Kata*, which is like Toyota Business Practices, and the Coaching *Kata*, which is to teach "on-the-job-development."

Review the Three-Part Recipe – What Lean Leaders Need to Learn

The recipe for what leaders need to learn is really a three-part solution. It has been laid out well in practice at Toyota. First, there was recognition back in the 1990-2000 periods that there was a need to be more explicit for developing leadership within Toyota outside of Japan. There was a period where they had many Japanese coaches in North America in the 1980s, and the Japanese coaches were doing detailed coaching of every leader down to the team leader. They were the masters training the America apprentices. By the end of the decade, they had to start pulling them back from the United States and Canada to other places where they were needed. What they discovered was that even with the intense training many of the Americans still had work to do in the *Shu* stage. They were losing Americans who were relatively advanced in their learning to other companies, who wanted former Toyota leaders, and they had to bring in new people from the outside or they were promoting people from within who lacked the deep skill levels.

The first solution was to write down Toyota's core values. They were implicitly known in Japan by those growing up in the culture. They had been evolving since the founding as a loom company, but they never had to write them down because they were taught through the master-apprentice relationship. "Now we need to teach it in a less passive and more overt way. We need to write it down." Toyota growth and globalization led to an increasing need to write that down, which led to the booklet called *The Toyota Way 2001* with the twin pillars of Respect for People and Continuous Improvement. The foundation is the five core values we talked about: Challenge, go to the *gemba* and see, develop a kaizen mind, respect and teamwork.

They wrote it down, they described each of these values, they had sub-values, and they had examples, famous quotes from founders and leaders from the past. Then they had a training course and the training course was to learn the values through case studies so Toyota managers could apply the values and discuss them.

They started training from the top, executive vice-president level, and worked their way down to the group leaders. As they were rolling that out in the early stages of teaching the senior leaders, they realized was it was powerful. It was starting to get people to articulate and speak the same language of The Toyota Way, but there was not enough action. There was not enough "doing" to actually socialize these people so that the values became routines. What do you do to make these routines? They needed disciplined practice.

This then led to developing Toyota Business Practices (TBP), the eight-step problem-solving model discussed in Chapter Two, which continues to be the global standard for Toyota. For each of the steps there are defined values that you learn by doing that step in the right way. For example, the first step is defining the problem. One of the values of the company is customer first, and you should be defining the problem in a way that puts the customer first. What does the customer need from this process?

More recently, Toyota developed a formal approach to "On-the Job Development." It was developed in the United States because by now Americans had learned a great deal, and since they were not Japanese, they understood the explicit learning process needed by other countries. It has a lot of similarities to the Coaching *Kata* approach though it is not as detailed.

Changing Culture through Changing Behavior

I first learned of this model from John Shook who went on to run the Lean Enterprise Institute. He did not invent it, but he clearly articulated the thinking. He explained that the common approach (see Figure 5-10) is to attempt to directly change the way people think. We need to get in their heads. Then if they think the right way, they will act in the right way. The way we teach people to think is by telling them things. "I am the leader, I am thinking the right way, now I have to pour my knowledge into your head. The way I learned in school was from a teacher lecturing in front of the room, so now I am the teacher in front of the room." Guess what? It does not work.

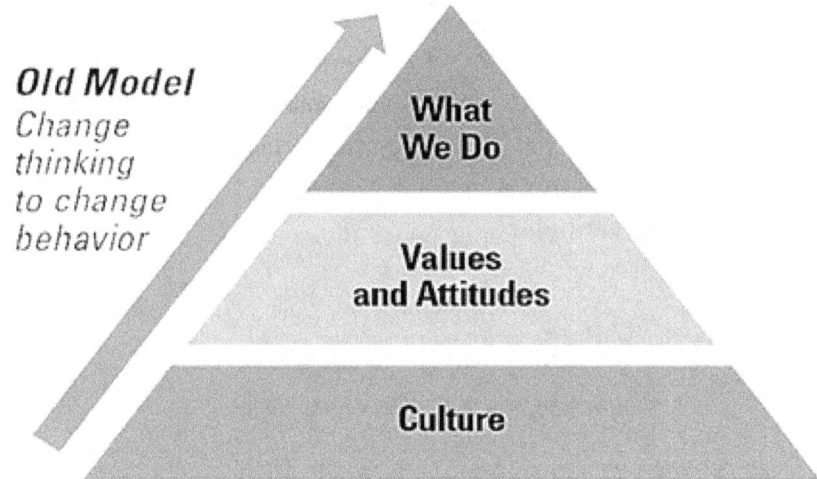

Figure 5-10. The Old Model of Thinking

Anyone who is familiar with Alcoholics Anonymous will recognize that changing behavior and thinking for any complex behavior pattern is a step-by-step process, one-step at a time, and will recognize that you need to meet with a coach, do something, and then come back and report to the coach and support group. That is also the model that they found worked back in WWII to change eating habits and became the basis of weight watchers. That model works for Lean Leadership.

What John further explained is that if you want to get to culture, start with what we do (see Figure 5-11). The new model is change behavior, and as people directly experience a new way of working, leading, and behaving, their way of thinking changes. The alcoholic is starting to see how they can live a happy life without alcohol. They start to feel better and then it starts to hit them like "oh my gosh, all those things I have been told for years actually work, it is changing my life for the better." They could not understand it when they were constantly drunk, no matter what anyone said.

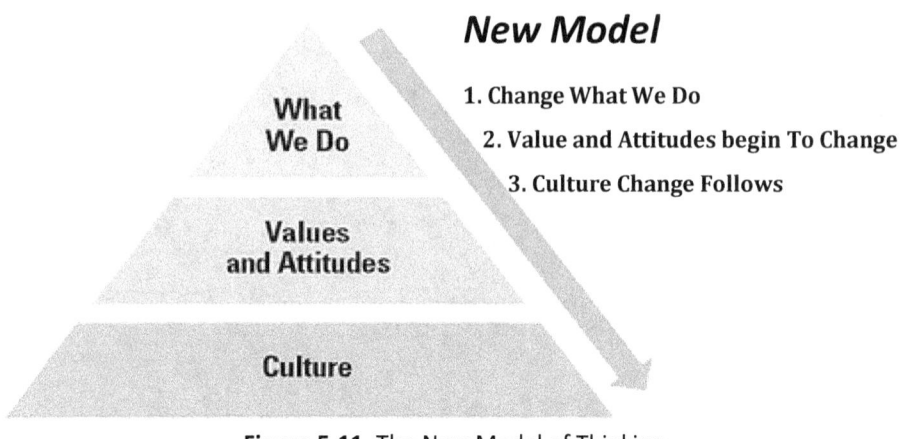

Figure 5-11. The New Model of Thinking

As you change behavior, your world view changes. John found a profound quote to describe this: "It is easier to act your way to a new way of thinking than to think your way to a new way of acting." This is very much The Toyota Way, as Sakichi Toyoda learned through hard work guided by his father. Somehow, this philosophy got lost in most American companies and we adopted the model of trying to change behavior by telling people things.

How can this Apply to Developing Others in Your Organization?

Rate your organization's leadership

Now we are up to the point where you can assess how you are doing compared to this idealized image I gave of Toyota. Let me just say that not every leader who went through The Toyota Way training, Toyota Business Practices training, and On-the-Job Development was a star. Some learned deeply, while others only superficially. After the early stages, there was a small group at the North American level who were coaching and the assumption is that the leaders will then coach the next level and you will over time need less staff support. Is it true that everybody was perfectly trained and did a great job of coaching? The answer is no. Toyota is far from perfect, but they try and the effort they make is heroic. In fact, it is remarkable compared to what most companies do.

I am asking you to assess your organization under the assumption that in most cases you have pretty big gaps. In the last chapter, you defined the ideal state for your organization. What would an ideal leader look like? Now I am assuming some things in my questions here. For example, I am assuming that in your ideal state those leaders are going to be teachers and coaches. I would not expect you to disagree with that, as it is a fundamental assumption of Lean Leadership. This is the *Shu* stage where you are the student and I am the master. I am telling you that leaders should be teachers and coaches, but exactly what the cores values are that your leaders are modeling can be subject to some variation. What, in your words, words that are meaningful to you, would an ideal leader be doing, thinking, and saying to develop others? Then, based on that ideal vision, what is the current state of your leadership? (See Figure 5-12).

Current state of Leadership in your company

Figure 5-12. The Goal

1=Critical Gap, 2=Major Gap, 3=Some serious Gaps, 4=Minor Gaps, 5=We are there

Toyota might have more minor gaps, and you might have more major gaps. However, is it a critical gap? Is it a really major gap that is urgent? On the other hand, is it a serious gap that is not quite so urgent? Is it pretty minor? Alternatively, are you there? If you say you are there on even one of these things then I would say you are rating yourself too high, because nobody is there. On the other hand, if you have a few minor gaps then that is great. Most of you will score anywhere from one to three on most of these items.

1. Are leaders developed to be teachers and coaches?

Are leaders at all levels of your organization skilled and active at teaching and coaching improvement? If you say we are all doing that then I would suggest you go to the *gemba* and look some more. Go back to the basics. Stand in a circle and watch. Tell me if they are really teaching and coaching.

2. Leaders at all levels value people development enough to give space and time for learning by doing.

When we were working on *Toyota under Fire,* I interviewed Akio Toyoda and asked him what they learned from the recall crisis, from the reaction in America, from all the negative publicity that Toyota got? I also noted that there were some analysts arguing that Toyota's problem was that they were growing too fast. Did Akio agree with that?

He said, "No, I do not agree we were growing too fast. Growth is good. I would say that the rate of growth was faster than the rate of people development." Toyota was falling down in how well they were developing people as they were rapidly growing, and bringing in a lot of new people. He would not concede that it was impossible to develop those people at the right rate. He would just concede that they were not doing it well enough, and they needed to do better.

Akio gave me an example of when he was first hired into Toyota. His dad agreed he could come work at the company, but only if he started at the bottom like everyone else. His dad wanted him to take the toughest assignment possible, and the toughest assignment was in the Operations Management Consulting Division, (OMCD), the boot camp for learning the Toyota Production System.

That is where the tough sensei are. They send you to a supplier, they give you a seemingly impossible challenge, you are in over your head, and you sink or swim. What Akio Toyoda said is that "with the assignment I got with a supplier, when I was first assigned there to understand the root cause, it took me three months." He said, "If my boss had worked on the root cause, he could have easily done it in three weeks. His boss could have done it within three days. The head of OMCD could have done it in three minutes."

You have a huge gap of three months to three minutes. What do you do if you are the head of OMCD and you have a bunch of people working on projects, and they are taking three months to do what you can do in three minutes? That can be very frustrating watching them flail around and in the meantime projects are not advancing and you have your boss on you because they want results. What is the natural response? Tell them the answer. Give them three days then tell them the answer. Akio Toyoda said that by the year 2000, when Toyota was growing fast, this was happening too often. The coaches that were supposed to be coaches were giving the answers too readily. They were not giving people the space to struggle so they could actually learn how to identify the root cause.

As a countermeasure, Toyota started to go back to the basics of how to teach, how to coach, as well as adding layers of management. For example in engineering, they ended up in the growth period with perhaps one manager for every 20 to 25 engineers. This is not a good ratio for coaching, so they added in a layer of management with the goal of one assistant manager for every five engineers, going back to the way they used to be.

3. Leaders at all levels are actively engaged in selecting and developing future leaders based on abilities in leading, teaching, and coaching process improvement.

Not all people are created equal. Not all people are going to be learning at an even pace, not all people are equally motivated and determined and purposeful. You have to watch people, and you have the luxury, if you were watching them at the *gemba*, to see them in action over a long period of time. This is not the three-day interview process where you have to judge a person and make a big commitment to hire them based on seeing them in artificial situations for a few days. You are now getting to see these people over time. You are deciding who should be promoted based on their ability to follow your company values, their ability to execute, their ability to lead and teach others and their potential. Who is ready for an assignment to take on more people to coach and teach? Who needs to stay where they are because they need to develop their own capabilities before they can take on responsibility for others?

4. Leaders at all levels are modeling the core values of the company.

The selection and development process takes many years and if your organization did not already start this ten years ago expect low scores in this case. Expect lots of ones to threes. The scores of one are obviously going to be a higher priority than the threes, and if you do have minor gaps, feel proud of yourself and fortunate because it is so unusual.

This is just a general, qualitative assessment of leadership in your company. If you decide to turn this into a survey and do a formal survey of hundreds of people you are probably going too far. If you decide "let me get a team of people together and we are going to each individually rate where we are. Then we are going to have a discussion amongst ourselves to try and come to a consensus on these five things," that would be a very good process.

In summary, please rate the following:

1. Leaders are developed to be teachers and coaches.
2. Leaders at all levels value people development enough to give space and time for learning by doing.
3. Leaders at all levels are actively engaged in selecting and developing future leaders based on abilities in leading, teaching, and coaching process improvement.
4. Leaders at all levels are modeling the core values of the company.

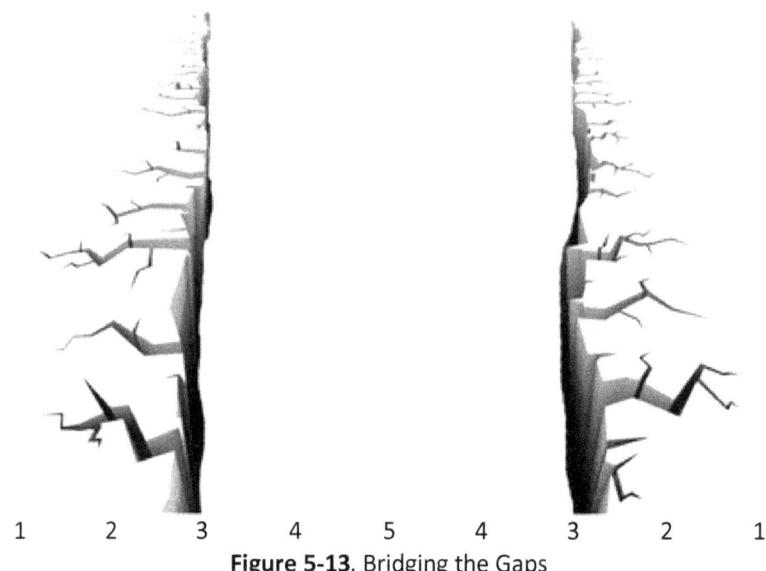

1   2   3   4   5   4   3   2   1

Figure 5-13. Bridging the Gaps

What is your next step toward attaining Lean Leadership?

Summarize key points in your vision of a Lean Leader. Look at the gaps (see Figure 5-13). Then ask yourself how you might apply this to your organization. Are you ready for a formal training process in On-The-Job-Development or the Coaching *Kata*?

- o Summarize key points you heard about how to coach others as a Lean Leader.
- o How might you apply this to your organization?
- o What is the targeted/measurable project that you can work on as a first step and what would the plan look like?

Now as you think about how to apply this to your organization, think about the improvement process. Do not start by listing brainstormed ideas of 100 ways of how to apply this to your organization. Actually, think about where your organization is compared to where it should be as we just went through. Think about how to break down that big gap into a targeted, measurable challenge you can work on as a first step. Then work through the improvement process as we have discussed.

If you carefully follow the PDCA process, you will come up with good first steps directed toward your vision. You will make progress. The problem is not "I am here, leaders are not Coaches, they do not know how to teach, they do not know how to problem solve, and I want to be there." The problem is "I see an ideal vision, I see how far we are from that vision, and I need to have a clear first goal post for my first set of steps." If you think about it that way, it is manageable, not so overwhelming. The more you practice the more it becomes deeply rooted in your organization.

CHAPTER 6
SUPPORT DAILY KAIZEN

Bringing Lean Leadership to Work Groups

Review of Self-Development and Developing Others

In Chapters Four and Five, we looked at developing self-developing leaders who can then teach and coach others (see Figure 6-1). We started the first two steps of our model. I asked you after each of these sessions to first think about how these ideas of leadership compared to the reality of your organization and in the first step think about self-development and steps that you could take to begin to improve your skills, mainly in problem solving. In the second step, I asked you to think about how you can start to coach and develop others. I hope that you have been practicing some of this. You assessed yourself, you saw gaps and opportunities, and I hope you are engaged in the hard work of improving your skills.

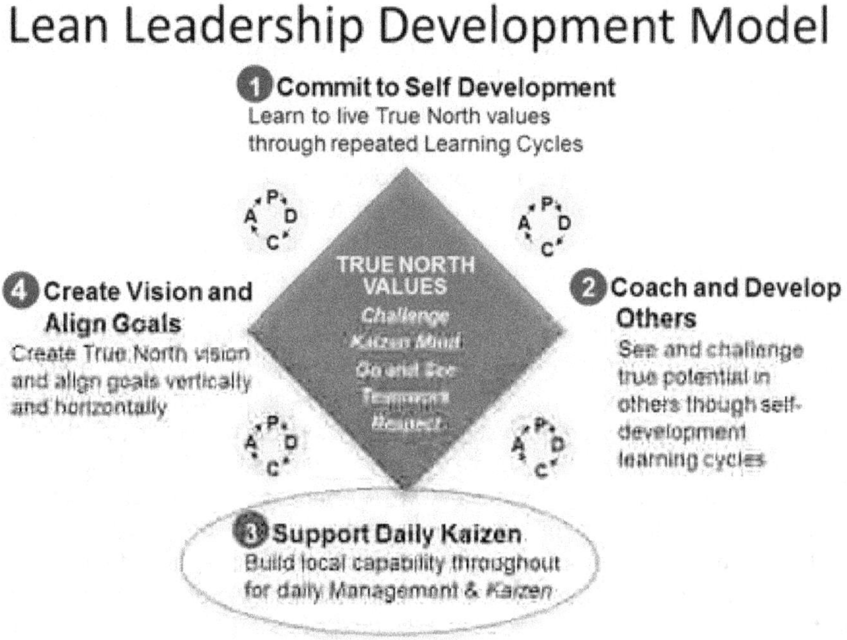

Lean Leadership Development Model

1. Commit to Self Development
Learn to live True North values through repeated Learning Cycles

TRUE NORTH VALUES
Challenge
Kaizen Mind
Go and See
Teamwork
Respect

4. Create Vision and Align Goals
Create True North vision and align goals vertically and horizontally

2. Coach and Develop Others
See and challenge true potential in others though self-development learning cycles

3. Support Daily Kaizen
Build local capability throughout for daily Management & Kaizen

Figure 6-1. The Lean Leadership Development Model (The Diamond Model)

Normally what happens in an organization that we work with is that we are brought in at a high level, possibly a vice president level or above. Then we are delegated to a manager or director of Continuous Improvement. We work directly with the Continuous Improvement group and they become our students, and we coach them so they can develop themselves. In each project group there is a leader. It could be a leader of a software development process or a manufacturing process, or a customer service center, and we develop that leader by coaching them through actual improvement projects using the PDCA method. We are developing the coach, we are also developing the manager, and we are starting normally from the top down. By top down we mean in the middle of the organization, let's say the manager of a department is the top of that department.

Let's assume we are successful in doing that. The coaches in training and leaders have begun to learn. The people in the project department have gone through some training and been involved in Kaizen activities. Let's say there is a department of thirty people, and that is a lot to coach, so we would often focus on one area of that department and on the people involved in a particular process. Then we would begin to move across the department to involve more and more people at the working level.

At some point, the leaders have been developed to the point where they can lead improvement toward challenging targets, and their group has enough experience with kaizen that the work group is relatively self-sufficient. At this point, they can have daily meetings to discuss the results of the previous day and what they can work on improving today. That is what we call daily management or daily improvement. It is the local capability throughout the organization for daily kaizen, and it takes some steps to get there. This is particularly true when we are starting from scratch with an organization that has not done a lot of improvement or perhaps they have used a mechanistic approach and only the black belts are leading projects. Now we are trying to penetrate into the line organization and start to develop the managers and supervisors and then the people who are doing the core work.

The process, as I described it, is starting at the middle and working down. Ideally, we would have started with developing the top, but certainly, we want to get them committed. In reality, we may need to get some success at the working level before we can get the attention of the top to suggest, "Hey, It would be nice if you showed up sometimes at the *gemba* and let people know why you are here." This is what we are trying to do. Unfortunately the mistake that we see very often is someone from the top gets the idea of "Continuous Improvement" and they have read my book or someone else's book and they like the idea, and they particularly like the idea of people at the working level solving their own problems. The problem is that they do not understand how to get from where they are to a culture of Continuous Improvement, or understand how much of their own involvement it takes.

The Challenge of Doing it Right, Not Fast

We worked with a big organization where the COO was very excited about Lean. We took him to visit another retail chain we had worked with that was pretty far advanced with Lean, and he came back and said, "I want that. I want what they have. I want their system." But the system that he wanted had been developed over about five years. They learned through a lot of growing pains to get to where they were, but he wanted the results now—instant pudding.

One of the things he noticed is that the supervisors met with their people around metric boards, and they all had the same headings for key performance indicators on the metric boards. He also saw they had figures that show "here is my target, here is how I am improving towards my target," and there were areas where they were writing out suggestions from employees and implementing those suggestions. That is what he wanted. However, what he was seeing was a point on a serious journey.

Then what do you do when you go back home if you are a COO of a major retail chain? These guys do not think they have a lot of time and they like to act. What you do is you buy a lot of boards. We had not done anything with him. Our contract did not even start for a month. He said excitedly in a phone call, "you guys are going to be so excited. I went out and bought 150 boards, I am having them put in every department, and we are going to have standard metric categories. We are not even going to wait until you come. We are starting now."

My reaction, not to him on the phone, but my thinking process was "Oh my gosh, what are we getting ourselves into? What are these people going to do with these metric boards? They have no skills. Nobody is working with them. Nobody is coaching them." It is like buying a golf scorecard for someone who has never touched a club and expecting them to get a great score. That is an example of a common mistake. What is tangible? What you can see are the boards and the metrics. You can see people having meetings. An executive in charge can also mandate that from now on, every morning for fifteen minutes, every department is going to have a meeting around the metric boards.

I heard a story from a different company about someone who worked in a plant where they had their version of the Toyota Production System, and he talked to some of the hourly workers who were saying, "We come into work every day and we have more work than we can handle. We know that we are going to be in trouble by the end of the day. Yet we have to stand in front of the stupid board in a meeting for fifteen minutes." Obviously, that is not what you want. You do not want to have people standing in front of boards and a supervisor, untrained, going through the metrics saying, "You know what we have to do guys, now get to it! By the way, get back to work!" What this chapter is about is how you can get to real daily improvement as opposed to a bunch of metric boards and a bunch of people who are wasting their time standing in front of them.

Toyota work groups are at the heart of Continuous Improvement

Daily Huddles around Metric Boards can aid Effective Work Groups

How do you answer that question, "why are we wasting our time in this daily meeting?" The answer is, use the time effectively so people are not wasting their time.

The reason they are wasting their time is that the supervisor has not been trained on how to effectively run a meeting, effectively use the metric board, or effectively improve processes. Someone just stuck the boards out there. Really, the question should be going to that chief operating officer, not to the people at the working level. We are just seeing the consequence at their level of a bad decision made at the top by someone who is thinking in mechanistic terms. "I saw people meeting around boards. They were making lots of improvements. I want lots of improvements, so I will get boards." This is simplistic cause and effect thinking—the boards cause improvement. There must be some magical treatment of the boards—a brain stimulating coating perhaps. What he was missing was the five years of work that went into training and developing these people so that the supervisors really understood how to be effective in leading Continuous Improvement.

I will rarely hear complaints from working level people if they are improving something. They can see that we had a meeting, we saw a problem, then throughout the day, there was somebody working on it and we came in the next day and it was improved. It might be an ergonomic issue of excessive reaching down to get parts. " I came back the next day, and the parts were presented at the right height so I no longer have to reach down. Now I am going to be motivated to go to those meetings." When there is an effective process then the board becomes an aid to that process. The board is not the cause of Continuous Improvement.

Visual Controls so No Problems are Hidden

The purpose of the boards is to provide visual control and, as we learned in Chapter Three, visual control is really a way to show the gap between where **you want to be** and where **you are**. Where you want to be is represented by a standard. It could be a standard of quality. It could be a standard for how you perform the work, the sequence, or the knacks that you use to perform the work. It could be a target for productivity, for safety. It can be any kind of aspiration or goal—this is what I would like to achieve. I would like to cut my accident rate in half. I would like to double my productivity. The metric board should be showing you in a simple, clear way where you actually are compared to where you want to be.

Any visual control is intended to do that. For example, a Kanban square is a form of visual control. Think of a supplier-customer pair. We ask a supplier to build a part or generate information when there is an empty square. The standard is a maximum of three units of work-in-process inventory (see Figure 6-2). If all three squares are filled then you should stop building. The kanban square provides a simple yes-no answer to the question of whether I produce the next unit. In Figure 6-2, we see that all three squares were filled and then another part was produced and stuck outside the three squares. This is clearly out of standard, and it is easy to see. **In this case there is clear overproduction, the fundamental waste.**

Use visual control so no problems are hidden

Used in the work environment and tells us how work should be done and if there is a deviation from the standard.

Figure 6-2. An empty kanban square is a visual signal to authorize production and in this case there is overproduction of one unit.

If you can see that there is a problem, you can ask why. Number one, why is the work backing up here and not being consumed at the expected pace by our customer? The second issue is that the people in the cell who have a clear signal to stop work are continuing to work. Put simply, visual control is a communication device to tell us how the work should be done, whether we are deviating from the standard, and whether we have skilled, motivated people with real leaders who are acting as leaders. Then they will do something about the problem.

The Work Group Structure

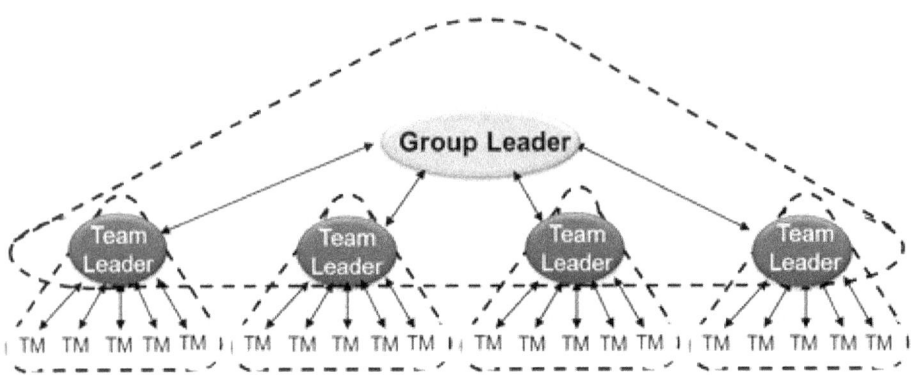

Source: Liker and Hoseus, *Toyota Culture*
Figure 6-3. The Linkage between the Group Leader, Team Leader and Team Members

This is the typical organization structure (see Figure 6-3) in a Toyota plant and it is used throughout the company globally. I have seen it in call centers for Toyota, for customer service. I have seen it in engineering where the team leader becomes an assistant manager for a particular part of the car. In the factory, it is the most consistent and structured, particularly in repetitive processes. The most basic concept is that if you are managing a group of people, and if your job is to check that they get the output expected and then punish the guilty when they do not, you can have twenty, twenty-five, thirty people reporting to one person without any problem. As long as you have very clear standards, very clear measures, you do not have too many problems, and there actually is production happening properly, the supervisor can run around punishing people when they are messing up and not producing. That's the command and control model.

If, on the other hand, you are shifting to the Lean paradigm and you expect your managers to be coaches and teachers, seeing problems as they occur and helping solve the problems as they occur, then the popular idea of a "flat" organization may not be effective. Toyota has concluded that the ideal ratio of leaders (coaches) to learners is one to five. That's one leader per five people who are doing the value added work. That does not necessarily mean promoting a bunch of people to manager.

In the factories Toyota created a role called "Team Leader" made up of hourly production workers selected for their leadership potential. The group leader seeks out team members with potential, encourages them to go to team leader training, and then mentors them over time until they have the skills needed to lead a team of four to seven people. They pay the team leader a little bit more per hour and they guarantee them overtime so they can come to work early and make sure everything is set up right. Production starts at the go sign, and then proceeds smoothly right from the first minute. They are also the first responder's to andon calls from one of their team members. I am getting behind, I am getting ahead, or I see that I might run out of parts.

For whatever reason, I see I am out if standard, I pull a cord, a light goes on, and music plays and somebody has to come to help, and the team leader is generally the first to come. This of course means the team leader cannot be working production or they will not be able to respond to the andon.

Finally, the team leader stays after the shift to make sure everything is prepared for the next shift and they may be working on an improvement project. They also have some discretionary time during the day, when there are no andon calls, to work on improvement projects, or to substitute to free up a team member to work on an improvement project. Often a company asks me how they can get hourly workers to work on improvement during the day since everyone is working all the time, and with a team leader role they would have someone available.

Visual Controls and the Andon System Support Improvement

Creating a Buffer to enable the Andon Process

Sometimes Just-in-Time is misunderstood to mean zero inventory. Certainly one-piece flow is the ideal, but in reality, there are inventory buffers strategically placed where they are needed. The purpose is to buffer against variation. Zero variation and the buffers are not needed, but without variation we also would not need an andon system. I was doing work for one of the American auto companies and they had been working a lot on Lean in the factory, but they had not taught Lean to the manufacturing engineers who lay out the factory and set up the equipment. They asked us to work with the manufactory engineers so they could actually design in Lean lines. One of the things we discovered is they had taken the line stopping system too literally based on a superficial understanding. They had seen it in Toyota plants on tours and they assumed when the team member pulled the cord the entire assembly line immediately stopped.

When the andon cord is pulled, a light turns yellow, and the production line continues to move until the vehicle gets to a certain "fixed position" entering the next workstation. Up to that point, whoever responds to the andon call has the right to pull the cord a second time and override the line stop. If nobody pulls the cord a second time before the car moves into the next zone the light will turn red and the line will stop, but not the entire plant. Actually, a segment of the line will stop, as there are strategically placed buffers between segments of the line that will allow the next segment to continue to produce until the buffer runs out of vehicles.

These manufacturing engineers did not understand the fixed-position line stop that allowed the lines to continue into the next zone and they were not aware of buffers Toyota kept of automobiles between segments of the line. We were in a strange position. We advocated stopping when there is a problem, and we were challenging the engineers, "Are you crazy? You actually want to stop the line immediately when there is a problem?"

"Of course, doesn't Toyota stop their line?"

"Not immediately."

When we explained the system, I remember an America engineer responding, "Toyota cheats. They claim to stop the line when they have a problem, but they do not really do it. They build in buffers and that's not real Lean."

I responded, "Its real sanity is what it is. It is common sense. If you have one hundred processes in series and you are instructing all team members to pull the cord for any little problem and the line immediately stops then what is the probability that you will ever make a car?"

What is important is that production can stop and that leaders take the andon system seriously. If it is a problem that can easily be contained by the team leader, while the line is running, then contain the problem and let the line run. If not, then let that segment stop and the buffer may provide 8-10 minutes of relief until the next segment stops. This is not a lot of time to fix a serious problem so line stoppages do occur. If the line never stops then reduce the buffer size.

Continuous Improvement means…a little better every day

What we mean theoretically by Continuous Improvement is in a literal sense every second, every microsecond you are improving. Obviously, that is unrealistic. On the other hand, if you do improvement once a quarter when the engineers come for a project that is far from Continuous Improvement. We like to think of a reasonable definition as improving something in each area of the organization every day.

Source: Toyota plant
Figure 6-4. The Continuous Improvement Board

The metric board from a Toyota plant is showing the key performance indicators, the metrics, for one work group (see Figure 6-4). This was actually a new version of the board at the time, and it was organized around *Hoshin Kanri*, which I will be talking about in Chapter Seven. When you read the board, you will notice that there are five areas of metrics: safety, quality, productivity, cost and human resource (HR) development. The particular measures can change over time. For example, at some point you are very focused on a morale survey for HR Development. At another point, you are focused on training people so everyone learns four jobs. There is going to be different things you measure depending on what you are trying to improve for each of these areas.

At the top of the board is the most general outcome measure. For example, in safety, it might be the number of recordable incidents, or the actual accidents that you report to the government. Then as you go down the board, the metrics become more specific and more focused on the process itself. You may determine that the best way to reduce injuries is to have an early symptom investigation process, where if somebody has a symptom, before they actually get injured, you go in and find the root cause of that. For example, their wrist might be hurting a little bit or their back is hurting, and you can act immediately instead of waiting until they are in the hospital for wrist or back surgery. You might measure symptoms then you might go down to find the root cause and the root cause is that the tools are not well placed and they are not grabbing the tools in the right way and you start to measure whether the tools are positioned properly so that the worker can have a neutral wrist when they do their job. When you have neutral wrists on all your jobs, then you are green.

As you work, your way down the metric board the information shifts from high-level outcomes to more detailed and specific measures of the process and perhaps A3 reports of the improvement process.

Creating a teacher who creates a critical mass of Lean Thinkers

Group Leaders Run a Mini-business, with Support

Managers need to be trained to develop group leaders who develop team leaders and team members. In the early stages of self-development and developing others, usually we are focusing on managers and then we're going to work with them to develop group leaders, probably in a controlled area like a pilot for learning. Then we will begin to spread that to other areas.

It is not as clear-cut as that, but that's the ideal way. You create the teacher who creates a student who creates a teacher who creates a student and it just keeps on going like that. At that point we have a critical mass and, when somebody is hired in, you have a lot of teachers to indoctrinate them into the culture.

The work group owns a set of processes. If you are the group leader, and if it is an equipment-intensive area like metal stamping, you have a certain number of stamping machines and they are yours. Your job is to make production. Your job is to have high quality. Your job is to keep team members safe. Your job is to ensure the machines are operating at a high level. You are responsible for making sure you can quickly change the dies on the stamping machines because you are being asked to make a small batch instead of a large batch. That is all the responsibility of the group leader. The group leader is in effect the owner of that mini business—of those 10, 12 stamping machines.

Group Leader responsibilities include:

- Make Production
- Ensure High Quality
- Be Safe
- Operate Machines at high level
- Quick Change Over
- High Morale

So what is the role of support groups? For example, what is the role of maintenance? The role of maintenance is to support the group leader. The group leader is a customer of maintenance, and you need to be a good service provider as a maintenance person, but also good service providers need good customers. For example, maintenance will ask the group to do preventive maintenance every day. "Check this fluid level, check the filter, change the filter," you expect them to do that in a Toyota plant, and if they are doing that the uptime of equipment goes way up. If on the other hand the maintenance person asks them to do that and the group leader does not take it seriously and does not lead the group to have the discipline then machines are going to shut down and the maintenance person is going to spend a lot of time babysitting them, and you will need more maintenance people.

At Georgetown, Kentucky, over the long run, all of the standard Key Performance Indicators (KPIs) improve. Every year there is a new set of challenges to get to another level and the workgroups by and large will either meet or exceed those new levels and then the next year there is another set of challenging improvement targets. When they introduce a new product, it disrupts the process, some of the KPIs may go down, and they have to bring them back up so it is not a linear progression, but every year wherever they are starting from, by the end of the year they are generally better. They are very consistently improving because they have developed effective workgroups with the right training, with the right support from management and from the support groups.

Creating a Critical Mass in a Large Organization

Let's say I am a plant manager knowledgeable about Lean and now run an existing plant of 700 people that is starting almost from zero on Lean. Lots of supervisors are trained in the old way; workers have not been involved in Continuous Improvement. How long would it take to actually get to the point where there is some semblance of daily improvement with effective meetings and actual kaizen going on at the plant, where I can walk anywhere and I am going to see vital improvement activity? I would say if you are really skilled as a plant manager, in two to three years you could achieve a novice level of improvement capability throughout the plant. To get to the point where you have really well developed group leaders and team leaders who you can count on to achieve the targets would take at least five years.

It is a big commitment and that is assuming that the group leaders and team leaders stay in place. If you develop them and then there is a downturn in your sales, you may be ordered to cut people dramatically. Whom will you cut? The first roles that often go are the team leader roles because they are not needed for production. You need some supervisors, but you do not need a one to five ratio of team leaders to team members to get product out the door. The role goes away and immediately kaizen goes backwards, and the team leaders were also your future group leaders so you do not have a bench of potential group leaders ready to promote. That can make everything fall apart and the businesses that have a three to five year cycle of having downturns and doing major workforce reduction followed by growth and rehiring are constantly in an unstable state. They get to a certain point, then they go backwards, then they get to a certain point and go backwards.

If that great plant manager after three years is so good that she is promoted, she is moved to another job, another plant, she goes away and someone takes her place who does not understand how to be a Lean Leader, there will be degradation in the plant. For some period of time, if the groups are functioning well, they will continue to function well but the engine will start to run down.

Toyota thinks long term and they take the time to develop well-qualified group leaders, team leaders, managers, in all positions. When they launch new plants in America, they already have a lot of experienced people in existing plants. They will assign one of the existing plants to be the mother plant for the new plant. For example, when they launched a plant in Mississippi to make the Corolla the Canadian plant that already builds the Corolla became the mother plant, picked some of their best managers and group leaders, and sent them to Mississippi. This allowed them to immediately begin to develop the team leaders even while equipment was being laid out and before actual production started.

Role of B-labor at Toyota to Supplement the Work Groups

Toyota's Classification of Plant Personnel

> **A-Labor:** Production team members who do value-added work
> **B-Labor:** Production team members who are taken offline
> **C-Labor:** Support Staff
> **D-Labor:** Management Team

Toyota classifies people in factories using an A-B-C-D system. The A-Labor are the people who do value-added work, the people who work on cars. Then they have B-Labor who are production workers taken offline to work on a special kaizen project. They are not doing value-added direct labor in this time. They often become team leaders when they return to production. C-Labor would be the support staff, like maintenance people. D-Labor would be the whole management team, which is somewhat interesting because you usually think of an A as a good grade and a D as a bad grade. In this case, the A is really saying the most important people are those who do the value-added work. The lower your grade, the harder you have to work to add value. If you are a D you had better be doing something to help the A laborers do their job better, or you are not adding any value. That is why you need to spend time at the *gemba*.

The B labor are pulled off the line for kaizen, and they are typically on an assignment for two to three years. As an example, Toyota is constantly launching new models. As soon as a fully redesigned Camry is launched into production, the product engineering team is already working on a one-year set of improvements, and a two-year "face lift," which is a significant change in the way the Camry looks, and then typically in four of five years there will be a brand new Camry. Who is responsible for all these production changes? In a typical plant, it is engineering. It might be engineering at the corporate level, production engineering, and there might be manufacturing engineers in the plant. They are busy, and they are launching the product and getting equipment set up and they are doing it in parallel with production and the production workers are not very involved.

In Toyota's case, one group of B labor are called the Pilot Team, pilot standing for pilot production, which is before you go into full-scale production. They are working in the pilot stage on the next new model launch, or the next new set of changes, and again they are production workers. They are developing the initial standard work, working on line balancing, and working on tool and equipment layout. They are even looking at the new model when it is just a concept represented as a clay model. That is correct. Hourly production workers may be flying to Japan to see these vehicles when they're in the earliest stages of development and giving input. "That is going to be hard for us to stamp out. We're going to have wrinkles in the steel body. That is going to be hard to weld together because of the way you designed it right here."

This is a developmental assignment. Usually after three years on the Pilot Team, they will go back as a team leader, or maybe even a group leader, or get moved to some other special assignment.

Every general manager will have several hundred people at least. They will have a certain number of B-Labor slots in their budget to staff their kaizen teams for whatever they are responsible for. They might be the general manager for the stamping plant. At the stamping plant, there is some number of workers, such as 5 to 8 workers with an engineer running the team and they are working on kaizen projects. Production worker kaizen is not only coming from the production team members making suggestions. It is also the team leaders, group leaders, and these B-Labor teams who are doing bigger kaizen activities.

Let's now consider an example of a B-Labor team that made a revolutionary change in the body shop of Toyota's Georgetown plant—doing it through incremental kaizen.

Creating a Material Flow Revolution (Minomi Case)

Minomi means parts without containers

In *The Toyota Way to Lean Leadership*, we have one long example of kaizen that had a major impact on the Georgetown, Kentucky plant in the body shop where they weld together the body parts, and it was by using a system called Minomi, which means, "move the parts without the containers." Normally when you have a part, you put it into some sort of container along with other parts. If they are big and heavy stamped body parts, a forklift might be needed to pick up the container to bring it to another area where the parts are going to be assembled and then it is put somewhere. It might be placed on a tilt stand so gravity shifts the parts down and they are easier to reach. There was an innovation in Japan focused on eliminating containers completely.

Figure 6-5. Dana Truck Parts Plant – Axle Subassembly Delivered Without Containers (Minomi)

The photograph (see Figure 6-5) shows Minomi in a Dana truck parts plant. When Gary Convis joined Dana as CEO, he brought in former Toyota employees and they were working on Minomi in some of the plants.

In this case, you can see that these axle subassemblies are put on roller conveyors; they are not put in a container. They are put on a cart, then the cart is being wheeled, shown in this second picture, by an automated guided vehicle (AGV) that takes it to where it is going to be assembled (see Figure 6-6), and then the parts just flow naturally on the gravity rack so there is no human intervention needed.

Figure 6-6. Automated Guided Vehicles bringing Axle Subassemblies with no Containers at Dana

Now what is the advantage from the worker's point of view? Before they had a big container and were reaching down into the container to get these parts. Normally in a Kanban system where you have containers of parts you want to have at least two bins. One is taken away and replaced, and while it is being replaced, you are working out of a second bin. If you have large bins, let's say they take up four feet of floor space, then you will have one four-foot container next to another four-foot container and there is at least eight linear feet that you have to walk up and down in order to pick the parts. Then you have to walk the parts to where you are going to assemble them. The standard work will vary if you have to walk two feet to get one part and later four feet to get another part. In addition, reaching down into a container when you are getting the bottom parts can be a poor ergonomic design and damage your body. That does not happen with well-designed Minomi. In the Minomi system, the worker stands in one place and the parts come to the worker, and the parts are always coming to that one point, so when you have standard work it's the same timing for every cycle.

Bringing Minomi to Body Welding in Georgetown, Kentucky

When Gary Convis was President of Toyota's Kentucky plant he learned about Central Motors, a company that is part of the Toyota group in Japan. They specialize in making steel car bodies, and they make an incredible variety in the smallest, densest space of perhaps any body shop in Japan.

It was known as one of the most efficient body shops and Gary visited and he discovered Minomi, and he was blown away by it. "It's just amazing." He started imagining how efficient they could be in Georgetown, Kentucky using Minomi. Now a non-Lean Leader would send a few engineers over with the orders, "We want Minomi everyplace. Figure out what they did and order the equipment and put it everyplace." Gary was better trained than that in Lean thinking. What did Gary do? He returned to his plant in the U.S. and assembled a small team of mainly B-labor, hourly production and maintenance team members, with one engineer named VJ. VJ happened to be a fabulous engineer, maybe the best in the plant. He also happened to be a little bit abrasive, and not a people person. Knowing this Gary gave VJ the assignment to work with a team of hourly welding workers and sent the group to Japan for up to two weeks, which in itself is a big deal. How often does an American company send hourly laborers to Japan?

Their job was to go and see in Central Motors. When they thought they had seen enough come home and try something at first in a pilot area. In Phase One, V.J. and the team were so impressed by what they saw they copied it. What Central Motors was using is what you might think of as a meat hook system. Imagine hooks with cow carcasses, or chickens, or turkeys, and they are hanging on a conveyor by hooks and then as you take these chickens off to do work on them the gravity is feeding the next chickens down. In this case, instead of chickens, they were stamped metal parts, parts of the body, hanging from these hooks, and the hooks were on a narrow roller conveyor across the top. As the worker takes the next part then the part behind it will flow down by gravity. Once the rack on wheels is loaded with parts, you just push it to the welding line and you never need a container. Even though it was working well in Central Motors, they put it in place in Kentucky and it failed.

Why did it fail? First, when they moved the carts with hanging parts they banged into each other, which caused little dents and nicks. At Central Motors, those dents were being fixed as the parts were held together and welded since their welding system had pneumatic fixtures that with a lot of force would push the parts together ironing out the defects. The system they had in Georgetown, Kentucky did not have that kind of force and there were bad parts being created. The second problem was that as these parts were swinging in the breeze, workers might put a hand in between these parts and hurt their hand and it was a safety issue.

So that was Phase One, the copy did not work. In Phase Two, they had to think about a countermeasure. An innovative idea was to change the concept from holding the parts from the top on a hanger to securing the parts from the bottom like fingers holding them up. They began to think about a DVD holder where you stack the DVDs and you have holders that are holding them in place from the bottom, and that is essentially what they did. They welded onto a piece of sheet metal fingers that held the parts in place like you would slide a CD into the holder. It worked fabulously and the parts were more stable.

Then, interestingly, Phase Three came about when the Central Motors people heard about this and they came over to Kentucky, and concluded, "This is a better system than we have" and they started to experiment with it back in Japan. One of the things they discovered was that they could automate with a robot the process at stamping of unloading then loading the parts onto the cart. The robot could easily pick up the parts, feed them onto the cartridge, and eliminate a person needing to unload the stamping machine. Then TMMK copied that so they could reduce some additional labor in stamping. Now we have learning from each other. It was not all ideas from Japan to the United States. Also, stamping was now involved.

In Phase Four, Kentucky extended the automation to material delivery from stamping to welding by adding automated guided vehicles (AGVs) as we saw in the Dana photo. The parts were removed by a robot from the stamping press and put into the rack, which was slid onto a cart, and an AGV pulled the cart to the correct location in the welding department.

In Phase Five, and note, this was taking place over years, not months, they added in what Toyota calls the set-parts system (SPS). In this system instead of bringing parts A, B, and C in separate batches if each product takes one of A, B, and C and there are different variations of each of these parts, then you bring the specific A, B, and C needed for one product. In this case, instead of bringing a cart of doors and a cart of hoods and a cart of smaller parts that make up the structure of the hood, they would bring a cart with the right hood and outer door metal and smaller parts needed for a specific car. The team member then picks from a cart exactly the parts needed, like an assemble-your-own piece of furniture that you might get from Walmart.

Again, a person was bringing that at first, and eventually in Phase Six, they replaced the person with an automated guided vehicle. Now this did add some labor as a person placed the set of parts on the cart taken by the AGV to the production line. But the advantages in productivity of the line outweighed this cost.

As they were expanding this to more parts and areas in the plant, they needed more AGVs. That is when they got a big benefit from the B-labor; because one of the very practically minded hourly workers asked the question "why are we paying so much for the automated guided vehicles?" which were costing, $30,000, or $40,000 a pop, and he suggested, "We could make these ourselves for a fraction of the cost."

After all, they were trained in welding, so they could weld together the carts, which they were doing anyway. What they were buying were the little mobile robots, and the key was the programmed computer board in the robot that tells the AGV "stop here, start here, unload, stop there, and so on." One hourly worker happened to be a good computer programmer as a hobby and said, "I would like to try programming one of these things myself. Why don't you just get me an unprogrammed computer board?" He figured out how to do it.

When their first homemade AGV was built, there was a big celebration. If you can imagine having balloons, and food, and drink, non-alcoholic drink, and people all coming together, and Gary Convis, the President, came down, stood on the cart, and let it pull him around the line. From then on, it cost just a few thousand dollars to make the AGVs, a huge gain. It was done by team members used to getting their hands dirty and making things work.

Then finally, Phase Seven was connecting this to the supplier. They were getting the parts in big bins and then converting them to the Minomi system, but what if the suppliers could actually start to sequence parts, and that again is an evolution that takes time.

These were broad phases. Within these phases, there are many individual kaizen activities necessary to get to the point where they had a quite automated system bringing exactly what is needed in the amount needed to the right place. The worker just takes what they need from the cart. It improved the productivity of the welders. It improved the productivity of material handling, and it also reduced greatly the time and expense needed to change over the production lines for introducing new products.

Minomi Project Results

So what was the result of this Minomi project led by a small team of B labor workers who reported to one exceptional engineer, VJ? They eliminated 40 forklift trucks, freed up over 100 line jobs, and the team learned to build and program their own AGVs reducing cost throughout the whole plant wherever they used an AGV. These results were based on just half of the stamped parts and the kaizen continued beyond this point. In the other half, they would get another 100 line jobs and another 40 forklift trucks reduced. Another key result was leadership development. VJ himself, as he led this activity, blossomed as a leader.

I walked with VJ after these phases were completed and they still had different parts of the welding line in different stages of evolution and the comparison was striking. The thing that struck me most as we walked around was that VJ knew everybody, and everybody was calling out to VJ because they wanted his help. "VJ, this Minomi system you put in, we have this idea for improving it." VJ was writing down these ideas as we walked and he was high fiving people and shaking hands. He looked like the most popular guy in the plant, and here was a guy who a few years earlier was not known as a people person. Now many welders wanted to be on VJ's team, so he was able to select from a list those who he would allow on the team based on stringent requirements.

The reason they wanted to be on his team was the phenomenal level of training and development they got in kaizen. This all blossomed because Gary Convis, who actually would meet weekly with VJ's team, really took this seriously. Gary Convis, the President who had 6,000 people reporting to him, personally was involved in every stage of the transformation, and when he saw this in Japan, he did not make the mistake of copying the results. He set in place a process of kaizen to begin to experiment, and to learn over time. He developed and innovated this beyond what they originally saw. This is a great example of kaizen in action and the value of B labor and the way you develop a top-notch leader like VJ.

Results of Minomi Project

- Eliminated 40 forklift trucks
    - ➔ + 40 more forklift trucks
- Freed up 100 line jobs
    - ➔ + 100 more line jobs

Teams learned to build and program AGVs reducing cost from $25,000 to $4,000 and V.J. blossomed as a leader with a small team of hourly employees he trained and developed.

Standard Work to Support Kaizen in Work Groups

Standard Work for a Bus Route

In 2005 we had the opportunity to support Hertz in their Lean journey. One of the tools we introduced was standard work for each of the jobs you would see at a Hertz rental site. This was done through coaching internal change agents who worked with the people in each job to develop the standard work. One of the things Hertz does in the United States at many airports is supply a bus service to offsite rental locations.

They guarantee you will not have to wait more than 10 minutes, and in order for that to happen the buses have to leave at timed intervals and take about the same amount of time to make the route.

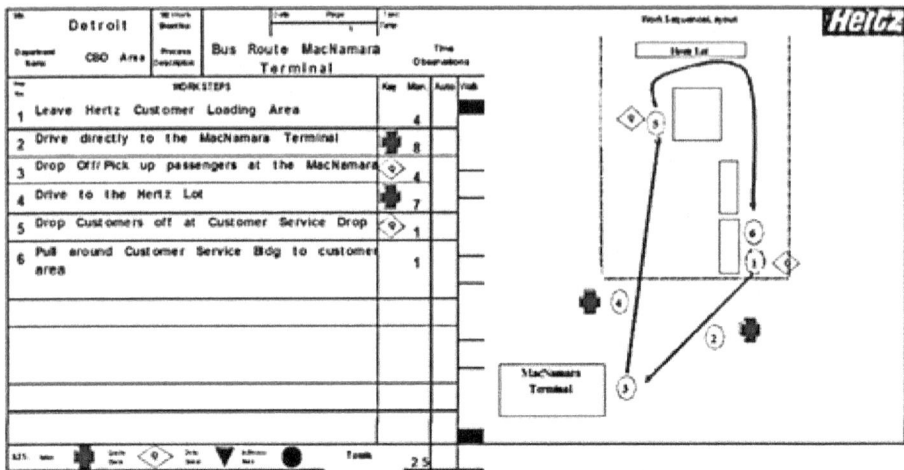

Figure 6-7. Hertz Bus Route Standard Work Sheet

This requires that all the bus drivers follow the standard work. In this case, we show the steps, for example, leave the customer loading area, drive to McNamara Terminal (see Figure 6-7). Each of these is a very clear step. We also show how long it should take, and we also show where there are potential safety hazards to be avoided and where there is a quality check needed, and we show the layout. This is a typical standard work sheet. The total for the route is 25 minutes so they would need three buses to meet the 10-minute guarantee.

Break down the work further for training

There is another chart that Toyota calls a job breakdown and is also sometimes called a work element sheet. The purpose of this chart is training. The standard work sheet gives you a picture of what you should be doing at a high level, and the timing, but to train you need to go into more detail to break down those big steps into smaller steps. For each of those smaller steps, show how it should be done. This should include key points and the reasons for the key points such as quality or safety. That is then the tool for training the bus drivers in this case.

Hertz — WORK ELEMENT SHEET

KEY POINTS:
- Safety: Injury avoidance, ergonomics, danger points
- Quality: Defect avoidance, check points, standards
- Technique: Efficient workment, speed as method
- Cost: Proper use of materials

IMPORTANT STEPS	KEY POINTS	REASONS FOR KEY POINTS
Step # 1 — Leave Hertz Customer Loading Area	1) Play "talking bus" 2) Check Mirrors 3) Raise bus if lowered 4) Open gate using opener	1) Customer safety, destination, and luggage warning 2) Watch for customers or traffic 3) Prevent mechanical problems with bus 4) Prevent bus delay and damage
Step # 2 — Drive directly to the Macnamara Terminal	1) Obey traffic laws 2) Yellow light stop observance. Brake unless unsafe. 3) Watch for merging traffic 4) Obey speed limit 5) Play "talking bus" as entering the terminal	1) Customer and Driver safety, as well as other traffic 2) Michigan Traffic Law 3) Customer and Driver Safety 4) Safety and Michigan Law 5) Give the customer vital information
Step # 3 — Drop Off/Pickup Passengers at the Macnamara Terminal	1) Aid Passengers needing assistance 2) Watch for proper luggage placement 3) Watch for approaching customers 4) Close door and activate "talking bus"	1) Customer relations 2) Customer safety 3) Customer service 4) Customer information
Step # 4 — Drive to Hertz Lot	1) Obey Traffic Laws 2) Yellow light stop observance. Brake unless unsafe. 3) Watch for merging traffic 4) Obey speed limit 5) Play "talking bus" as reaching Point 5 6) Watch for traffic pulling away	1) Customer and Driver Safety as well as other traffic 2) Michigan Traffic Law 3) Customer and Driver Safety 4) Safety and Michigan Law 5) Give the customer vital information 6) Safety of all concerned
Step # 5 — Drop customers off at Customer Service Drop Off Area	1) Visually inspect to ensure all luggage taken off 2) Watch for customer before closing door 3) Watch for pedestrians and vehicles 4) Obey 10 mph Speed Limit	1) Customer does not forget something 2) Customer safety 3) Safety and Vehicle damage 4) Hertz regulations
Step # 6 — Pull around building to Customer Loading Area	1) Park in Designated Area if 2 buses are in loading area 2) Pull up to the Pick-Up Area as soon as it is open 3) Lower bus (optional) 4) Leave Bus running	1) Customer relations 2) Customer safety 3) Customer service 4) Customer information

Figure 6-8. Hertz Bus Route Work Element Sheet

This is a blowup of part of the Work Element Sheet (see Figure 6-8). For example, before you leave the Hertz customer loading are, you play the "talking bus," that is the short audio file you hear when you get on the bus. You raise the bus if lowered for passengers with disabilities and open the gate using the openers. For each of these, there is a reason for that key point, and when you train a bus driver, you now have your agenda for training. You do this through repetition—describing, showing and letting the learner try it, then explaining more deeply with the key points, and letting the learner do it while explaining the key points. This is called the "job instruction training" method. The training was first introduced to Toyota by Americans who created "Training Within Industry," a program for the United States Defense Department during World War II. It is discussed in detail in *Toyota Talent* (my book with David Meier).

Work Element Sheet (WES) for Training

- Breaks the standard work into more detailed elements
- Includes Key Points and explains WHY
    - Quality
    - Safety
    - Knacks

Uses sketches to visually explain some work steps

A core job of a group leader is to be a trainer. If you are a group leader or a team leader, you are training the people to follow the standard work, you are auditing the standard work, and if you see deviations, you can ask why. The why might be that they have a better way, so you incorporate that into the standard work. It is actually giving these leaders a way of adding value through kaizen.

Solve Deviations from Standard One-by-One

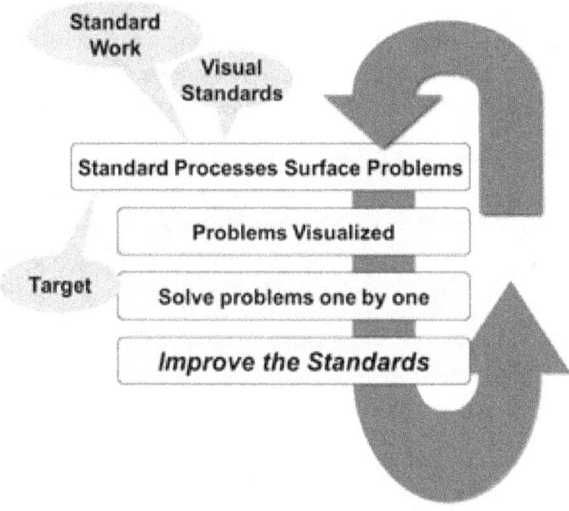

Source: Michael Balle

Figure 6-9. Lean Systems surface deviations from standard so we can solve problems one by one

By having clear standards (see Figure 6-9), and seeing deviations from the standards, the problems will visibly surface. The problem definition now is a deviation from the standard work. Then you can solve the problems as they occur instead of waiting for them to accumulate. Otherwise, you look back on three months of statistics and who knows what happened in the last three months? We are aiming ideally for one-by-one problem solving instead of batch problem solving which has many more opportunities for PDCA, which is many more opportunities for learning problem solving by the workers, the group leaders, the team leader, and the managers.

Roles and Responsibilities for Standard Work

All of this depends on people taking responsibility for developing and following and improving the standards. Who is responsible and what are the roles? The team member's main role, those who do the work, is to follow the standards. Do it the way it is written, but look for ways to make it better and to eliminate waste, and make proposals to change the standard work. The staff experts, the engineers, set up the preliminary standard work at new product launch, and in Toyota, we discussed the role of pilot teams made up of hourly production workers who are part of that process. The staff experts will also review any big change that might have a technical impact on quality, productivity, or safety. The work group leader can also pull in the staff members to help them when they are beyond their expertise. In addition, the staff expert will periodically audit the standard work.

The team leader is trained to use the job instruction method, the standard work broken down to the element level, to teach the team members, but they have to be certified as a trainer to use the job instruction method. They also create work element sheets, they monitor the team members, say auditing a different team member every day to see if they are following all the elements of the standard work, and they are working with the team members and group leaders to develop new standard work and finding new ideas for improvement.

Finally, the group leader is also monitoring the standard work through formal audits, and they will audit what the team leader has audited, sometimes with the team leader. They are evaluating proposals for change to the standard work, coordinating new product launches, coordinating all the training and team member development and some of the improvement. Everybody has a role that focuses around that standard work.

Even the managers and assistant managers get into the act. They do not get to sit in their offices and go to meetings all day long. They come down to the floor and they are checking that the standard work, job instruction methods, and kaizen are actually happening within their area. They also have to be skilled enough so that they can observe the worker to see if they are following standard work and they do that on a regular basis, and they are coaching the group leaders and team members and they are checking to see whether the standard work is static or whether it is improving.

Team Leader

- Trains Team Members in Standard Work using Job Instruction method
- Create work element sheets
- Monitor Team Members – Standard Work is followed
- Work with Team Members and Group Leaders developing new Standard Work
- Look for ways to eliminate waste

Group Leader

- Monitor Team Members – Standard Work is followed
- Evaluate Team Members proposals for new Standard Work
- Coordinate new product launch
- Coordinate all training and Team Member development
- Look for ways to eliminate waste

Managers / Assistant Managers

- Insure Standard Work and Job Instruction methods are followed throughout the shop
- Periodically check Team Members are following Standard Work on the floor
- Review and initial all changes to Standard Work

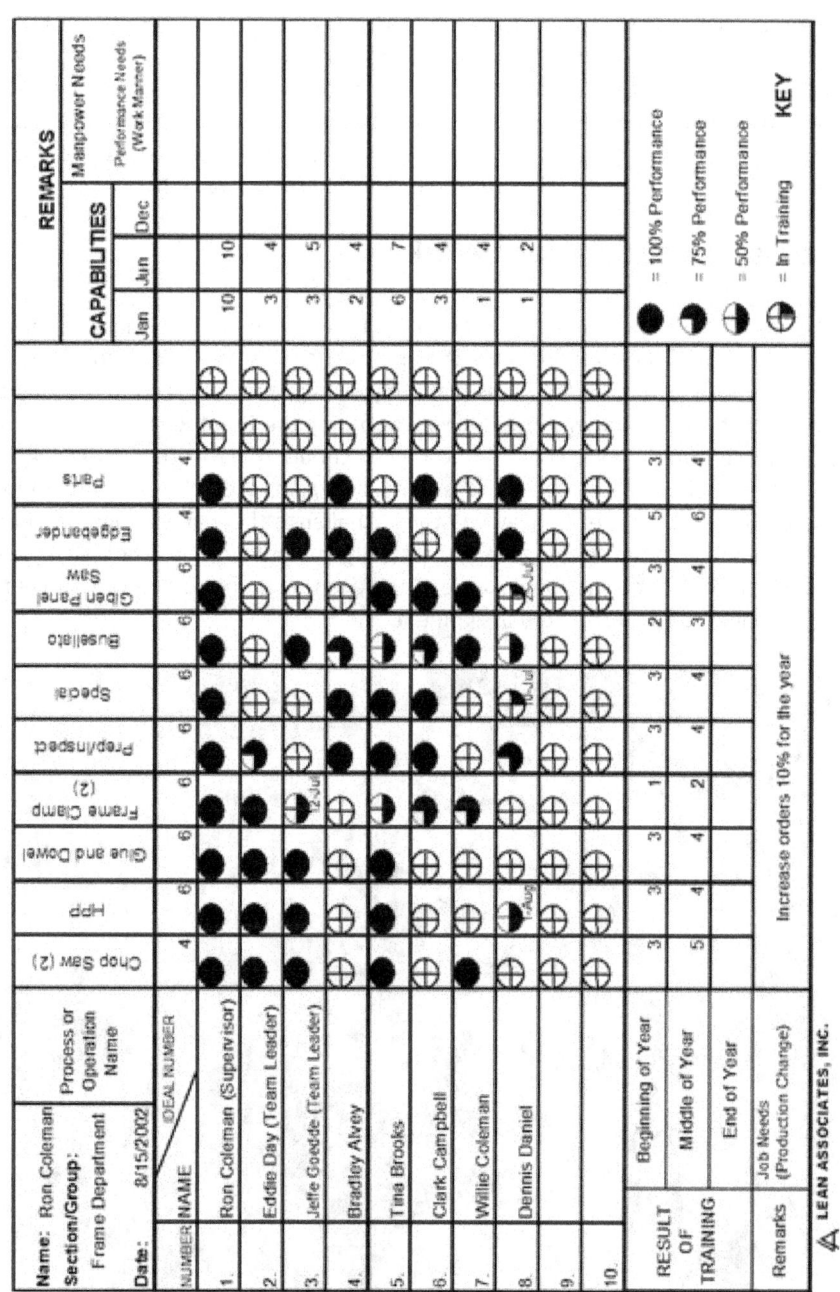

Figure 6-10. Multi-Function Worker Training Sheet

The standard work and job instruction training is also used as to keep a record of who is certified in what skills (see Figure 6-10). The multi-function training sheet displays team members and if they have a full black circle, they can do that job at what is defined as a 100% performance level. You can see that different people are trained to different degrees in different jobs. This is a great tool for figuring out whether you are meeting your labor needs. We can show how many people should be trained in each job and how many people are trained. It is also a tool for actually assigning people. If somebody does not show up one day and we have to shuffle people around the group leader can look at this and easily see who is qualified to do each job.

What is Leader Standard Work?

In *The Toyota Way,* a manager is a teacher, and the teacher in a martial arts sense acts as the master and the subordinate is the apprentice. This particular photo (see Figure 6-11) was taken at the Toyota Texas plant. It just happened to be somebody who was teaching me how they taught problem solving during the Great Recession. This is when they had team members coming to work even though they were not making trucks. They were teaching them new skills every day. Again, the role of the mentor is to challenge you – challenge the way you think, challenge the way you act – and to give you assignments and to then watch you carefully, much of the time not giving you any feedback at all and letting you struggle. Then eventually they will give you feedback, and they will give you a concrete assignment.

Figure 6-11. Learning at the *Gemba*

The master-apprentice relationship that was very common a few hundred years ago never left Toyota. When you are assigned a new job there is somebody to teach you and it is usually your boss. If you are on a special project, it might be somebody who is an expert at the Toyota Production System. You treat them with the respect that the apprentice would treat the master.

For example, when Steve St. Angelo went to Georgetown, Kentucky as Executive Vice President to eventually become President, at first he was still an apprentice, and he had a variety of masters – Japanese, as well as Gary Convis – who were teaching him to become a president in the Georgetown, Kentucky plant. Despite decades of experience as an executive at GM and NUMMI, he willingly subordinated himself, and he was also learning from all the workers as he was learning their jobs. That kind of one-on-one coaching is the way you learn on the job, through On-the-Job Development.

Lately there has emerged in Lean a popular movement called "Leader Standard Work." In many cases, it is based on a simplistic assumption – if we get leaders to go to the *gemba* and give them some questions to ask or a checklist of things to look for they will emerge as Lean Leaders. In theory, Leader Standard Work is a good concept. What we are really referring to is repetitive patterns of activities that represent the current best known way of planning and controlling business processes.

Standard Work is the Routine Part of the Job

There is a part of every leader's job that can be made very routine. What we show (see Figures 6-12 to 6-14: from former Toyota manager Tony McNaughton) is that the percentage that is repetitive as compared to the percentage that is unique work particular to that job is going to vary depending on the leader's level. As you go higher in the organization more of what you have to do is react to unique circumstances and improvise to react in the proper way and the closer you get to leading the value-added team members the larger the routine portion of your job.

For example, consider the team leader in Toyota, (see Figure 6-12). They are off the line and they are responding to Andon pulls. The team leader can be trained in a lot of detail about how to respond to an Andon pull. What happens when the light goes on? Now you are responsible– the spotlight is on you as a team leader. The team member simply pulls the cord. He is done. He has called attention to the problem. What do you check for first? You can be trained in that in a fairly routine way, but in reality, every situation that you face on the line will be different and a high level of skill is required beyond rote routines.

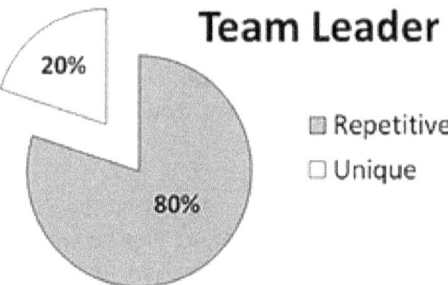

Figure 6-12. Theoretical Portions of Team Leader Work that are Unique and Repetitive

What happens if there is a missing part? What happens if the team member made a quality error? How do you judge when you need to allow the line to actually stop versus when you can pull the cord a second time and solve the problem while the car is moving down the line? What do you do if the problem is bigger than you are, you cannot handle it, and you have to call for help? There are defined routines for dealing with those situations even though there is also improvisation.

There are also routine things that you do as a team leader like check to see if the tools themselves are within the quality range. For example, is the torque on the torque wrench within the acceptable range? You are making quality checks. You are collecting data that is posted on the team meeting board. There are things that you should look for before the shift starts. You come early as a team leader, and everything should be set up right so that when the line starts everything is ready to go. Roughly, 80% of your job is fairly repetitive, and there is about 20% where you must improvise in unique situations. A machine fails in a way that you have never seen and you have to improvise. Even then, in a Lean system, near at hand is the Group Leader to help.

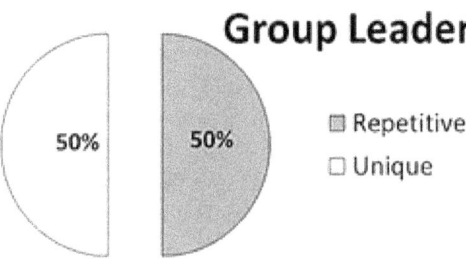

Figure 6-13. Theoretical Portions of Group Leader Work that are Unique and Repetitive

The group leader, we are suggesting, has more like a 50/50 split between routine and non-routine work (see Figure 6-13). The group leader is the first-line supervisor. A typical day might start by reviewing the logbook of notes left by the previous shift group leader. You then walk the line with team leaders to see the situation and what needs to be done to prepare it for the start of production. As team members arrive to work you greet them by name, look them in the eyes, and ask them how they are feeling looking for any abnormality. Sometimes a person is missing and adjustments to labor have to be made with other group leaders. You confirm checklists such as 5S and that protective gear is being worn. Then you develop a plan for the day including team meetings, safety discussions, and quality discussions.

During production more of the group leader work involves walking the floor and responding to abnormalities. There are also routine things to check like auditing whether workers are following the standard work and doing their preventative maintenance. After production stops, there is a variety of paper or computer work to do tallying, reporting, and filling out the log for the next shift. And that is when kaizen activities are often scheduled.

As you go up to a manager level we are saying that perhaps only 20% of what you do is repetitive and 80% is adapting to circumstances, adapting to people's needs. What we are really arguing with Leader Standard Work is that even a manager can take advantage of the 20% by standardizing it and making it very productive (see Figure 6-14). That is one day's worth of work out of a five-day week of activities that you can do relatively routinely, and that is the part you want to standardize. What you should be learning in that period of time is a routine way of coaching people to improve. The questions might be standardized but there is additional training needed to ask probing follow-up questions to guide the learner toward a deeper approach to improvement.

For the other parts, you need to learn from a mentor over many years through on the job development – the tacit parts of the job – the parts that cannot be written down procedurally. The tacit parts you learn through experience of dealing with many different circumstances. You develop a repertoire of skills that allow you to deal with that employee who is repeatedly absent. You deal with the machine that breaks down in a spectacular way and it could shut down production for the whole day. You deal with the vendor who misses a shipment. You can lead cross-functionally to achieve the breakthrough objectives needed to support the company strategy. You have done these things many times before. Even though each situation is unique, they are similar to what you have done in the past. You are developing a repertoire of skills for the 80% and the other 20% is relatively routine, specific, repetitive work where you actually can write down the procedure.

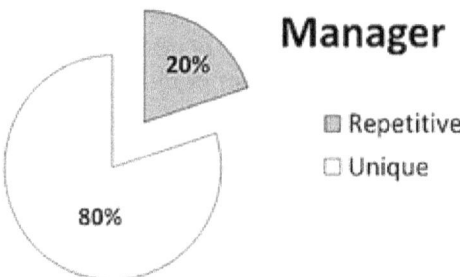

Figure 6-14. Theoretical Portions of Manager Work that are Unique and Repetitive

Leaders Standard Work is at the *Gemba*

Part of the routine work of a Lean Leader should be a daily visit to the *gemba*. We illustrate a daily round of a plant manager walking and checking the process in a factory example (see Figure 6-15). They will do it every day unless there is some emergency, and we note the area they have decided, "I am going to do a deep dive here today." "For this workgroup I am going to spend more time," and they will change that every day. Then every place they go there are things that they are looking for.

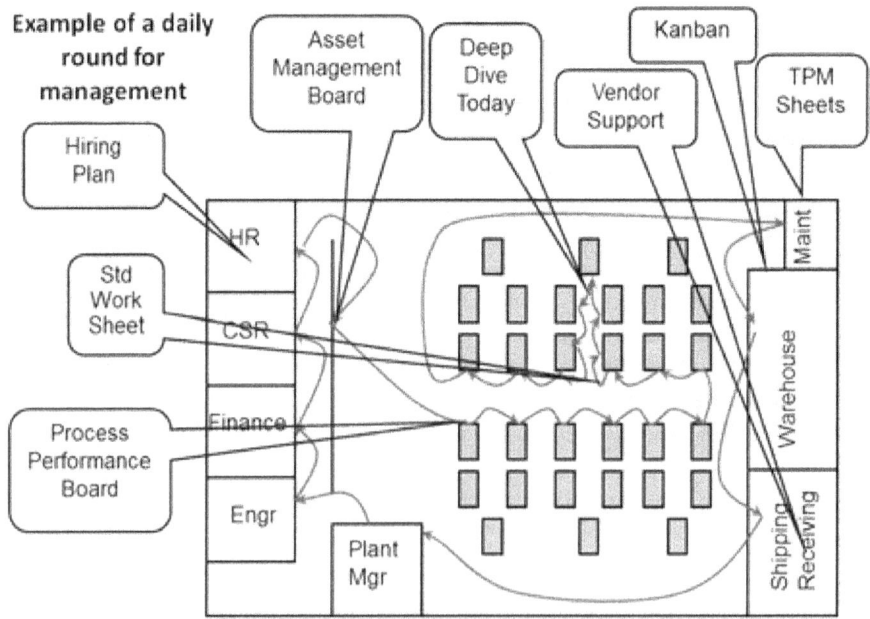

Source: Tony McNaughton, former Toyota Manager
Figure 6-15. An example of a daily *gemba* walk of a plant manager

They have determined something specific to focus on in every area they visit and that will change over time. For example, in Human Resources (HR), it might be the hiring plan and they are going to be asking questions about that. If it is visual and if they can see the status, then it is much easier for them to ask the right questions and challenge the thinking of people.

Scripted standard work for the leader is useful, but it is only a first step until leaders naturally become Lean Leaders – until they have developed to the point where they just do this and they do not need it written down and they do not need it to become formal written standard work. Leaders at the *gemba* should be doing more than walking around. They should be systematically checking the process and coaching the people. Carefully defined standards and visual tools to clearly show deviations from the standard facilitate this. There needs to be a plan for the walk and a clear purpose. Then the manager becomes a teacher and coach rather then somebody wandering about randomly barking orders.

The leader standard work we have described is a general walk around and check of the workplace—standard versus actual. The aim is coaching. The Coaching *Kata*, discussed in Chapter Five, provides another type of leader standard work. It is designed to develop deep routines for coaching improvement projects focused on defined target conditions. The focus is on the coach-learner relationship and it is more rigorous for developing improvement routines then general walkabouts to check the workplace.

Tying it all Together

Figure 6-16. A factory setting where all of the pieces are in place

Standard Work, Visual Management, and Leader Standard Work are all interrelated. Standards provide aspirations to strive for—to reduce variation and perform at a high level. Visual management is a tool to easily see deviations from the standard for problem solving. Leader Standard Work is a way to develop leaders so they have routines for checking the systems and people at the *gemba*, and depends on Standard Work and Visual Management so the leader can coach with a clear focus based on facts.

Let's consider one factory where they had all these pieces in place. They have a visual board with all the key documents for the work group. We see a team leader in the area of the work cell (see Figure 6-16), and you can see there is a lot of visual management.

On the visual board they post the standard work (see Figure 6-17) for each job, a stack chart with the current labor balance, a training matrix to see who is trained on what, and there are also trend graphs that show how they are doing in audits of standard work by shift over time. It is easy to see how valuable this board is to a manager or group leader doing their standard work to coach the work group.

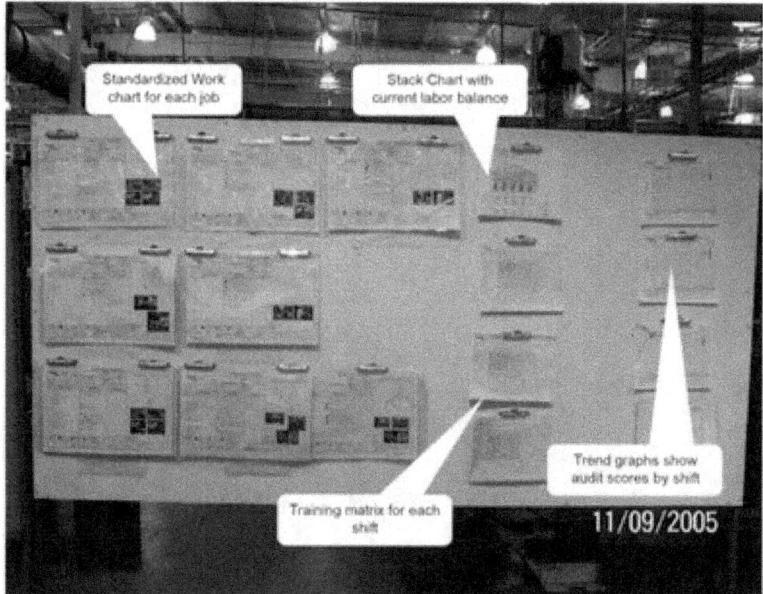

Figure 6-17. A Visual Standard Work Board

This is an enlargement of the standard work sheet that has to be signed off by the group leaders and team leaders in Toyota's terms (see Figure 6-18). In this case, there are three shifts and all three shifts signed off on this. They are saying, "I agree with this. This is how we are going to run this job," and then as it changes they all have to sign off that they agree to the changes and then they have to train to it using job instruction training methods.

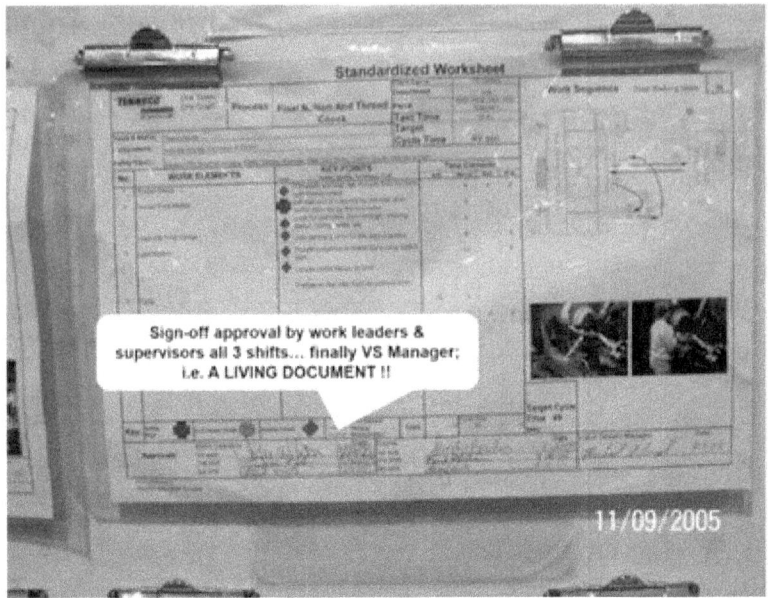

Figure 6-18. Standard Work Sheet

Then we see a simple audit card (see Figure 6-19). Notice that it is just yes/no questions. "Is the standard work in the correct place? Yes or No?" "Is it up to date and approved? Yes or No?" In this case, it has not been approved yet. To get a total score you simply add up the yes responses. It is intentionally very simple. You could put it on a five-point scale (a score of 1-5), but then it is more complicated, and if standard work is done right, either it is there or it is not. Either it is in the correct place or it is not. It is either up to date and approved or it is not. It is not the degree of being up to date that is being measured. Then you can graph the total score and find areas that are red, yellow or green.

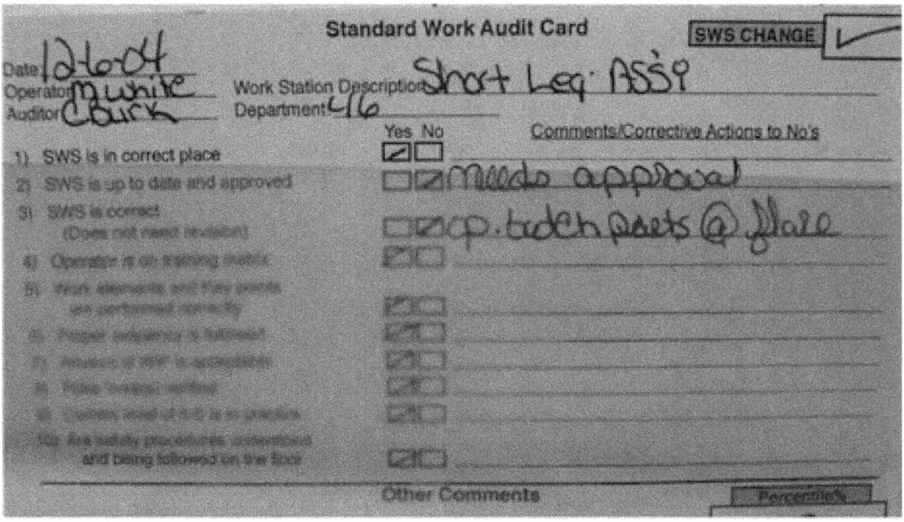

Figure 6-19. A Standard Work Audit Card

What is the Current State in your organization?

What we are talking about is how you get to the point where you have daily kaizen in your company. One of the key points here is that it is very difficult, arguably impossible, to systematically improve a process where there are no standards because a problem is defined as a deviation from the standard. The standard could be standard work where you do the steps in this order; it could be that tools should always be placed here, as in 5S; or it could be a technical quality standard. The standard could also be an aspirational target on a key performance indicator like the old standard was 10 defects from this department per shift and we want to get to a new standard of five defects per shift. It could be a number on a chart or it could be something physical that you can see such as the maximum number of bins of work-in-process inventory allowed.

Then the whole team has to understand their role—the engineers, group leaders, team leaders, team members, and managers. Everybody has to know their role in developing, checking, maintaining, and improving upon the standards to meet the goals the company needs them to reach, and the work group structure is where a lot of kaizen happens. Kaizen of that particular work area is mostly the responsibility of the work groups. Please rate these statements as they apply to your organization (see Figure 6-20)

> **Current state of Daily Kaizen in your company?**
>
> 1=Critical Gap, 2=Major Gap, 3= Some serious Gaps, 4=minor Gaps, 5=We are there
>
> 1. First-line Supervisors and Team members are organized into work groups.
> 2. Standardized work is present and updated regularly.
> 3. Standardized work is the basis for employee training.
> 4. Key Performance Indicators are visible to each work group with clear accountability for reaching challenging targets.
> 5. Engineering projects are viewed as long-term kaizen activities supported by team members.

Figure 6-20. Questions for Assessing Daily Kaizen

In Number 1, we are simply stating you have work groups which many organizations do. I would rate this highly only if you have a ratio of leaders to team members similar to what Toyota recommends—about 5-8 leaders for each team member. Otherwise, here are not enough leaders to coach and support the team members.

Number 2 is saying that standard work is present and updated regularly. It may be present but it is not as likely that every place you go it is being updated and used as a tool for kaizen.

Number 3 says standard work is the basis for employee training. You have something like the work element sheet, with key points and reasons used in a very structured way like job instruction training to train all of your employees. That is also less likely.

In Number 4 we expect both that Key performance indicators are visible to each work group and there is clear accountability for reaching challenging targets, and finally for five an engineering project is viewed as a set of long-term smaller kaizen activities supported by the team members (as we saw in the Minomi case). You have a big goal and a lot of small steps to reach that goal.

I would be very surprised if you were to score very highly on all of these. You might be able to point to an area of your organization that gets a number of fours and is doing very well and many other places where you are less than that and you are barely getting started.

Interestingly, there is variation in a Toyota plants as well. There is variations across group leaders depending on how well trained they are. There is variation over time if a plant has gone through a lot of turmoil because of a major new model introduction and everybody is working overtime and producing like crazy. You might see that the standard work does not get updated, the job instruction training method is not used in a disciplined way, and kaizen goes down, and that is a point where you will hear in Toyota "we need to go back to the basics."

After you have evaluated yourself and you see where your gaps are then think about some of the key points you have learned here about daily kaizen and how they might apply to your organization. Every organization is different. Standard work for non-repetitive jobs is not going to be as detailed, you may have more difficulty creating charts that look just like the ones here, and the takt might not be as clearly defined. How can you define standards that are meaningful, useful, and visible within whatever your type of work is? How can you then use standard work and KPIs to create a functioning daily management system so that management at all levels are involved in improving the value-added work?

CHAPTER 7
CREATE VISION AND ALIGN GOALS THROUGH *Hoshin Kanri*

Create the Vision and the Capability

The Lean Leadership Model Building to *Hoshin Kanri*

If you actually could do in real time all the things we have talked about, you would now be self-developed and you would be spending every day walking through the *gemba*, coaching by asking great questions, checking the process, there would be visual management everyplace, you would have clear metrics, you would understand your processes and all the leaders in your organization would too. As a leader your job would be walking around and checking the process and the people, and figuring out who might be ready for a more challenging assignment, and who is struggling with a current assignment. You would be continually improving the way you solve problems, the way that you reach challenging goals and your organization would be getting better and better, and in the meantime, your competitors would not have this capability so they would be falling further and further behind.

That would be Nirvana and it is not going to happen in a few weeks or a few months, but more like five to ten years. As we go through the model, just keep in mind that what I am really trying to do is familiarize you with the model and a way of thinking about the key importance of self-development, developing others, viewing people as your most valuable, appreciating asset and having the kind of discipline of a great sports coach, or a great symphony conductor. What you are trying to do is develop all the instruments in the symphony and then get them to play in harmony.

Now we will discuss the last part, playing in harmony. You have been working on yourself, developing others, and you now have a few string quartets that can go off on their own relatively unmanaged. They can put together rehearsals, practice sessions, and they are getting better and better. The percussion section is doing that too. Each section of the orchestra is improving themselves and making suggestions to you on how to improve the way you conduct.

The problem is they are not all playing the same piece. There is a Bach concerto being played by the cello group and a Mozart sonata being played by the violins; each department is playing their own piece, and together it sounds terrible.

What is *Hoshin Kanri*?

You really need to get them moving in the same direction now that they have the skill level and passion. They want to be a team. They are ready to be a team. You have to find one piece of music at a time and you have to work with the orchestra now in a different way. Your job is to prepare them, help them prepare themselves so they are in harmony, in time, and they are coming into a piece at the right time and the right volume and together they are making one sound.

In Japan, they came up with a term, *Hoshin Kanri*, part of a national movement back in the 1950s and 1960s focused on quality called Total Quality Management (TQM). The Hoshin is the direction. Sometimes they use the analogy of a compass. We are all playing the same piece, moving in the same direction, and the Kanri is how you do it. In leadership development phases one to three, you have been developing the capacity to do it, so you can figure out the how, but you still need the what. You still need the direction. You still need the clear purpose to align people.

Which comes first?

There is a chicken-and-egg problem. How can people focus intensely on improving the business without a shared vision? On the other hand, you are probably worse off if you give people the vision, but they do not have the capability. For example if the violinists are terrible and they cannot hit the notes or the drummers are drumming to the wrong beat no amount of great conducting is going to compensate for that. *The Music Man,* in which a fake conductor led unskilled children to play great music, was a great film, but not realistic. On the other hand, if you have highly skilled musicians and they are all playing different pieces, then it sounds awful and they are not satisfying their customers.

So what comes first? Is it the vision and clear purpose and alignment so that you get people to start to focus and find ways to solve problems, improve processes and improve themselves, or is it improving people so that they have the capability to participate in *Hoshin Kanri*, an aligned vision and goals?

Figure 7-1. The Lean Leadership Development Model (we are focusing on step 4)

The Lean Leadership development model (see Figure 7-1) seems very simple and sequential. You get the people developed first, and then you roll out *Hoshin Kanri*. If there is one thing I have learned, it is that any linear view of the world is going to be wrong. The world is always more complicated than that.

This chapter focuses on the fourth phase, and I am going to assume phases one through three have been worked on, not perfectly, but at least with a good first pass. Think of this as a cycle that is going around and around and each cycle you are learning through the PDCA process. You are planning, you are doing, you are checking, and you are acting. You are getting better; your people are getting better; there is more enthusiasm; there is higher morale. At some point, you are ready to pull on a string and at least start to get these people aligned towards a common vision, and in addition to that, your senior management is at least doing a decent job of crafting a vision, and leading a process to get everyone aligned to figure out: "What should I do? What does the vision mean for me?" It does not have to be a perfect process. In fact, at first it is likely to be clunky with lots of fits and starts, which is after all how we learn anything new.

Hoshin Kanri to focus energy on aligned learning cycles

Hoshin Kanri focuses on aligning. Align that great knowledge and skill you have developed for improving things so that everyone is improving the right things for the business at the time, and the right thing for the customers at the time, and there is a coordinated focused effort. You do not want one group focused mainly on safety, another group focused on customer satisfaction, and another group on productivity.

You are not going to get synergy that will deliver value to the customer and help the company be focused. You will not get safety throughout. You will only get safety in pockets just as if you will only get productivity in pockets.

That is why you need to create a vision and align goals, and that will be easier to do the more deeply you have done steps one through three. If you have people who are ready, are good at learning, teaching and improving, then all you really need to do now is harness that energy like a laser beam and get it focused. If you do not have the energy to harness to begin with you are not going to get focused improvement. All these things ultimately fit together, but there is somewhat of a logical order. As you go through this, you are going through learning cycles. You would like those learning cycles at an individual level to be as rapid as possible so individuals get quick feedback—the faster the PDCA cycles, the faster and deeper the learning. They will add up to bigger and bigger learning cycles.

If you look back and you were to say, "What is the process by which I learned my first complex musical piece?" that might then look like a year-long learning cycle. However, embedded in that learning cycle there may be hundreds of learning cycles if you did practice drills and then broke the musical score into measures that you drilled over and over. Learning cycles are an abstract construct. You can go through a learning cycle in a minute if each minute you try something intentionally, you do it, and then you check what happened and based on that you adjust. Every time you play a scale that could be a 10-second learning cycle.

The point is that you need a method of learning, called "deliberate practice," where you are intentionally trying to learn something. You know the purpose. You then have developed something to do to try it, and when you make an error, when a sound does not come out the way you want, you figure out why, and then you can make an adjustment and try again. This is the cycle of deliberate practice. A coach may be needed to help identify the cause of the error and adjustment necessary.

The opposite of deliberate practice is playing around. You can play around without getting much better, but in playing around you just make interesting sounds, and you feel good because with enough repetition, sounds will start to get better. Eventually you can play a piece at a low level of quality but you will probably not get better than that.

As leaders develops skills to lead improvement you can reach higher and higher levels of coordinated improvement through *Hoshin Kanri*. It is also called "policy deployment" in some English language books. Everybody who learns about it is anxious to get started right away, but it is really hard to find examples where companies are actually doing it top to bottom and have gone through phases one through four enough times that they are good at it.

The Japanese companies experienced with *Hoshin Kanri* have settled on one-year cycles, an annual plan. Maybe in year one you are not ready for any *Hoshin Kanri*, even a very weak version, though your improvement projects have clear challenges tied to business needs. In year one you are focusing on steps one through three. Some organizations might focus on steps one through three for several years before they try *Hoshin Kanri*. At some point, you are going to try it and when you do try it, just think of this as your first experiment, and something that you are going to be working on for the rest of your career to improve upon.

Hoshin Kanri at Toyota

The problem of aligning people toward common business goals

How do you Develop People with the skills and motivation to become aligned toward a Common Vision?

This is the age-old management question. I bet you could find it in Greek writings or perhaps earlier. Leaders were scratching their heads and asking, "Why don't people do what I need them to do, and do it well and do it with passion? I am telling them what we need to do to be successful. Why don't they just do it? Well, people are naturally resistant to change. They were not raised right. They are lazy." The definition of being a leader is you have followers, and if they are all coming together toward your vision that is heaven.

If I presented this opportunity to any CEO in the world, they would agree: "We want it." Then I might ask them: How do you get it?" They will probably have eloquent answers, but mostly based on a simplistic view of motivation and capability. They might say something like "I tell them what I need and motivate and inspire them, and we have a positive work environment and treat our employees well, and I expect them to do a full day's work for a full day's pay and to work to achieve the business metrics we set for them." That is great, but how do you do it? It does not really answer the question of how you do it. It still assumes that if you have the right environment and the leaders make it clear what they need somehow people will find a way to get it done.

Underlying this whole book is the proposition that there is a set of skills needed for improvement that can be deliberately learned as you deliberately learn any other skill. It does not happen just because of charismatic leaders who give impassioned speeches, treat you well, provide attractive pay levels and a safe work environment, and then make the objectives clear. People also need a structure to develop plans that align, then they need the discipline, skill level, and leadership to execute on a daily basis. In short, well-conceived plans are needed that are executed with motivation and skill at all levels. The plan cannot be static since the world is far too complex. In fact, the planning and execution need to continually evolve through PDCA.

Hoshin Kanri History at Toyota

Toyota began the journey to *Hoshin Kanri* in 1961. Major companies in Japan already used *Hoshin Kanri* as part of Total Quality Management and by that time Toyota Motor Company had accomplished a great deal. TPS had been developed within Toyota and it was functioning quite well. Their direct suppliers were mostly trained in TPS. Engineers who got their hands dirty were continually improving the design and launch of new vehicles.

They had a lot of smart, hardworking people but leaders of Toyota still realized "we are not a modern global company. We are a really good local company and if we want to achieve our goals and be a successful automotive company for the long term we need scale, and scale comes from globalizing."

They decided that they needed to modernize their operations and then President Eiji Toyoda, cousin of Kiichiro Toyoda, identified two fundamental needs. First, they needed to clarify targets; in particular, Toyota was not competitive in quality at that time. Their quality was getting better, but there was a gap with the American automotive makers. By clarifying targets, it did not mean he needed to polish up his speech as the President and make his speech clear; he needed to have targets on metrics which were meaningful to the people doing the work. Second, they needed a management system to promote cross-functional cooperation. It was not enough to give orders that cascade down the hierarchy vertically within chimneys. Sales, engineering, purchasing, marketing, and staff organizations needed to identify common goals and work together toward meeting those goals. The customers buy a car that starts with conception and ends with delivery to the customer. They are not purchasing services of independent functions.

Just waving your hands and saying, "we need quality, we need fewer defects," would certainly not be enough. Even holding people accountable to targets for defects and customer satisfaction was just scratching the surface. I am still going to be in the stamping department, stamping body parts and saying, "so what does he want me to do? We have a defect measure, we know how many defects we create inside the factory, we know how many defects are getting to the customers, and we know they are not satisfied with the body. There is too much air noise leaking through. We know all these things. What am I supposed to do? What am I supposed to work on?"

An outcome metric like defects is too global to really help people at a local level identify what to do, and then Eiji Toyoda also recognized that even if he could do number one well, it was not going to work unless he could promote the second fundamental need, cross-functional cooperation. Quality, Human Resources, Maintenance, and Engineering all needed to work together to achieve quality. Toyota discovered *Hoshin Kanri* in the 1960s, and began to implement it with a more concrete goal than "we want excellent quality." The concrete goal was to win the Deming prize. Deming had become a quality guru in Japan teaching statistical process control and the philosophy of building in quality, not inspecting in quality. He was highly regarded by

Toyota and Japan established a prize in his name, which was extremely tough to win. Eiji Toyoda set the challenge, "we are going to win the Deming Prize for quality as a concrete target to focus our efforts as a company." They accomplished the goal in 1965.

Toyota *Hoshin Kanri* – History

1961: TMC identified need to modernize management operations to compete globally
Eiji Toyoda's two fundamental needs:

- Need for top management to clarify targets (especially quality) and engage employees.
- Management system that promoted cross-functional cooperation.

1965: Toyota wins Deming Prize for Quality

1972: *Hoshin Kanri* matured as it is practiced today.

Visual Metrics Aligned from Top to Bottom to meet Annual Plan

One of the early things that you can do to start to get people aligned is to post metrics out in the workplace that are aligned from top to bottom. We have already talked about the importance of visual metrics in Chapter Six on work groups. We talked about how the work groups need to meet someplace, visually see how they are doing, and step-by-step develop plans for improvement and that management should be coming around and checking on the process, on people and how they are doing in achieving the metrics. The metrics give you a starting point. "What is our target? Where are we? Where are we red, the gap between the target and the actual," and then you can begin coaching.

During the recession, in February of 2008, I visited Toyota's plant in Indiana. They had been operating for about eight years making trucks, minivans, and large SUVs and they were winning quality award after quality award. During the recession they had to shut down for three months because they had too many trucks and demand had dropped so much, and then the recession hit and they were operating at about 60% capacity for another eight or nine months. During that time, they did not lay off regular employees, but they turned the plant into a kind of university to teach the Toyota Production System for three months, building no trucks or large sport utility vehicles, and then after that, team members were alternating between working half time and learning.

One of the things they were focused on was teaching *Hoshin Kanri* using the floor management development system (FMDS) which we talked about in Chapter Six—a system of getting people to meet every day, identify problems to work on, and do kaizen every day in small loops—PDCA, PDCA, PDCA. They introduced for the first time FMDS visual boards aligned from the work group to the senior management level (see

Figure 7-2). They were developed about 10 years earlier in Japan and the boards are organized to facilitate *Hoshin Kanri* and teach people to follow Toyota Business Practices. To my surprise, they acted as if this was all new. I had been seeing this around Toyota for 10 years. Why was this great plant with so many quality awards talking about *Hoshin Kanri* and the floor management development system as if it was a new thing?

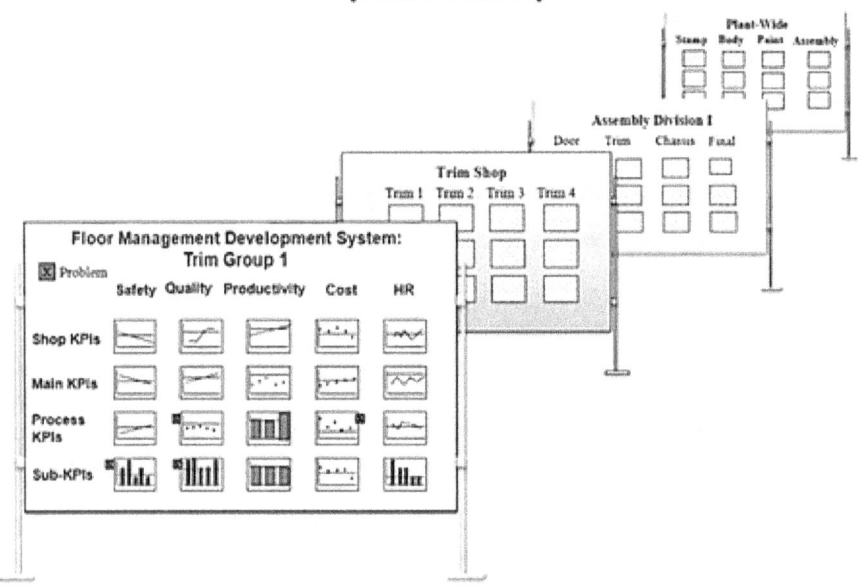

Figure 7-2. Visual Boards that Align top-level Plan to Shop Floor Metrics

The answer was "We have been engaging our employees in kaizen. Some of our hourly workers are better than the managers at kaizen. We were selling so many vehicles and working overtime regularly and neglected training on these newer tools. What we have really never done was to take the time to systematically put in the whole process of *Hoshin Kanri* so that there was true alignment throughout this plant. We are doing that now that we have the time."

They had just recently installed Floor Management Development System (FMDS) boards for each work group led by a group leader and team leaders (see Figure 7-3). As an example, if you are a group leader over one of the parts of the body shop that say welds the doors; on the top row of the board, you have got the main metrics used throughout the body shop for safety, quality, productivity, cost, and human resource management. Those are standard categories and link directly to the hoshin boards for the head of the body shop. They are generic outcomes.

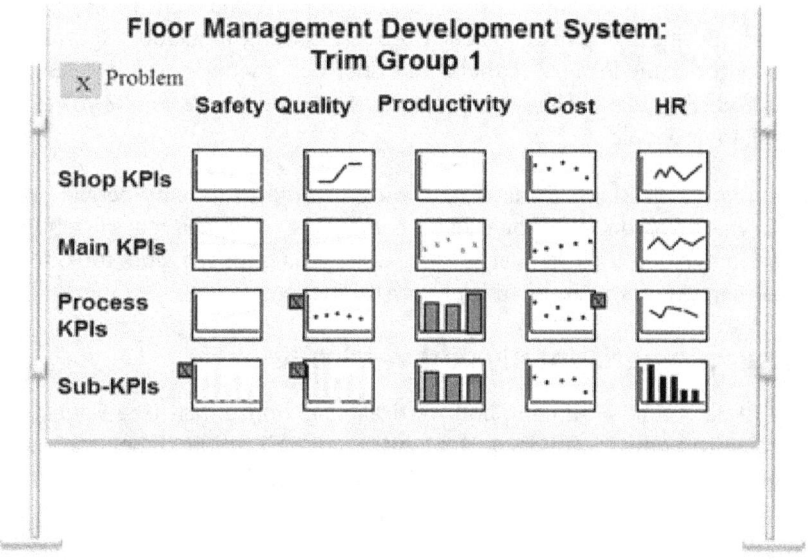

Figure 7-3. Floor Management Development System Board

The Indiana plant signed up for targets needed by the President of the company, and also had internal targets related to training and development while production was shut down or slowed. One area of emphasis was quality. They decided to pull ahead their expected quality targets for the following year and achieve them one year earlier since they had the time to focus.

The top-line metric was defects per 100 vehicles produced which was the overall plant measure. As I said, defects produced is a generic outcome. Then as you go down the board, you have to translate that. One area of defects they discovered in the Indiana plant was what they called "mutilation" of the car body, a dramatic sounding term for scratches, bends, and dents on the car body and they located the source of many of these in the body shop where stamped parts are welded together. Now we have a more shop-specific KPI called mutilations and a target was established for reducing these defects.

In the body shop there are inspection points in which they can identify instances of body mutilation and the specific process that caused these. The work groups responsible for those jobs will now focus at the process level on those causing the largest number of defects.

Now they are doing something like the Improvement *Kata*. They observe the current operating pattern of these jobs, set the next target condition, identify potential obstacles, and begin to experiment with countermeasures. They are at the level of cycles of PDCA. They may record what they are doing at the bottom of the FMDS board or use a separate flip chart or white board for this. In the Indiana case, when they focused at the process level, they used a flip chart and went through the eight-step Toyota Business Practices for each process causing mutilation. It was the first opportunity for group leaders, team leaders and team members to learn TBP, so they were both getting the quality improvements to meet the *Hoshin Kanri*, as well as developing their people.

The was a great blessing... to have the luxury of time to develop people. Ironically, while this was going on I was speaking to companies which had mass layoffs because sales were down and I would hear, "there was nothing for the work force to do." To them, learning was not doing anything worth paying for.

Align people horizontally and vertically

The ideal state is total alignment, both vertically and horizontally (see Figure 7-4). The hoshin come top down, with dialogue at every pair of levels, and then the checks roll up the organization That is the vertical. The horizontal is the coordination that must take place across functions, departments, and physical locations.

The Hoshin Kanri process should lead to discussions across the organization, always with a clear leader. Gary led the warranty claims reduction process out of the manufacturing hierarchy in North America and had to pull in leaders from other organizations all over the world. This was horizontal alignment at its best.

Even in the case of welding no group is working in isolation. One thing they might discover is that some of the parts come to them from stamping misshaped. It could be that the parts come to them and they just do not fit together very well for welding purposes. The parts have been stamped within tolerance, but they are at the outer extremes of tolerance. They may fit forcefully, but they are not fitting easily and they are going to put pressure on the welds possibly damaging them over time.

If I am a group leader in the body shop, I only have control over what I do, but the problem originated in the stamping department. Ultimately, I may need help from product development because they have not set their tolerances right so that the parts are usually fitting, but sometimes they are not. How can I do that? How do I get that horizontal alignment across these different functions? That will require elevating the problem to a higher level. You do not want a welding group leader running around to find the right people to talk to in other departments to convince them to change their process or product specifications.

The horizontal alignment is going to happen across management, and the vertical alignment can happen through that hierarchy with the FMDS boards. The managers in all these departments have quality targets in their *Hoshin Kanri* plans for the year so they will naturally have a degree of alignment. A new cross-functional team may get formed focused on eliminating body mutilation led by product development, stamping, or welding and those team members may get some additional targets added to their individual *Hoshin Kanri* plans.

Figure 7-4. *Hoshin Kanri* Horizontal and Vertical Alignment

That means everybody needs to be skilled in problem solving. How do they get skilled in problem solving? Toyota has a simple answer for that too. It is On the Job Development (OJD). They have bought in. It is in the water in Toyota. If you are coached through OJD to follow the spirit and practice of Toyota Business Practices you will naturally want to work with other departments to achieve the company goals, and you will have the skills to do it effectively.

The company wants to be more competitive in quality. They know what they need, and ultimately it is total customer satisfaction. This needs to be broken down into actions within functional departments and cross-functional activities. Then those departments and cross-functional teams have to break them down into actions at the granular level, execute, and then check how they are doing. They do this by checking and adjusting, thereby contributing to the higher level Hoshin. You are going down in a breakdown and up in the contributions which include checking. The breakdown includes all the planning, that includes how we are going to do it, then executing, and then the benefits go upward. We have a nice model, and it is a powerful vision. This is what we would look like if we were the perfect organization. Everybody would be doing this. The real challenge is to turn the vision into reality.

How *Hoshin Kanri* and Daily Management Work Together

The *Hoshin Kanri* Annual Cycle at Toyota

Hoshin Kanri is an annual cycle designed to support the rolling five-year business plan and the global vision of the decade. The cycle itself at a macro level, not surprisingly, follows Plan, Do, Check, Act. Over a three-month period, you develop a plan in preparation for the year. Toyota is on a fiscal year starting April 1st. The President gives a speech in the beginning of January laying out the top level Hoshin. It starts with discussing our vision for the decade, our five year plan, where we are on the five year plan, where we have been, the current situation, what our competitors are doing, what environmental challenges we face, and what new things have come up, say a tsunami this year, so there are new challenges. Our competitors are launching vehicles at a historic rate and we are behind. Whatever it is, the President paints a picture of the challenges the company faces, and then focuses in and says, "This is what we need to accomplish globally by the end of this year. This is our annual plan for the company."

This then launches a complex and rather exhausting effort, which in Toyota has become very routine, of breaking that down by function first at the very top global headquarters level. Globally there is a head of R&D, there is a head of sales, there is a head of logistics, there is a head of finance, a head of quality, a head of human resources, and then they begin to break down their plans and it gets allocated within regional functional groups. What is North America going to take on? What is Europe going to take on? Then it finds its way to individual units within regions like the technical centers, the sales unit in that region, and the regional manufacturing organization. It flows down, and what is flowing down are two-way discussions about what we need to sign up for in order to achieve the annual objectives for the company, then how are we going to do it? What is our initial plan? What are the levers we can pull that we believe will allow us to achieve these results?

That is all happening in the Plan stage. As I mentioned, it starts in January, and all this is cascading down, all these two-way discussions, called "catch ball" and all this thinking and planning is happening over a three-month period. The fiscal year starts April 1st and now we go. Somebody shoots off a gun to begin the race. Now we are starting to execute on the *Hoshin Kanri* plan. Then there is constant checking, constant action, PDCA all the time, but at the halfway point of the year, six months in, there is a big corporate checkpoint for the whole world for Toyota. At that point, everybody has to be checking and report up and the company finds out where they are. At that point, there is an opportunity for some adjustment. For example, let's take the tsunami and Great East Japan earthquake that led to severe parts shortages. That happened in March and by then the *Hoshin Kanri* plan was mostly finalized without considering the effects of that earthquake and tsunami. That has to be brought into the plan and some things must be taken off the table.

In this checkpoint for six months, we are reflecting on where we are and figuring out what we need to do to adjust for the rest of the year. At the same time, this begins the process of planning for the next year. A major catastrophe like an earthquake may mean some items will be pushed into the next year.

Therefore, we have to begin collecting data about where we are and thinking about the targets for the next year. For the improvements so far, we may be in the Action stage of PDCA so we need to stabilize so the improvements are sustained.

People throughout Toyota would agree that three months, starting in January, is not a long time to develop such a complex plan. They also will tell you, "we have been thinking about the Hoshin since last August. We have a good idea of what we are going to be asked to do. We are already working on it."

This is how the annual *Hoshin Kanri* cycle works, and at a company level you can see this as one big Plan, Do, Check, Act. Here is our annual plan, we execute, here is what we have achieved, here is what we still have to do. Within the annual PDCA, there are embedded PDCA loops at smaller and smaller levels, through the country level to the plant level for the year, to the quarterly level, ultimately to the minute-by-minute level in the work groups. If there is a defect or something going wrong that you notice you are trying to fix those problems through PDCA. There are embedded PDCA learning cycles from top to bottom.

The Critical Relationship between *Hoshin Kanri* and Daily Management

The *Hoshin Kanri* is harnessing the energy of all your people to use the planning and executing discipline that they have been working for years to develop, and the daily management system, what Toyota calls the Floor Management Development System, is guiding the work groups up to management in daily PDCA. To get the full benefit HK and FMDS need to work together. The *Hoshin Kanri* sets your big picture objectives and then you are translating that into specific actions through daily management.

The first question you need to ask is, what do we need to do? You need to answer that question for the company, for each department, and ultimately each work group. The end result of the answer to what you need to do is a set of objectives translated to measureable targets. The second question is how should we do it? What is the process we are going to use to get closer and closer to hitting the target? We are now not even hitting the dartboard, let alone hitting the target. To do that we need daily activities that give us practice and get us closer and closer to hitting that target. Finally we need to know how we are doing and what the results are, and for that we need to have the process of daily review of Main Key Performance Indicators, Sub-Key Performance Indicators, down to an individual process that we are working on right now. Again, from the big picture down to the microscopic details for solving a particular problem right now.

How should we do it? The management of that and the how are we doing are obviously interlinked. Steps two and three are constantly going on as we have our daily meetings, do kaizen, constantly check how we are doing and identify the next step.

Hoshin Kanri and Floor Management Development System Harness the Energy of Work Groups

What do we need to do?

(Company –Department –Work Group)

- ➔ Hoshin – Objective and KPIs

How should we do it?

(Process)

- ➔ Floor management – Daily Activities

How are we doing?

(Results)

- ➔ Main KPIs, Sub-KPIs, Process KPIs,

I have talked about *Hoshin Kanri* as separate from daily management, but intimately connected. By *Hoshin Kanri*, we mean the planning and checking process, at a big picture level from the President down to the worker and every level in between, and the daily management process is what you are actually doing on a daily basis. For example, you are standing in front of the FMDS boards with your team and discussing, "Here is where we have some weaknesses, here is what we need to work on today. This is how we are doing on this particular process of installing the instrument panels." That is the very detailed discussion in daily management and the activities we are doing every day.

You can think about these as two different things and some companies do. We have observed that companies that implement *Hoshin Kanri* with weak daily management systems to translate the objectives to actions experience a saw tooth effect. They make big improvements on a metric executives emphasize, perhaps quality. Then executives have cost pressures and that becomes the new imperative. Quality goes backward. On the other hand, daily management without *Hoshin Kanri* can be effective in sustaining improvements, but the improvements will not be dramatic. However, if you integrate the two you will get very nice results as shown in the trend chart (see Figure 7-5). What we show here is a big step forward, followed by a smaller or more flat adjustment period. For example, we decided that we are going to reduce defects by 10%. We change many things. We change tools, we change how we train people, we work with our suppliers and they change their process. We are even giving some feedback to product development so they are going to make the next version of the model easier to build.

Lots of things change. Lots of people have to change the way they do their jobs. There is communication that has to take place daily across departments, a whole new set of tasks. After making all these changes, we need to stabilize and sustain the changes. We are still going to be finding little things every day to improve, but we are not yet going to be tasked with another major challenge.

For example, by 2010, there was a very strong Yen in Japan and a lot of analysts said that this was almost a lethal problem for Toyota. They make so many cars in Japan that when they export them it is hard to make any money at all. They might lose money because the Yen is so strong. Toyota does not accept that it is hopeless. They figure that they need to work on it. To work on it, they established a target of reducing costs by 30% in Japan over a three year period—10% a year. There are a lot of fixed costs that are hard to change and a limited amount of variable costs to work with. It comes back to fundamental redesign of the whole vehicle and how it is put together and many changes in the factories. They had to rethink everything to get another 30% in an extremely efficient company..., they did it, and then Prime Minister Abe instituted policies that greatly weakened the yen and Toyota was extremely profitable.

That is a big change, and you are not going to be doing that every year forever. There is going to be periods where you have smaller objectives to sustain what you are doing, recharge a bit, and get ready for the next big mountain climb. Again, the Hoshin can give you these big challenge, and then you need to use daily management to make the many small changes needed to achieve the challenge and to stabilize the process.

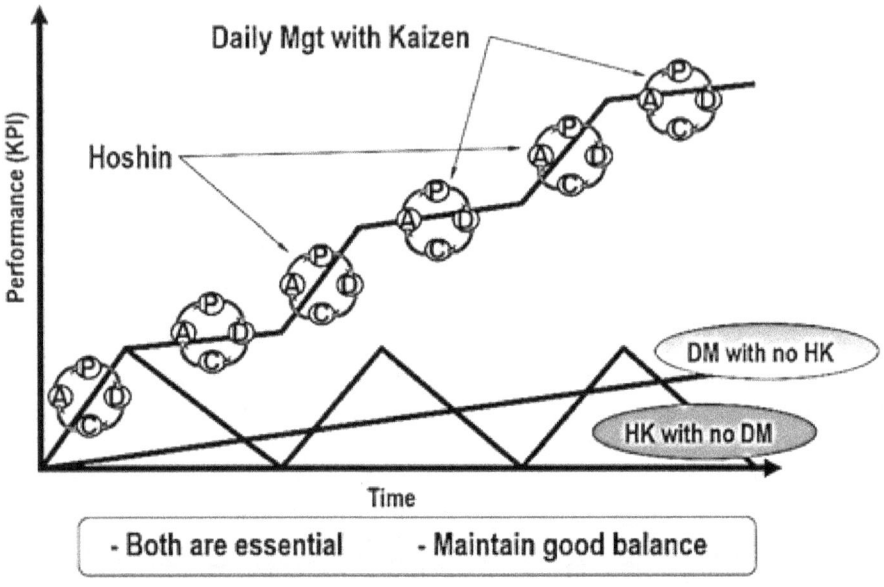

Figure 7-5. *Hoshin Kanri* and Daily Management work together for breakthroughs and sustainment

Philosophy in *Hoshin Kanri*

The Philosophy underlying *Hoshin Kanri*

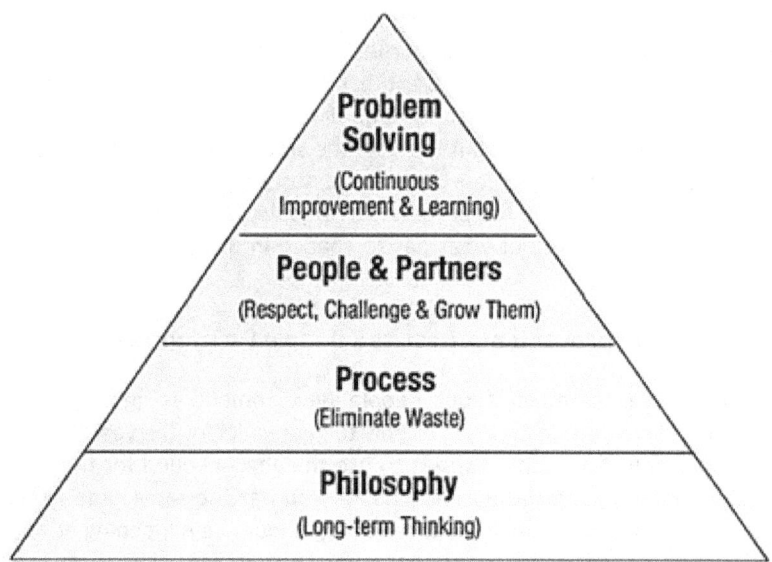

Figure 7-6. The Toyota Way Model.

Let's go back and talk philosophy, which in my Toyota Way model is the foundation (see Figure 7-6). The foundation of philosophy is always values. What do you believe? What is driving you? What is important to the business? What is important to the company? What do you believe about customers? What do you believe about people? What do you believe about leadership? The answers to these questions give you the foundation to talk about Toyota's five values—challenge, kaizen, going and seeing at the *gemba*, teamwork and respect. You then need to have some sense of direction and the initial step is going to be a broad vision, and Toyota has a 10-year global vision posted on their website. Obviously, a 10-year vision has to be very general because so much changes in the world.

You need to get cooperation from all your employees. If you have horrible employee relations because you have been beating up people as a way of managing for years you have to start to repair that and develop some trust which probably means working on smaller projects, without *Hoshin Kanri*, to get people experienced with improvement and to believe failed experiments will not be punished. In addition, you need to start to coach and change through leadership development cycles. You are right back at self-development, and you need self-development by leaders at all levels, ideally starting at the top and working down.

- Core values are the Foundation
- Starts with Vision for future (e.g., 10-year vision)
- Cooperative effort with all employees

Then you need to have a clear sense of purpose for *Hoshin Kanri*, and in Toyota's case, like in any other company's case, they want results. They need the results for business, but they go beyond that, because results without actually improving and stabilizing the process are unsustainable. They want to avoid the saw-tooth effect. They want results and they want a repeatable process to produce sustainable improvement, and they know only people can improve the process. The people need to be developed so they can check the results, figure out what has to change in the process, and make those changes.

Purpose: Process Improvement x Results x People Development

True *Hoshin Kanri* is as much about people development as getting results. The philosophy underlying *Hoshin Kanri* is not only to get results for the year. That is part of it, but the philosophy for *Hoshin Kanri* is to use the goals needed for the business to satisfy customers and keep the business healthy and at the same time improve our processes and develop our people. All three things should be happening at once and if even one of these has not happened than the *Hoshin Kanri* has failed. If one is zero, the total is zero, like multiplying not adding.

The core belief is that a good process will lead to good results. In other words, I can first start with the results and then say, "what do I need to do to get these results?" That leads to simplistic approaches like only cost reduction matters so my engineers and black belts do projects that give me a high return on investment, and when I get the results, I am happy. Again, Toyota believes that the only way you can sustain good results every year that keep on getting better is to have repeatable, defined processes, which are continually improved by the people responsible for running them.

In short, when you are working on the process, part of what you are doing is getting a return on investment and other things you are doing, like training people and daily maintenance, do not have an immediate measurable benefit. You do them because you know you need equipment functioning at a high level. You know you need top-notch people who are motivated and trying to help the business by doing daily kaizen. You know you need meetings around the metric boards each day. You know you need a team leader and group leader who know how to coach. All those elements have to be in place to get the desired results so you are working on all those elements, without expecting a direct return on investment every time I train somebody, or every time I authorize overtime to maintain equipment.

Comparison between MBO and *Hoshin Kanri*

Management By Objectives has Become Command and Control

Every company has objectives in some form. The most common is often referred to as "Management By Objectives." What that looks like is discussions from the top executive level to the supervisor level about measureable objectives. It sounds like *Hoshin Kanri*, but the similarity ends here. The discussions are, almost exclusively, about what results we are trying to get, the outcomes. The outcomes are associated with rewards and punishment. Either you meet this and you are going to get that great bonus and be up for that promotion, or you fail and there are consequences.

In sum, it is fear, recognition, and rewards, and it is tangible. This is going to be the tangible result for your career if you achieve the tangible results. That has led, for example, to the ABC system that GE popularized. You have the A employees who get exceptional raises and bonuses. You have the B employees, who are doing a good job and getting an average raise, and you have your C employees who need improvement and they are going to get punished. If they are a C employee for two years in a row, they are going to get fired.

Every group of whatever number, say its 10 people, needs to have at least one C employee, and at least say two A employees, and everyone else is in the middle. You are forcing each manager to define the winners and the losers. This fits the management by objectives philosophy, which is fear, rewards, and clear targets and then let it rip. Let them do their thing and the people will be motivated enough that they will achieve the results.

When we look at the characteristics of Management by Objectives it is short-term focused. Senior management dictated the results required in a short time frame, and will be checking on you. It is not linked in your mind to some broader vision of your company in 10 years. That is the furthest thing from your mind. What is on your mind is: "I have to make the numbers because I am being evaluated when the deadline comes at the end of the quarter."

I should point out that one of the advocates of Management by Objectives was Peter Drucker, one of the top management thought leaders of all time. As he described MBO, it involved participative management, dialogue, and empowerment. It was much more like *Hoshin Kanri* then like MBO as it is often practiced. At some point, the original intent of MBO got lost in the practice.

Management by Objectives Characteristics

Short-Term, No Philosophy

I say that, "there is no philosophy," but what I mean is there is no defined philosophy of how you lead people and what your values are (see Figure 7-7). You could summarize the philosophy by saying "survival of the fittest, and achieve results at all costs, and results are what we are being pressured to achieve in the short term, often by a board of directors, outside shareholders, or some investor."

Results Oriented Evaluation of Effort

"We are only going to evaluate results. I do not care how you do it. Just get it done. Obviously, you do not violate ethical principles. You do not steal, rob, break the law, or put people in physical danger. We care about safety, we care about our ethical system, but other than that, there are no rules. Just get it done."

Top Down, Directive Communication

Communication is top down. You may be polite, nice, and listen to people's concerns, but the objectives are the objectives.

Primarily Authority Oriented

Your base of power is your formal authority. You are in a position of handing out rewards and punishment. You have the carrot and stick, and these are your most powerful tools.

Management by Objectives	Hoshin Kanri
Short-Term, No Philosophy	Long-Term, Strong Guiding Principles
Results Oriented Evaluation of Effort	Concerned with Results and Process with Focus on People Development
Top down Communication	Top down Direction Setting and Bottom-up flow of Information and means
Directive	Participative
Primarily Authority Oriented	Primarily Responsibility Oriented

Figure 7-7. Comparison between Management by Objectives and *Hoshin Kanri*

Hoshin Kanri Characteristics

Long Term, Strong Guiding Principles

There is a set of guiding principles, a long-term vision. The guiding principles are about customers, people, respect, the soft stuff, and we are concerned with not only the results but also the process and the focus on people development.

Concerned with Results and Process with Focus on People Development

With *Hoshin Kanri*, we are focused on developing people at all levels, developing a basic trust, and people are continually, not just at the end of the quarter, but continually working on improving certain things that they believe will lead to the results. They might be wrong. They might have to readjust what they are working on as they learn, and that is what makes it a learning process.

Top Down Direction Setting

The top is setting direction. The business needs will not emerge from a democratic process. It emerges from deep analysis of your competitors, of new technology, of opportunities in the future, of where you want to go as a business, as what your business model is going to be. Strategic planning has to come from the top and senior executives need to determine what the business needs to be successful. It is a business need, it is not nice to have.

Participation through bottom-up flow of Information and means

When you start to cascade that down, if the reactions you get are "no, we cannot do that, we can do half of that, we can do a quarter of that," the business is not going to get what it needs. Once those top-down directions are created, you are going to get those results. It would be very difficult to convince Toyota in a given year, like in Japan, when they set a target of 30% cost reduction over three years, that they should compromise and settle for 15% in three years.

Greater effort is spent on discussing the means then debating the targets. "How are we going to do this?" There is a lot of planning about the methods that are going to be used. "To achieve higher productivity what are we going to measure that is meaningful for our operation?" In paint, it might be equipment uptime. In assembly, it might be labor hours per unit, if you are in sales, it may be the time it takes to close a sale.

It is a participative process in that everybody is involved. They are actively involved. They are thinking, analyzing, looking at data, coming up with plans. It is not participative in the sense that people can block the goals and say, "no, 30% is ridiculous. I think we should do 17%." It is not that kind of participation. It is participation more over the allocation of targets across the organization, but even more so on "how are we going to do it?"

Primarily Responsibility Oriented

It is primarily responsibility oriented, and that means people are signing up, putting their name by an objective, and leading that effort rather than people responding to carrots and sticks from their boss. In Toyota, they do not have a lot of contingent rewards. "You do this, you get this. You do this, you get this." There is a bi-annual bonus in Japan (annual in some countries), tied to how the company does and how the plant does. It is more global bonuses, and there is some percent as an individual bonus at the management level tied to the *Hoshin Kanri*. They rarely fire people so you do not get on the C list for two years and get fired. They do not force distributions. If everybody is excellent, everybody is excellent. They primarily are interested in intrinsic motivation. "I am part of the team, I am getting paid well, I am doing my job and an important part of my job is achieving these targets for the company."

Radical Lean Transformation: Dana Chassis Parts Supplier

There seems to be a misunderstanding that *Hoshin Kanri* is really something you drive down to the floor level where small improvements are made, which is true, but that is only part of the story. You want the shop floor workers to be involved in Continuous Improvement. You want them to be working toward defined goals that collectively help the business. That is all true, but there is a management hierarchy from the president to the CEO down to the worker, and every stage of that hierarchy should be actively engaged in Continuous Improvement. As you move up the hierarchy, the scope of the projects you personally lead gets bigger and bigger.

You will find in Toyota that the majority of high-impact changes are led at the level of manager or executive. At that higher level are the larger projects that involve hundreds or even thousands of people and many pieces of equipment. Note that there are still many smaller improvements at lower levels that support the larger goals set at the higher levels. In addition, there are staff functions like production planning that lead big improvement activities. They are focused on things like leveling the schedule, overall material information flow to suppliers, and they have a much broader scope of responsibility in their Hoshin items with much larger dollar, quality, and safety implications, though they do depend on alignment and support from the work groups to deploy these larger changes.

Perhaps we like to think of *Hoshin Kanri* as something you delegate down, like passing a hot potato, because it lets us off the hook. First, the President has it, then he passes it to the Vice-President, then he passes it to the general manager, and he to the manager, and you pass it down ultimately to the work group, then they are working on improvement and their improvements bubble up. All those layers in between are abdicating responsibility, because they should all be working on improvement of a broader scope.

When Gary retired from Toyota he spent time participating on Boards of Directors. One of these companies was Dana, and Dana was in trouble. They had earlier declared Chapter 11 bankruptcy and emerged from it early in 2007 just in time for doubling of US gas prices followed by the Great Recession. Dana supplied chassis components to the automotive and heavy truck sector. One sector of customers built large commercial trucks and the automotive customers built small passenger trucks, and almost every week it seemed another big supplier in the automotive world was going bankrupt. Dana had overcommitted and became one of the casualties.

Gary was on the Board of Directors when they were developing an aggressive plan to emerge from all of these crises, and it was a good plan. They were hiring a CEO to lead the turnaround but at the last minute he changed his mind. The board then came to agreement with Gary that he would be the acting CEO and he took over for one year. He accepted the job of leading this battered and beaten down company to recovery.

This was a real crisis and it was possible that Dana would end up being shut down as a company. They were governed emerging from Chapter 11 by a board of debtors, banks, and a private equity company that helped bail them out. At key milestones if they did not meet their targets for things like free cash flow then that board had the right to sell off parts of the company and even dissolve the company.

Dana Snapshot

- Founded in 1904
- Based in Maumee, Ohio
- 2009 Sales: $5.2 Billion
- 22,000 employees
- 96 major facilities in 26 countries

It was a big company, 5.2 billion dollars in sales, 22,000 employees, and 96 major plants in 26 countries. This was back in 2008, and they had to go through a radical transformation. John Devine, the Chairman of the board, who was the former CFO of Ford, then General Motors, hired Gary. He was a heavy hitter. He knew how to reorganize a company from a financial viewpoint and that was critical. Reorganize means closing things, and selling things, and consolidating things, and pushing on suppliers, and consolidating suppliers, and limiting pension programs and cutting employees. He knew the dark side of a turn around, but he was forward thinking enough to realize that in this industry, in particular, automotive passenger trucks, the quality standards and pressures for technological innovation had gotten so high that you could not simply cut your way to success. You still needed operational excellence.

It had become a basic requirement for being in business. You need to deliver really good products on time, you hold the inventory your customer does not, super high quality, and you also need R&D to give your customers new technologies that they cannot get from other suppliers. They divided the labor. Gary's job focused on operational excellence and to deliver cost reductions, and the chairman's job was to lead the financial turnaround. John Devine brought in friends from Ford who were skilled at restructuring union contracts, consolidating plants, renegotiating salaries and benefits and the more traditional restructuring.

Gary in the meantime began hiring people he knew from his time at Toyota who had expertise in operational excellence. As a Toyota-trained leader, he naturally headed out to the plants to do *gemba* walks and suggest major improvements while assessing the strengths and weaknesses of the leadership in place.

In summary, here is the background.

2007, February: emerged from Chapter 11 bankruptcy

2007, Summer: Dana US sales decline when gas prices double in the US

2008, October: Lehman Brothers Crisis

2008, April: Gary is named CEO.

2008, Fall: Great Recession continues to keep sales low and facilities underutilized.

You might expect based on this in "2009, dissolve the company, go out of business." In fact, quite the opposite happened.

Turning around a company is not something new. There is a major industry of turnaround experts and private equity that buys and turns around companies. The traditional skill set is financial management. Bean counters pour over the numbers figuring out what to eliminate. What you can eliminate means, "we have this number of people in this labor category. We did a benchmark study and found out we have 30% more people in this labor category then competitors. So we eliminate 30% of the people," then we expect the leaders in that group to figure out how to get the 70% of people to do 100% of the work. Amazingly, people seem to settle in somehow and get the important things done. They may not have great quality, or great processes for doing it. They may be working like crazy, fighting fires constantly and under extreme stress, but somehow they get it done if they want to keep their jobs.

One of the private equity people assigned to Dana explained: "You do not get new results from the same old management that got you in trouble in the first place." One of the first things you do is shake up the executives, fire most of them, and bring in a new team who can deliver the results. Then you restructure, which is a nice term for sell off and close a lot of things, lay off a lot of people, take people's pensions away from them, and decimate the company. That gives you the cost reductions you need. Now that you have done that, the company is decimated, and a lot of the intellectual property that is in the heads of people is gone, a lot of the most skilled labor is gone, and the next challenge is to stabilize the business.

You somehow have to get truck chassis components made with an unstable organization. You have weakened the organization, but you have at least survived, and your breakeven point is lower. Now you need to renew the business. As you begin to make profit with a lower breakeven point you will start to hire in new people, and you can hire in younger people who cost less and know less, but they are also energetic so it is a new challenge. This is the traditional approach to a turnaround, but it violates all The Toyota Way principles for creating an excellent enterprise.

How do you develop Lean Leaders in a Crisis?

How does Toyota create consistently high quality, while delivering on challenging objectives like 30% cost reductions? They do it through leadership, and the way they develop leaders is through the model that we have been learning. Leader Self Development, Coach and Develop Others, Developing at the grass roots level a system of Daily Kaizen, and aligning all the actions through visions, through goals, through metrics, through plans. Then the result is that you have a highly adaptable organization with deep leadership capability, a strong bench because you are teaching group leaders, managers, general managers. At every level, people are developing a strong capability to lead, teach, and to take on their own improvement projects.

That is great, but the typical answer to the question of how long it takes to get there is on the order of seven to ten years, and you still are at kind of a base level even if you do this consistently. By this time, a company in crisis is out of business. What you need to do in a crisis, and what Gary and John Devine did as a team, was to follow both paths at once. John Devine was leading the traditional restructuring process, and Gary was leading the operation excellence process. Through operational excellence, you can get savings if you approach operational excellence with that focus. If the life or death issue is that the cost structure is too high, you can break down that problem just like the warranty reduction, and begin to filter down those objectives and you can end up with two things that really matter. One is cost reductions. The other is inventory reductions, because in this particular case, inventory is money. It is cash flow and you need the cash because you have incredibly high interest rate loans that you have to pay off. Every dollar you save pays off loans with loan-shark type rates.

In a sense Dana was taking two paths: Toyota Way leadership development and restructuring complementing each other. There were tough-minded leaders with spreadsheets making transactional decisions about purchasing, and consolidating buildings. For example, Dana had R&D in one building and corporate headquarters in another and they moved R&D to the corporate offices and moved out of the R&D building saving money.

On the other hand, if you are interested in operational excellence for the long term, you want to develop leaders. The first step in developing leaders is identifying future leaders. Who is going to be able to function in the future Dana environment that will be based on Continuous Improvement? You need to equip those leaders with the training, and the coaching, and the tools. I am not going to sugar coat it. Identifying future leaders means the ones who do not get identified get pushed into a different role, perhaps taking a demotion, or they end up being pushed out of the company, or they voluntarily leave when they get the demotion, but a lot of the current leaders end up going away somehow. That is not the pretty side. It is very convenient if we do not care about those people to pick the cream of the crop, periodically have a purge, and get rid of the people who for some reason do not have the leadership capability to drive strong improvement. In a crisis, it may be part of the necessary pain.

Then what you want to do is get to the point where you are building operational excellence through daily kaizen and you are continuing to develop leaders. Now you are in a position not of taking this decimated, broken organization and trying to fix it. You are in a position of re-growing the business with a whole new set of leadership, some of the old leaders who are renewed and some new ones, but a leadership body that has a lot more strength to drive Continuous Improvement.

That is the ideal, that you have these parallel paths so after you have gotten to the point where you are going to live and not die as a company, you can continue the process of building operational excellence. During the period of restructuring and layoffs, and severe targets, it is like boot camp in the marines. That is when leaders are going to develop skills at a rate they never thought possible and come out the other end as transformed leaders and people. You are also going to get the organization to pull together to survive. You will have a level of teamwork that you would normally never have. You are actually emerging stronger instead of weaker. This was done remarkably well by Alan Mulally leading Ford through its near bankruptcy during the Great Recession.

First-Year Actions taken by Dana: Focus on Developing Leadership

Gary's decades of Toyota experience led him to create an operational excellence leadership team with a Global Vice-President of Operational Excellence, there was a reporting structure, and people at the regional level and then people at the plants reported up to him. They reduced the number of group presidents from about a half dozen down to two people, each running a business sector—commercial truck or light truck. The goal was to have one Dana with one unified focus leading up to the CEO level. The Dana Operating System (DOS) was patterned exactly after the Toyota Production System (TPS).

They also needed standard, global key performance indicators. Gary was accustomed to having those at Toyota, and he was used to looking at standard reports and he could very quickly assess the state of the business at any level: North American level, Plant level, even deep down to department level. He could not do that at Dana. It was as if suddenly he were half-blind, and he was thinking, "I cannot lead this way," so he had to create that system to have the visibility to see the problem areas.

Then he decided, as any Toyota leader would, that his resources for Continuous Improvement needed to be internal, committed and owned by Dana, rather than outside consultants. He found people that he already knew from his broad network and gave them 10 month trial contracts as outside consultants so they could prove themselves before being employed internally. Most became regional Continuous Improvement directors and their jobs were to enhance the management capability of the leadership in the plant by doing projects. They would do very aggressive multi-week kaizen activities in a department that was a bottleneck and completely turn it around. The leaders of the plant, including the plant managers, had to personally lead those activities.

They would have other plant managers from other plants come and participate in those activities. When they held big, radical kaizen events, they would assign different areas of improvement to different plant managers from various plants and they could not leave the plant until they achieved 100% of the objectives that were set at the beginning. Some people were there for a week. Some people were there for four weeks, but they wanted to instill the discipline that the only measure of success is 100% achievement of the target. It was a very intense boot camp, with very experienced people leading and coaching them.

A summary of the first-year operational excellence actions taken across all Dana plants, led by the CEO and staff, is summarized (see Figure 7-8). This set the foundation for further development of the Dana Operating System.

Dana Background
Actions Taken: Focus on Developing Leadership

- Formed Operational Excellence leadership at presidential level reporting to CEO with 100% global plant focus:
    - Created Dana Operating System (DOS) patterned after Toyota Production System
    - Established 12 standard global KPIs in six categories
    - Formed core internal Dana Lean Consultants
    - Enhanced plant leadership management capability, methods, and tools.

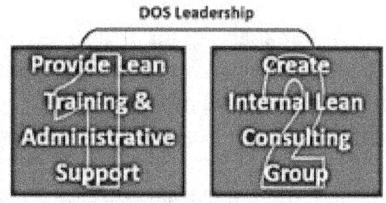

Figure 7-8. First Year Actions for Dana Operational Excellence

Seven-Step Process to Launch the Dana Operating System

The Dana operating system is the whole Toyota production system but they needed to break down the problem into manageable steps (as you would with Toyota Business Practices). The initial focus was to get transparency on how the plant and each department in the plant was operating. That is where the key performance indicators came in, and they set up one area physically in each plant which they called the Dana Diamond area. That is where the metrics for the whole plant were and daily plant manager meetings were held.

They developed a global communications system where the KPIs in computer databases could be rolled up to the CEO level and broken down to any level. At the regional level, they had live meetings to discuss performance. At the global level most of the communication was virtual including conference calls. For example, the main person that had been assigned by the private equity company as part of the turnaround had experience at Danaher, which has the Danaher Business System—a very strong corporate-wide lean program. They are aggressive about getting results and this person had learned that. His job every Thursday of every week, and sometimes into Friday, was to talk to the 90+ plant managers one by one to find out what they did the past week, what problems they were working on, what results they got, and grill them. "What was the problem when this machine went down and we went to half day production? Why did that happen?" They might give an answer like:

"There was one robot that broke down, and it was an old robot."

"Why did that old robot break down?" Through questioning the former Danaher coach was teaching them the problem solving process. It is not acceptable to say a robot broke down. Robots do not have to break down. They can be maintained. That might lead to a preventive maintenance program. He was coaching the plant managers to become Lean Leaders. He was taking them through the development process using coaching in the weekly phone calls.

The plant managers could also go back to the regional Continuous Improvement champion and say, "we have got a problem with maintenance. We agreed to develop a total productive maintenance program, but we do not know how to do it. We need your help." This is going on week by week by week, not quarter by quarter. There was standard training developed in problem solving, process improvement, kaizen and basic lean tools. That was the real skill they needed, problem solving in a disciplined, structured way. They needed to sustain the program through visual management and visual pull systems.

Launch Phase 1 of the Dana Operating System

1. Visual transparency (KPIs, Diamond area)
2. Global communication
3. Study values streams & opportunities to improve
4. Stabilize cells (flow, visual management, hourly tracking)
5. Team leaders: eliminate waste, learn by doing
6. Problem solving training, process improvements and Kaizen
7. Sustain improvements (visual management, pull system)

Visualization and Meeting Management Standards

Where do you start? From Gary's point of view, it seemed obvious that you start by developing leaders. What leaders do you focus on? He focused on the top, which is what Toyota does. They start with the top and the top then has responsibility to become the coaches as it cascades down, with expert support. His main targets of teaching were at the executive level and at the plant manager level, and the plant manager of course was expected to teach and develop people in the plant and there were a lot of initiatives to develop people working in production.

For example, as they freed up people through productivity improvements, say they had 10 people and they did radical kaizen, and ended up with three people, they would keep one extra person behind to be trained as a team leader. They had a general policy that you do not lose your job because of the Dana Operating System. Everybody displaced was put in a new position, sometimes on a kaizen team, until the order came down from the transactional, financial side of the house, that you need to layoff this number of people. That was the reality. They were trying to separate the needs of the business to survive from what they were doing in the kaizen effort. Those who were displaced through kaizen were not necessarily the ones who were laid off. For example, if they were put in a team leader role or kaizen role they were highly valued and probably would survive.

You can imagine that it is not 100% possible to convince people the layoffs are separate from lean, and some people were saying, "Right, we are not going to lose our job because of the Dana Operating System. Lean did it to us and lost us jobs," but a lot of other people understood the realities of the business crisis and appreciated that when the kaizen activities eliminated seven jobs by Friday, all seven people were still employed on Monday.

The first step was again to get line of sight visibility based on Key Performance Indicators with leadership from the CEO down communicating performance relative to targets ultimately to the work group level. Gary did not want to simply impose the KPIs he used at Toyota. He wanted some ownership and he wanted it tailored for this business. What he did was pull together the regional executives and challenged them:

"we need to come to agreement on major key performance indicators that all of you are going to be judged on, and that is what I'm going to see and what you are going to be looking at every day."

They came up with these categories: safety, quality, efficiency, productivity, cost, and inventory. Then they came up with specific measures and picked one plant in each region to pilot the KPIs. Based on what they learned from the pilots they made adjustments (PDCA). Finally, they decided and announced, "These are the standard measures for every Dana plant in the world." The piloting and evaluation took place over several months, so if anyone has seen the TV show "24" where the whole show is 24 hours and they save the world in 24 hours and every minute counts, it was sort of like that. It was happening at an accelerated rate.

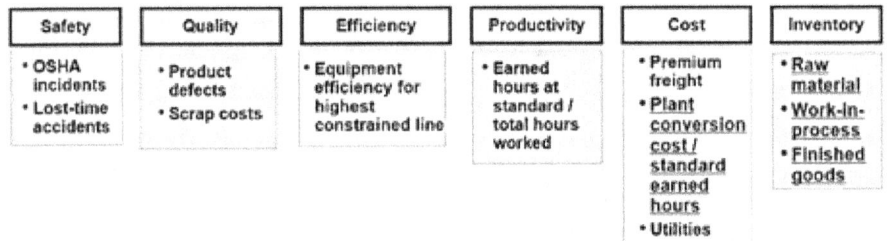

Figure 7-9. Dana Global Key Performance Indicators.

The illustration above (see Figure 7-9) showing the underlined metrics highlights those key indicators which were going to help save the company. They needed safety and quality and they significantly improved all those things. For example, scrap costs were very high in a lot of plants. The scrap costs were a key cost reduction measure, even though they fall under quality. Equipment efficiency, to keep the equipment running, was necessary for productivity. There were a lot of relationships between indicators, but the main thing they were interested in was cost, which was measured as plant conversion cost. This takes out the cost of raw material and anything coming into the plant, and focuses on costs controlled and owned by the plant manager. All the costs, including energy, the cleanup crew, the cost of production, the cost of defects are part of plant conversion costs and could be subject to kaizen.

The total plant conversion costs are then divided by standard earned hours, as a way to standardize this by volume, so for example, your plants with twice as much dollar volume product should not be compared on cost itself to a plant half its size without some adjustment. They standardized by what you should be producing—you should be producing this number of products, which should cost you this amount of money based on standards. Conversion Cost was a major focus, and Inventory was the second major focus. Every dollar in inventory is a dollar that could be used to pay down the debt. In a sense, this was like MBO and targets for cost and inventory were set at Gary's level, but as they worked to achieve these targets the leaders were being developed to understand lean and the problem solving process.

Daily KPIs are tracked at each plant

Results displayed in common area:

→ Broadcasts the challenge
→ Encourages commitment and ownership

Figure 7-10. Dana Diamond Area.

Here is a picture of one Dana diamond area (see Figure 7-10), and you see that there are scoreboards and they are tracking all the KPIs, and it is very visual. If you zoomed in you could easily see the gaps between target and actual on a daily basis. At a plant level, you can tell how you are doing on a daily basis. In a major department, you can also tell on a shift basis. If you walked out to a department you could see actual versus planned production by the hour.

Performance became transparent. Everybody in the plant could see it. If you notice in the photo, there are no chairs because people are expected to stand up walking the wall and different people are responsible for different performance indicators, and they are reporting out. "Here is what happened today, here are the problems we had, here are our countermeasures, here are what we will be working on tomorrow."

The data were entered into a web based system and Gary was able to use his computer to view how the whole company was doing and drill down to the plant level and even down to the department level. Simply having metrics does not guarantee anything. What it guarantees is you have pretty displays to show people when they visit the plant. What matters are the actions that come from analyzing the data. You need some process of checking the measures, finding the key gaps, prioritizing, then coming up with countermeasures and putting those countermeasures in place and seeing what happens.

At the executive level, every month they reviewed the performance of all the plants (see Figure 7-11). At the regional level it was every week by a Group Vice-President and an Operations Director, and looking beyond the data they visited plants in their region regularly. At the plant level, the plant managers walked the floor daily. We talked about having standard work for a manager of walking around and checking the process and going where there are problems and deep diving. The KPIs provide a signal detector pointing to the area's most in need of being visited. What happened today, what is the root cause? What are we going to do about it? Is there a good thinking process in place for solving the problems? Who needs to be trained better because they are not achieving their targets? Then the area manager at every shift met with their direct reports, and ultimately the team leader, which for Dana was a new hourly role.

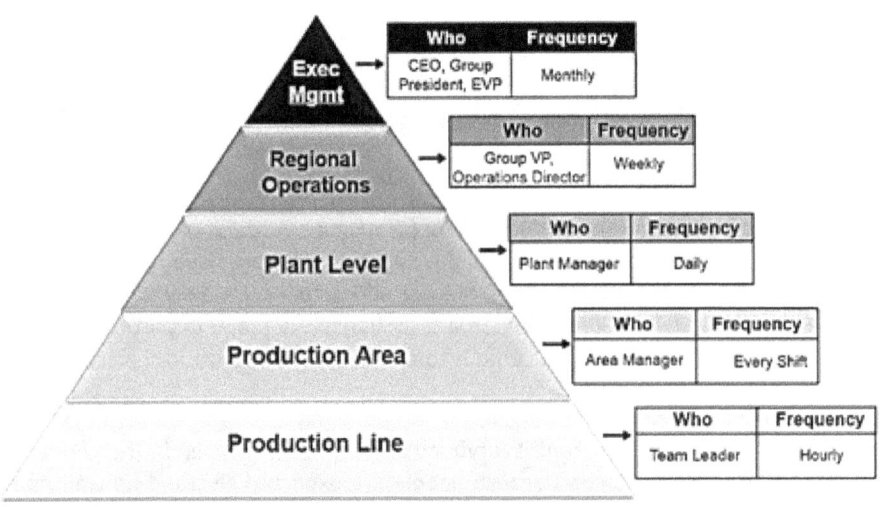

Figure 7-11. Standard Meetings by Responsibility and Frequency.

In each department, they also tracked progress through hour-by-hour boards. Every hour they show what they were supposed to produce compared to the number of good parts produced. Any gap is a powerful measure, because if you can see the gap between good parts produced and parts expected, then you can solve problems hour-by-hour, and those problems are going to cover everything. Quality problems will affect that number, machine downtime will affect that number, and somebody who is poorly trained who is not meeting the standard will affect that number. It reveals issues in quality, productivity, and safety. All those things will show themselves in your ability to produce good parts that you are expected to produce each hour. As you get closer to building each hour exactly what is planned you are moving toward perfection.

Years 2-5: Dana Operating System Implementation Roadmap

In the first year it was very top down. There was not a lot of dialogue (catch-ball) between layers of management. Rather Gary dictated: "This is what you need to achieve in all these areas." Experts Gary hired were coming in and helping, but the plant managers were driving it and accountable for results.

They also looked ahead five years in developing and implementing a Dana Operating System road map. The first year was mainly to stabilize the process and start to generate savings. That started with Key Performance Indicators and a lot of problem solving. It was a very short-term focus, though laying the future foundation for developing leadership boot-camp style. As the five-year plan progressed (see Figure 7-12), and there was less pressure for short-term results to save the company, the focus shifted to developing a true operating system for the long term, though business results were still expected. They began training people in all the tools of the Dana Operating System, developing training modules, developing and deploying standards, and the motto became "let's develop a basic flow, get parts flowing the way they are supposed to with as little interruption from waste, from inventory for example, as possible."

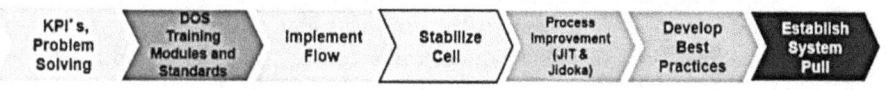

Figure 7-12. The Dana Operating System Implementation Roadmap (Years 2-5).

They set up cells, and then focused on stabilizing the cells through standard work so they could consistently produce to the customer demand rate (takt). Then they were ready to move into Just-in-Time, pull systems, delivery of parts on a more frequent basis, and finally getting to total system pull. Of course, this was a theoretical road map and there are always variants. Some plants were doing pull in the second year, and even in the first year in some cases, so they did not necessarily follow this path linearly.

Within a stabilized cell, the improvements get broken down into even more detail. They have 11 steps (see Figure 7-13). They use value stream mapping, they develop standardized work, they look at the details of how parts are being presented to operators, and they look at 5S. They also developed daily audits to sustain the process. In addition, there are a lot of details in each of these steps.

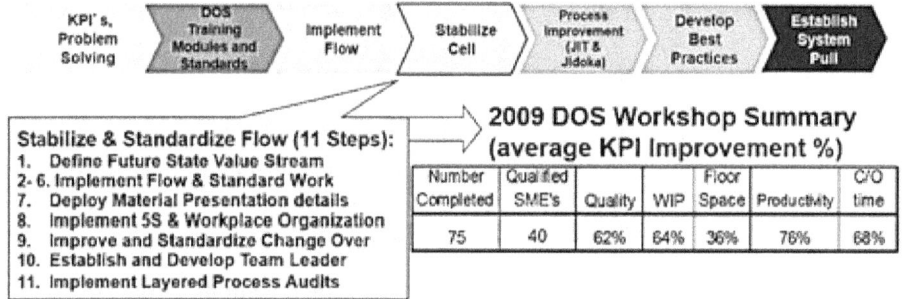

Figure 7-13. Some Results of Implementing the Dana Operating System.

Plans are nice, but how did they perform in results in the early stages? The answer is very well. For example, in 2008, before most of these lean efforts, they had 63 days of inventory. By 2009, they cut about 40% of the inventory, so were down to 25 fewer days on hand, and that translated to 273 million dollars less tied up in inventory, which is literally 273 million dollars you can bring to the bank to pay down your high interest loan. By 2010, they saved another hundred million dollars.

The aggressive kaizen workshops that I talked about were a way of getting quick wins, and very quickly training the plant management through immersion. The plant management led the workshops, with help and support from the coaches. They did many workshops (kaizen events) in 2009, 75 of these in one year. Plant managers also were required to free up people's time to create subject matter experts in each plant, which are experts in each of the modules of DOS. There was a standardized work expert in the plant, a pull system expert, a value stream-mapping expert. They had to be developed from existing staff in the plant and Gary recalls a lot of complaining by plant managers who said their staff was spread so thin they could not possibly do it.

However, they did it and as the process became more stable and predictable, fire-fighting turned into planning and they could more comfortably staff the plant.

Quality was pursued along with cost reduction and improved in one year by 62%. They also freed up one third of the floor space in their factories. They improved productivity by 76%. The time to changeover tools in machines was reduced so they could make smaller batches—a major source of inventory reduction. These numbers reflect radical change, not numbers you are going to get from bottom-up suggestion programs. This required top down aggressive leadership and drive.

Globally 2009 DOS efforts delivered important results

→ -Exceeded Conversion Cost target of $170 Mil Reduction (2010 Target to reduce 5% from 2009 actual)
→ -Exceeded Reduction targets for Inventory cost & Days on Hand

Tools to Plan and Sustain Kaizen at Dana

A key tool to sustain the momentum was a simple A3 report (see Figure 7-14). It was used at many levels and in both manufacturing and R&D. We show here one that was initially a planning document to create a charter for the kaizen team and then became a high-level problem solving A3 as they got results and filled those in.

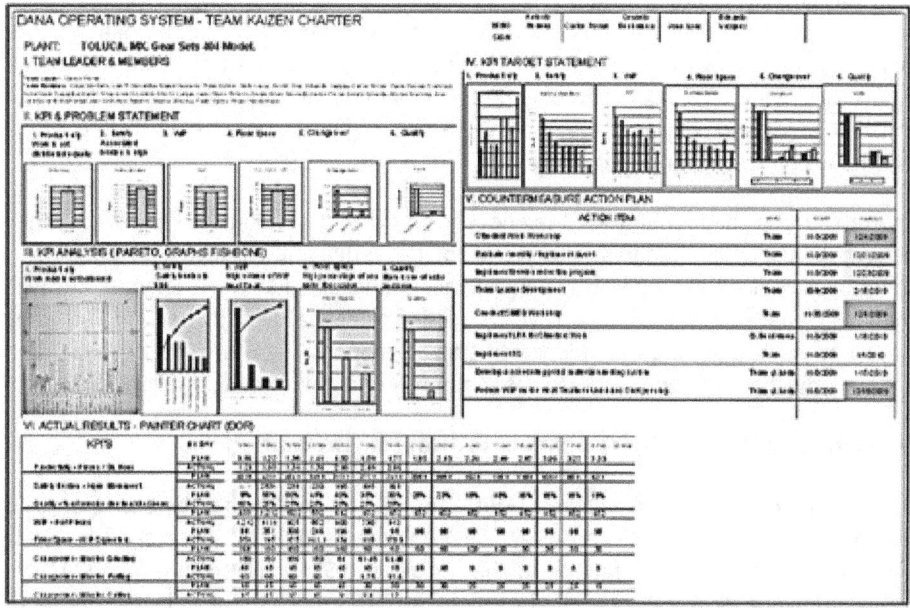

Figure 7-14. Proposal A3 for Planning Dana Operating System Activities and Expected Results

The proposal A3 was also used at the plant level as part of their beginner version of *Hoshin Kanri*. So for example, when Gary would do a review with each plant manager, he would want to see their A3 plan. He would tell them, for example, that by this date he expected a 5% reduction in plant conversion costs. He would not ask their opinion. He would tell them what he expected. Then he asked them to come up with a plan for doing it, and they had to develop an A3. Then he went through red lining the gaps he saw in the plan.

He was sitting at headquarters in Ohio at the time, and they might be in China, and they sent Gary the A3 by email and he was going through it with them by phone. He rattled off problems he saw in the plan, in most cases knowing the plants from visiting them, and immediately his assistant who was recording this sent an email summarizing Gary's observations and the agreements. Then the plant manager had a task to fix the A3, to improve the plan, and that did not end until it was a good plan from Gary's point of view and the point of view of the Operational Excellence leaders. This was another way to teach the importance of having a good plan and what having a good plan really means—one of the most critical parts of PDCA.

Value stream mapping was a powerful tool particularly to reduce inventory. By diagramming the material flow, and making it visual, the waste became apparent. A future state map is another type of planning document. They did it by hand with cutouts that they could move around. That is very important compared to say doing it on a computer, which people often want to do. Teams cannot work effectively as teams if they are standing around a computer and having somebody with a mouse or a cursor trying to create this box, or move this box, fumbling around while you are standing and waiting as opposed to writing something on a post-it and slapping it on a board. Afterwards, you can then put the resulting drawings on the computer and you can circulate it and communicate, but the process of developing the maps should be a very hands on, active, engaging process.

Then to sustain the momentum, they needed to do a lot of audits to keep score. They needed to coach the leaders who were not delivering the results. They needed to sometimes replace the Operational Excellence managers that were selected because they might have been great in a Toyota supplier plant that already had TPS, but they were not doing a good enough job with transformation. There is a lot of people and process adjustment needed to keep the momentum for improvement going.

Dana Results through three years of radical transformation

In 2009, they had a remarkable year. With the help of Jon Devine, the chairman, and his cost reduction strategies, despite a 35% volume decline, they managed to break even on the profit and loss statement. They also raised $250 million in new equity from freed up inventory. They reduced their debt by $250 million. They cleared the debt covenants. The covenants are the formal legal agreements with the people who own the company, the banks, and the private equity owners. You have covenants that say, "We will get our debt to this percentage of our total income of the year, and if we do not you can shut us down." They were successful in meeting these aggressive targets and they ended up reducing their inventory by over 35 days.

By 2010, Dana was on the road to financial health, and they had added many new products so a similar effort was happening in Product Development. They were at a record pace getting new products into production. They had developed new customers. One thing Gary could do with his Toyota pedigree was talk to the Japanese companies like Toyota, Nissan, and Honda, and they started getting business they were not getting before because when, say, Toyota's purchasing people would come into the plants they would be impressed and note: "this is really good progress! I am amazed by what you have done in this time." They also were now investing capital in new product lines and new equipment. The turnaround in a short time was amazing and they did it while developing Lean Leaders rather than decimating their human resources.

Great 2009

- Actions offset 35% year over year volume decline.
- Raised $250 Mil in new equity.
- Reduced debt by $250 Mil.
- Cleared debt covenants.
- Reduced inventory by over 35 days.

One measure of success, the most visible, was an increase in stock price of 1365%! They were recognized in 2009 as the global parts supplier with the highest total shareholder return. I am not saying this is all because of lean. The large majority of the cost savings came out of the more traditional cost reduction, consolidation, plant closures, large layoffs, and all that. The contributions of Operational Excellence were first significant cost savings as well as freeing up cash. Second, while they were achieving these incredible cost reductions, they were building capability instead of reducing it. They were building product development capability; they were building strategic planning capability that they did not have. They were marketing more effectively to customers. They were building better quality products with far fewer people with far less cost in the plants. Everything was getting stronger and better. They were not destroying their intellectual capability and they were not destroying their physical assets.

By 2010, Dana was financially healthy and growing with new products, new customers, and capital investment!

With the Right Philosophy it all Comes Together

In summary, when you get beyond lean tools to actually developing leaders, you build an incredible, rock solid foundation. Organizations are dynamic, not static. You do not put in place a pull system and expect the pull system to continue running at a high level. You expect the pull system to deteriorate unless it is continually adjusted and maintained. How does that happen? Local leaders are driving it and driving it.

You need a long-term strategy represented in your vision and translated to a business plan. *Hoshin Kanri* provides the annual cycle of improvement in which all leaders have aligned, measureable objectives from top to bottom and sideways. The success of HK comes from highly developed leaders who learn how to lead improvement. A long-term strategy is nice, but it is only useful if it is implemented, so you need to break it down into specific actions that can be taken by the right people with accountability. It takes individual initiative at all levels, but the individual initiative is going to be driven by the leadership.

It takes people development. You want people development to be the responsibility of the leaders of those people, not the responsibility of human resources or the Continuous Improvement department or the quality department. All those departments can play a supporting role, but ultimately I report to my boss on a daily basis, and that is who should know my performance the best. If my boss is managing me by fear, "get me these numbers or else," I will do whatever I have to do to get the numbers, but will I develop anything more than my ability to play games? I am going to work really hard, but I am also going to learn how to play the numbers, to lie and cheat, and I get really good at that. Whereas what we want with people development is to have the ability to lead a team to actually find the real problems and solve those problems at the root cause so they do not keep coming back.

What is happening is that as you give people challenging assignments, like 5% cost reduction for the plant, then if those people are coached and supported correctly, not once a year in an offsite, but on a daily, weekly, and monthly basis, they will grow by taking on those challenging assignments and dealing with all the problems and solving them. They will gain confidence in their ability and develop deeper and deeper skills. Then they can contribute to the strategic roadmap to success, which is deployed through *Hoshin Kanri*.

Hoshin Kanri gives the challenging assignments. The strategy does not give you the challenging assignments without translating it into the right improvement targets, the right metrics, and the right plans at every level of the company and across the company. With this you can get:

- Individual Initiative
- People Development
- Grow through Challenging Assignments
- Contribute to a strategic roadmap to success

As Gary put it: "management has no more critical role than motivating and engaging large numbers of people to work together toward a common goal; defining and explaining what the goal is; sharing a path to achieve it; motivating people to take the journey with you; and assisting them by removing obstacles." That is a nice definition of Lean Leadership, and now the structure, the architecture that allows you to do that, that supports you in doing that, is *Hoshin Kanri*, the process of breaking down a problem and deploying it.

I somewhat crudely talked about how lean evolves, and suggested that there are two paths. One is with the philosophy we have been talking about; developing people, developing leaders; developing skills. One is without the philosophy, which is drive results; drive results; drive results. It is the difference between the *Hoshin Kanri* philosophy and the management by objectives philosophy. Normally what happens in a lean transformation is you go through a series of stages as you become more mature. Stage one is applying the tools (see Figure 7-15). Now, everything I have written talks about the weaknesses of a tool-based approach to lean, and here I am saying step one is to apply the tools. Is that a contradiction?

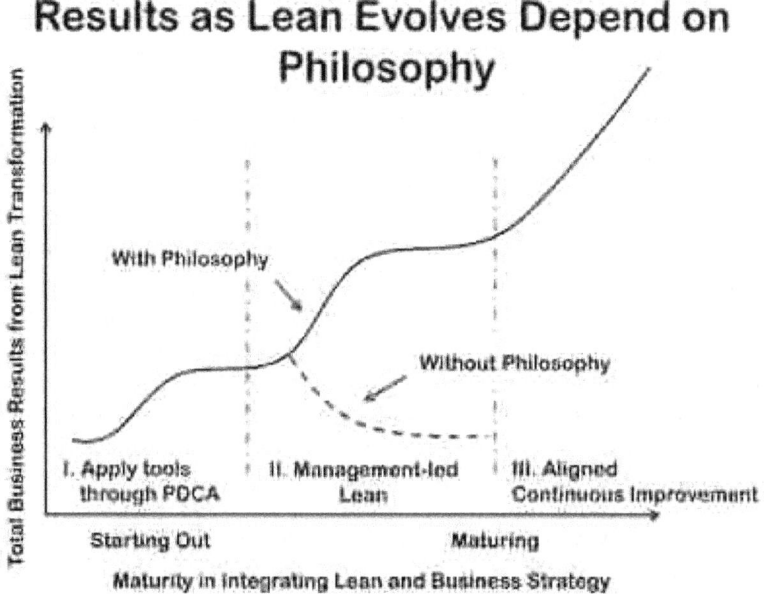

Figure 7-15. Results as Lean Evolves Depend on Philosophy.

The answer is yes, it is a contradiction if you stop at stage one, and only focus on implementing tools, but it is not a contradiction if you see applying the tools as the first stage of teaching, of learning. What is the first stage if you have a challenging task to teach somebody? Say if you want to teach them to play an instrument or to cook complex meals, or if you want to teach them to be a machinist or a carpenter or a plumber? The first stage is to start the student off with simple, routine tasks, and the master plumber is watching, and they are showing the learner the right way to do it and then they are letting the learner try, struggle but giving feedback. You learn how to use a wrench the right way and how to hold it. At that point, you are learning tools, and it is very basic, it is very elementary, and it has to be. In an organization with a lot of people who have never seen lean before, for example they are not doing daily problem solving, you do not just stick metric boards out there and assume they magically learn all these tools. You have to teach them like learning how to use a wrench.

In stage one; they are learning the improvement process while learning to use the right lean tools, with mentors, with "lean coaches." Call them what you want, but ideally, you have qualified people working for you, which is not always the case, or you may have to find consultants who are teachers rather than deployers. Even if the coaches are internal, they usually begin in a staff role supporting the top management leading as we saw at Dana. The top management is responsible; the expertise is coming from the side, from those process improvement specialists. The managers in between, in the middle, are just doing and learning at a very basic level.

At this point if I have a vision of Continuous Improvement, I know where I want to go next which is making the managers responsible for lean. In addition to having a small department of Continuous Improvement experts I have managers as lean coaches all over the operation, all over the hospital, all over the insurance company, or whatever type of organization it is. I have continuous improvers who are managers. They are not experts yet, they are still learning, but they have a level of skill so they can begin to develop others. Your philosophy is that you are going to have many managers who are all leading lean toward defined targets in their area with a good process, with a good way of working with and engaging their people. Still, it is very dependent at this point on management, particularly middle management. If you do not have the philosophy, or if your philosophy is "hire the consultants, delegate objectives down to the managers, measure them and then use a carrot and stick," what usually happens is you get an initial shot in the arm with the consultants and the lean experts pushing things, and then slip backwards. With the philosophy, you go to another level because you have so many people responsible for improving.

The Nirvana is when you have actually gotten to a daily management system, and everybody everywhere has targets, every day they are finding something else they can improve, they are adapting to changes, and their activities are aligned to broader business targets. Locally, you have management and leadership that are driving true Continuous Improvement that is aligned to the business objectives of the company. The implication is that you cannot get that alignment through a toolkit like *Hoshin Kanri*. You cannot jump to Phase III without going through phases II and II. On the other hand, if you go through phase one, you are not necessarily going to get beyond the tool-based approach unless you are using that period of time to develop the leaders that allow you to then progress to management-led lean.

Final Feedback: Deliberate Practice is not Fun

Final review of the Lean Leadership Model

Hopefully I have given you a lot to think about. Maybe you feel overwhelmed by all this information, but that is a good thing. We began with the model of Lean Leadership that goes through a series of stages and the final stage is *Hoshin Kanri*, but the final stage is really "align goals from top to bottom," with people at every level capable of achieving aggressive targets for improvement by creating sustainable, repeatable processes, not one-off fixes. Then we use *Hoshin Kanri* as a tool to create conversations leading to plans at all levels.

We start with a vision. This conversation is at the top level, based on environmental and competitive analysis, the development of the business model and strategy for where we want to go that then gets deployed downward. At every pair of levels there are discussions, proposals, critical feedback, adjustment to the feedback, and developing a target and plan, and then that is repeatedly broken down. By the time we are done, everybody has a set of targets that align to what the top needs, and they have realistic, thoughtful plans for how they are going to proceed, and they begin executing and as they execute they keep on checking and adjusting. From your point of view, I am asking you to think about your organization and whatever it is you are responsible for.

If you are in the middle of the organization and you lead a department, you obviously cannot develop a strategic plan for the whole company. You need to bite off what you can chew. Within what you control, what is your vision? Where are you trying to go? What is your true north? What are the critical steps that you can actually take over the next year? Then how can these be broken down into a manageable plan, one that is adjusted as you learn? It helps to talk to your boss and some senior leaders about their visions and your direct customers about their needs.

Then, what role will the senior leadership play in those improvements? They may well be giving you the targets in an MBO sort of fashion. Now you are going to take those targets and translate those in the right way into actionable plans, and you are going to surprise your boss, because no one else is going to do that, and you will stand out. You will do your best to enlist and engage senior leadership, and educate them as you are making improvements. They need to see results, but also understand the process needed for sustainable improvement.

Final Review

- What role will senior management play in your company?
- What is your vision?
- What are the most critical steps over the next year to move toward that vision?

I do not want to mislead you. This is not jumping to aligned metrics and Continuous Improvement everyplace in the organization. This is something you can control that is reasonable, but a big stretch for the year. Summarize this to your coach, like in Dana. There were coaches and all the plant managers were calling in every week and starting with "here is my plan," then "here is what I did this week, here is what I plan to do next week." I do not know what your cadence will be with your coach, but you should have a regular cadence. The coach should give you useful feedback, and unfortunately, useful feedback is critical feedback. It is what you can improve. The atta-boys feel good, but they do not lead to improvement. Criticisms are gaps that you can work on closing.

As we go through this, you may be thinking "we went through self-development, which Liker says can take years, through these four steps and each one can take several years, so this is a 10 year journey, but I have taken this course over a few months (www.ToyotaWaytoLeanLeadership.com)." What I am really proposing is that you work on a micro version of this four-step model within your area of responsibility, whatever it is. What you are going to do is try out all the four steps. You are not going to complete any of them in a year, but you are going to actually try the four steps, and increase your understanding of what they mean, and then next year you will do it again and keep on doing it. Hopefully, others will get interested and want to learn from you. Even if they do not, you will rise in the organization, or rise in another organization, and you will have a larger scope of responsibility, so you can do this more broadly.

Deliberate Practice

There is a lot of literature these days about how to develop skills and the key phrase repeatedly used is "deliberate practice." As a budding student of guitar, I have heard this all too much. When I am sitting there with my guitar, and I set aside one or two hours, I can play pieces I have learned and it is fun, but I am not learning anything.

Alternatively, I can strive to achieve a level of skill. Deliberate practice means I know what I am working on. As I am making mistakes, I am identifying mistakes, and I am putting in place countermeasures. For example, I started playing guitar about 35 years ago, but now I am taking lessons in a structured way to learn classical guitar. After taking almost two years of lessons, my teacher realized I still had problems with rhythm, with basic beats. I played eighth notes when I should have been playing sixteenth notes and I did not hold half notes long enough. My teacher instructed me to get an introductory book on rhythm that starts with just counting quarter notes, and play the strings open and just play the quarter notes. Then I played increasingly complex patterns of rhythms, and I was not doing anything with my left hand. My son, a musician, suggested I tap out the rhythms on the side of my guitar. That is deliberate practice. You know you are deliberately practicing when you are not having fun, but you are gradually getting better.

What should you do in the next year to deliberately practice?

"How does somebody learn something about the four steps through deliberate practice? Can you give an example of what someone in management would go through over a year?"

In guitar, we know how to teach it pretty well, and it is one person playing one instrument, but in a complex organization, defining leadership skills is a little bit vague. There are a lot more students to learn, and it is tempting to go for mass education in a classroom, but we know that is not how you develop real skills.

What Toyota determined was that the best vehicle for deliberate practice, if you want an organization with Continuous Improvement, is going through the problem solving process, repeatedly, on real problems, with a personal coach. It is why Toyota introduced Toyota Business Practices, the eight steps. Self-development should really focus on projects that you personally lead, and in the course of doing that project, you should be engaging a team like Gary engaged a team, but this will be a team that reports to you, or maybe there will be some other departments involved.

Your first step should be leading a team to solve a problem. This is not a problem you can solve in two days, but maybe a problem you can solve in two to three months, or longer if you are an executive, where you have to collect all the data, find the root cause, and go through all the steps and sustain the changes, and you need to lead that. The Improvement *Kata* is one method for doing that. You may be in a high enough position where you believe you should be able to delegate that, but in the Lean Leadership model you are not delegating, you are doing it. You are leading it.

As you develop skills by personally leading a team to reach a challenging target that will naturally spill over into step two of developing others, perhaps through the Coaching *Kata*. That is because to lead the project you are going to be developing the people working on the project as you are learning the skill. You have got to stay a step ahead of them and go through one step at a time. You need a coach. You may have a coach locally if you search or you can get one through the Lean Leadership Institute (www.LeanLeadership.guru). A friend of mine actually sought out a coach in the company from a distant corporate headquarters. She was at a branch location. She found this person, and on her own flew out, met this person, and asked this person to coach her. A lot of that coaching was virtual, but periodically, she would go to where her coach was. Find a coach, and take advantage of that to get useful feedback. It is called self-development because you must take the initiative.

If you can take a full year, you might think of the year in quarters. The first quarter, you are focused on the project, your own self-development and beginning to develop others. In the second quarter, you are focused on developing others, so now you are going to give an assignment to somebody that reports to you, then you work with them to identify a problem they can work on, and they are going to lead the improvement process and go through the steps, with you coaching them, they are going to be leading a team. Now you no longer have a team, just the person you are coaching. In step three, you are going to drive this down to the working level. You are going to want to have Key Performance Indicators, metric boards in one or a few departments, depending on how many people you have or how you are structured. You are going to want to set up a daily management system where you have targets and look at the measures every day with stand-up meetings, divvying out assignments and improving on a daily basis.

Finally, maybe in the last quarter, you will set objectives and do the planning for the next year. Perhaps you will develop a proposal A3. You may not have time to complete it, but you might be starting the countermeasures. You may only get as far as that A3 that ends up with the plan, assignments, and targets for improvement for the second year. That will then be the start of next year's work, and you then share that with your manager, even if they do not have ideal training as Lean Leaders. You are going to show them the A3, and take the lead even without their regular guidance. They are going to be very impressed, and it may pique their interest to do this in other places… or even to learn themselves.

Now, within each of those quarters, there are a lot of skills to develop. For example, observing the *gemba* and actually seeing the problems, prioritizing the problems, doing the root cause analysis. Each of these three things involves a lot of skills. Over the year, as you do this again with the subordinates you are coaching, and then you do it on a daily management basis, you are going to see this over and over again. PDCA, PDCA, PDCA. You are refining your skills with the help of a coach even as you coach others.

If you choose to learn based on the Toyota *Kata* methodology you have Mike Rother's website (http://www-personal.umich.edu/~mrother/Homepage.html) which is a wealth of information and can point you to you-tube videos, slide shares, live workshops, coaches, and even his own *Improvement Kata Handbook*.

With that, I would like to wish you well. By no means do I, in my wildest dreams, believe that I have taught you how to be a Lean Leader. What I hope I have done is given you a jump-start, a launching pad for getting started on this life long journey. That is the way I see it, and hopefully you also see it that way, and as you start to do, you realize where your weaknesses are, then it starts to become energizing as you realize you never stop learning. You are never done. There is always something else to look forward to, another level of skill, of accomplishment. A lifetime of learning is a lifetime of wonder!

- Focus on Project
- Focus on Developing Others
- Drive it down to the working level
- Set objectives for next year

CHAPTER 8
CONNECTING STRATEGY TO OPERATIONAL EXCELLENCE: The Scion Example

Every Improvement Starts with a Challenge

When we think about Toyota, very often we immediately connect Toyota with assembling cars in factories and do not think about the total organization. Toyota has every department that every complex global organization has and it starts with sales. Sales defines what the customer wants. Sales interacts with product development so that the right things are being developed. Sales markets and sells the cars, and sales even interacts with production control when they are developing a schedule so it meets both manufacturing needs and sales needs.

To wrap up this book I would like to illustrate the important connection between product strategy and operational excellence. I will do this with the value stream of creating a new product brand, from a sales point of view, using the Scion brand that Toyota introduced in the United States in 2005 as an example. This story also illustrates how even at the level of developing a new brand Toyota was following Toyota Business Practices led by exceptional leaders. They were defining a need, developing a strategy, and they were then connecting that strategy to the lean manufacturing system and logistics that would produce and deliver what the customer wants when they want it. I am not suggesting Scion is one of the most successful brands Toyota has ever created, but rather I want to focus on the *fit* between the strategy, the sales approach, and operational features.

Figure 8-1. The Scion Brand of cars; the xD, tC, and xB.

We show the three cars that were originally the Scion brand; from left to right they are the xD, the tC, and the xB (see Figure 8-1). They have developed new cars since then for Scion, including an inexpensive and small sports car, and product development is ongoing. From some viewpoints Scion has been a failure as their sales have dropped dramatically since the best year, which nobody in Toyota is happy about, but Scion still serves an important purpose. What is the purpose of Scion?

Every improvement effort should start with a clear problem statement or challenge. You should never start by having a senior leader say "sales, we need a new brand to attract young people, go do it." A senior leader might say, "We have a problem, and we need to find a way to address that problem." The context of the problem was Toyota's business model based on having a customer for life. That means that you buy your first car and it is a Toyota brand, and as your life situation changes, say you get married or have children, your children leave home, and as you age, you will always have a new product that will meet your needs. The entry point into the Toyota brand should be the young customer's first car, but it rarely was in the United States. The average age of Toyota owners in North America was too high, one of the highest in the industry, and many of the younger people thought of a Toyota as "a car my parents drive," or even worse "as a car my grandparents drive."

To increase market share in the future, looking ahead decades, Toyota needed to lower the age of entry into the Toyota customer value stream. Young people had to view a car available to them as something different from their parent's car. Toyota Motor Sales led by senior management, working together with product development, the R&D side of the house, decided the countermeasure should be to create a new brand. After a lot of research, a lot of discussion, a lot of analysis, they concluded that many young people in America were not going to think about Toyota as their kind of car, and that a new brand for young people was needed.

The next step was a deeper understanding of customer requirements. It meant that sales had to do an intensive study to understand what young people in America want in their cars, and this is a lot like the technical anthropologists at Menlo Innovations. The philosophy of Toyota is that you never learn enough about what people really want just by looking at data from surveys. Statistics never tell the whole story. You need to personally go and see people in their daily lives. They had people going out to beaches, going to museums, art shows, rock concerts, and any other place that young people hung out and a clear picture started to emerge.

One thing they learned was that young people in America liked the features in their parent's car and believed they should have them in their car as well. If the Lexus, for example, had a display that showed a rear-view camera, they would like that in their car, and they were not satisfied to hear "you're too young, you can't afford it." They wanted a lot of features with very high value at prices they could afford. Young people in America also wanted to express individuality. They grew up customizing many products like phones, clothes, and they wanted a car that in some way was unique to them.

While young people in America wanted to express individuality, they also had a desire to belong to a group. Many felt isolated, and part of that had to do with the computer technology we have today, even with online social networking. The Scion would ideally help fulfill that need of getting people together, physically in the same place, and online. Finally, they found that young people absolutely hated being treated unfairly. If my friend got this deal for their Scion, or even this deal for an oil change, "I shouldn't have to pay any more for the same service." Young people rejected haggling on price. When I was growing up it was almost like a national sport. You go to the car dealer and brag about the price you got, but young people in 2005 found that a hassle and unfair.

Want

- Loaded car with Lexus features at Corolla (or less) prices
- To express individuality (e.g., used to customizing everything)
- To belong to a group
- To be treated fairly—same service for same price

Do Not Want

- To haggle on price.

Scion Sales-Marketing Approach

Based on these requirements, the Scion brand and its key characteristics were defined. The approach Toyota took was consistent with The Toyota Way—teamwork, frugality, going where the customers are and seeing what your competitors are doing. A small team of five people, led by a vice-president, began developing the brand. Five people are not a lot for developing an entire brand for a major automotive company. Typically, offices are set up and dozens of people assigned along with their secretaries, and this was just five people. What these five people did was they left the office and went to see customers and they developed the customer requirements and they started to get ideas for the business model.

One of the key insights came when Jim Lentz, the vice-president responsible for Scion, visited Brazil. He had heard about the Chevy Celta, which was an inexpensive, basic car being sold in Brazil, but it had a lot of optional features and you could go on the internet and customize it. From the point of view of the factory making the car, there was only one Celta with one configuration. Then there were lots of accessories you could add after the fact at the dealership. You could even order those online, and the combination of accessories you order made the car unique to you.

That sounded like a winner. Jim Lentz wanted to see it first hand, so he got on a plane, went to Brazil, and concluded, "This is a great idea." That led to the Scion production logistics model, which was directly connected to the customer needs and the vision of the brand from sales. They called it "mono-spec."

According to Jim, "We decided to start with a basic model, with a few configurations. For example, there might be two different transmissions or two different size engines. From the point of view of the factory, there is very little variation so it is very efficient to build this car. Then the cars would be shipped to California. When they arrived at the center, they would be pooled, and as customers ordered their cars and before they were shipped to the dealerships, then that basic, vanilla car would be accessorized to order, and immediately delivered to the dealer, who might add some additional accessories."

This really was a case of mass customization. They have the basic, vanilla unit, and at the last possible point when the customer places the order they customize the car, and it requires a certain type of logistics model. They began with vehicles that already existed in Japan so there were no costs at first for new product development. This, and the factory efficiencies of making a vehicle with little variety, allowed the price point to be kept low with a lot of features standard.

Small Team (5 people) to develop brand

> Go and see customers, get ideas for business model
>
>> Key insight: Chevy Celta in Brazil—Web based purchasing of single configuration model accessorized at dealer.
>>
>> Scion Production Logistics Model:
>>
>>> -"Monospec"-Basic model with a few configurations at factory in Japan (color and transmission)
>>>
>>> -"Pooling" at port and accessorized to order

From the customers' viewpoint, they go online and select from many options. The table below shows examples of some of the original choices. Since then the list has expanded, and there are many third party add-ons available. For example, a carbon fiber engine cover will give you a sporty look; there is a tip you can put on the exhaust system that looks cool to some; you can select LED taillights that come in a variety of colors. These are all things that can be added to the car after the car is shipped from Japan and sitting in that pooling center at the port in California.

Accessorizing by Toyota
Exterior accessories

Carbon Fiber Engine Cover	$325
Exhaust Tip	$76
Rear Bumper Applique	$69
Rear Spoiler	$423
Fog Light Kit	$320
Carbon Fiber Window Trim	$299
Custom Grille	$215
LED Tail Lights	$375

Interior accessories

Cargo Liner	$119
Cargo Net	$65
Cargo Dover	$259
Door Sill Illumination	$265
C-Pillar Storage	$129
Floor and Cargo Mats	$155
Sport Steering Wheel	$279
Scion Security System	$469
Remote Engine Start	$529
Under Dash and Cup Holder Illumination	$299

The Mission statement below is not something that Toyota developed. It was written by a group of Scion owners and this was another part of the bundle that made up the business model. It was part of the answer to "how do you get these young people a sense of community?" What Toyota did was to engage new marketing partners that had different skills beyond advertising in magazines, the internet and television. This particular advertiser specialized in creating cooperative groups, and encouraging those groups to form throughout the country. This is one owner group, which Toyota helped fund, a leader stepped up, and the group began meeting to do whatever they decided to do.

This particular group said:

Mission Statement:

Scion Evolution (SE) was started to be an outlet for Scion owners to gather and share their passion for their Scions. It is with anticipation that SE humbly approaches this philosophy to enable Scion owners to contribute to the continuing belief in the Scion brand.

- ➔ Scion Evolution, Driven to Evolve, North Carolina Chapter (a Scion owner's club)

Now you have customers selling for you. There were also large events organized in different regions of the country to bring Scion owners together. For example, Toyota rented out Disney Land in California for an evening and only Scion owners could come, and they could get in for free, but they had to drive up in their Scion. Then they would auction off prizes, and celebrate being a part of the Scion community.

The early sales approach, what they called pure price within Scion, was setting a price for the car with a dealer. Some dealers will set different prices, perhaps based on where they are located. Once they set that price for selling the car with specific features, and even the service that comes after that, like an oil change, they agree to lock in that price for a year. Anyone who buys the product gets the same service and pays the same price.

They also unbundled marketing. Normally they would go to one advertising company and say, "do everything," but they discovered that to get an innovative approach to marketing suitable for young people they needed specialist companies. Some companies are good at social networking, some good at television ads, and some were good at creating the national events and clubs. Owner's clubs were organized by owners with support from Scion over social networks, both over the internet and also coming together face to face. Some groups would focus on music. Maybe it is country music in one part of the country, or rock in another. Then they had the Scion events, which grew to over 100 a month, to enable networking. For example, around Halloween, Knott's Berry Farm in California becomes Knott's Scary Farm, and they had a special event just for Scion owners.

Pure Price

→ Dealer Sets price for car and service then everyone gets same price

Unbundled marketing

→ Direct mailing, television, radio, events, and internet

Scion Owner's Clubs

→ Organized by owners with Scion support for social networking

Scion events (over 100/month)

→ Enable networking and belonging
→ Regional owner events tailored to local tastes (e.g., art festival) & generic events (e.g., Knott's Scary Farm)

To give a lot of value to the customer for a relatively low price, they decided they were going to use existing Toyota departments and staff and not create an entire bureaucracy around Scion. In 2007, the early days, they started with 19 people at headquarters and 40 people in the field who worked with the user groups and dealers, and that was it. That was the whole company for Scion.

Use existing Toyota departments-staff

➔ 2007 Headcount: 19 headquarter staff & 40 field staff

Use existing models from Japan

➔ e.g., bB to xB

Use Existing Toyota Dealer Network

They got a huge van and did a road show to sell the idea of buying into the Scion brand to dealers. It was not a requirement, it was an option, but most of the dealers in the US were excited about this opportunity to bring young people into their showrooms and got on board. They paid to create the Scion portion of their existing showroom. They had to train their sales staff differently and have different pricing policies, so there was an investment by the dealers.

Connecting Purpose to Results

What results did they get? This is going back to the early days. In the first year, they achieved all their goals. They wanted to bring younger people into the Toyota brand. At the time, the average age of 30 for Scion buyers was the youngest in the industry for any brand. A full 80% of these owners were new to the Toyota family. This was their first Toyota car. For those who already owned a vehicle and traded it in, in 80% of the cases they were trading in a vehicle from a different automotive company. They were getting what the industry calls "conquest customers."

In the early years, they had modest goals of 40,000 cars sold and achieved this. They were not expected to make a profit, but they did anyway. Scion sales peaked at over 180,000 per year but had dropped by 2013 to 68,000. New models were being introduced in 2015 and beyond, but it is reasonable to ask, "Is Scion a failed concept?"

This is a natural question if you think short term and do not understand the strategy. From Toyota's point of view, they were not evaluating it the same way. Number one, it worked in the first few years, they did a root cause analysis, and it was obvious that sales were down because the models were getting old, and they needed to develop new models for the Scion brand. Scion vehicle development was not a top priority particularly during the recession and various crises for four years. The time gap between new product introductions was a problem, but it was not a long-term problem that was going to kill the brand.

Mark Templin, vice president of Scion in 2007 when I did the interviews, explains the original objective in this way:

> "The metrics we think are important are not about sales or profits—that is not what Scion is all about—it is about opening the door to Toyota. We try to reach young people. The median age of Scion owners is 30 years old,

which is the youngest in the industry. As it turns out, we do make money selling Scion products and learning new ways of doing business."

They were also learning new ways of doing business. For example, they learned about new ways of marketing. Scion also excited a lot of the existing departments in Toyota Motor Sales. Interacting with young people was fun. There was a high level of energy of youth, and that actually helped the company as a whole to rejuvenate some of the energy you tend to lose when you become a large multi-national corporation. Obviously Scion would like to sell more vehicles to better serve its mission, but there were other indicators of success as well.

Scion Results in Early Years

- → Average age of 30—youngest in industry
- → 80% of Scion Owners new to Toyota family
- → 8 of top 10 were conquest customers trading in non-Toyoda vehicles
- → Investment paid and profitable by fourth year
- → But Sales were down in 2007 - Still Success?

Relationship between Strategic Innovation & Operational Excellence for Scion

Let's review how the pieces fit together, and how this relates to leadership. Number one, you start with strategic intent, which was a new brand with high value-added automobiles that could be personalized and created a sense of community, and bring young people into the Toyota market. That strategic intent then turned into innovation. The idea of mono-spec, some basic vanilla models that are customized through accessorizing, was one innovation. They got the idea from General Motors, and they modified it, but to Toyota, it was an innovation. The idea of pure price, the idea of unbundling the marketing approach, which then also found its way into other Toyota brands, and the idea of creating a community of owners were all innovations born out of the necessity of trying to achieve this strategy based on what young people in America really want.

These innovations by themselves had to be turned into operational excellence. In the words of Jim Lentz: "we then needed to deliver Toyota as a car to young people. That is what they want. Young people aren't particularly patient. Americans in general aren't particularly patient, so they want it now. We needed to have high quality, and we needed to not only have quality in the factory, but where the accessories are being added, either at the port or at the dealership."

One of the lean concepts that had to be used was Just-in-Time logistics systems so they could actually build to order at the port what the customer wants, the accessorizing, and very quickly get it to the dealers. They needed the Toyota production system in the factory to be able to build the model at a very low cost with high quality, so they had to eliminate waste, eliminate any excess cost. Pooling the cars shipped from Japan in California and customizing them there was a logistics innovation.

They needed to plan for future models to continue to adapt to customer needs. In Toyota, this is done through the chief engineer system. The chief engineer leads product development, working very closely with sales, and the chief engineer goes to the actual place (the *Gemba*) to see firsthand. In this case, the actual place is where the customers are using the car, for example, how they feel when they are driving it to the beach in California or how they feel when they are driving it to a museum in Washington D.C. The chief engineer had to be everywhere and see how young people in America live, and, working with sales, turn that into a new set of customer requirements.

Then the whole enterprise of Toyota had to cooperate. This was a tiny group that had to get the cooperation of sales, manufacturing, dealers, R&D, and they had to sell the concept and excite people, which meant that the original team developed through this experience their capability to persuade and to lead horizontally. All the parts of Toyota had to have the culture of focusing on what is good for the company, not just what is good for their department. This might be a nuisance for them in manufacturing, to make these particular cars, but it is for a particular purpose which will help the company long term, and that is where The Toyota Way culture comes in. The link between Strategic Intent, Innovations, and Operational Excellence is diagrammed in Figure 8-2.

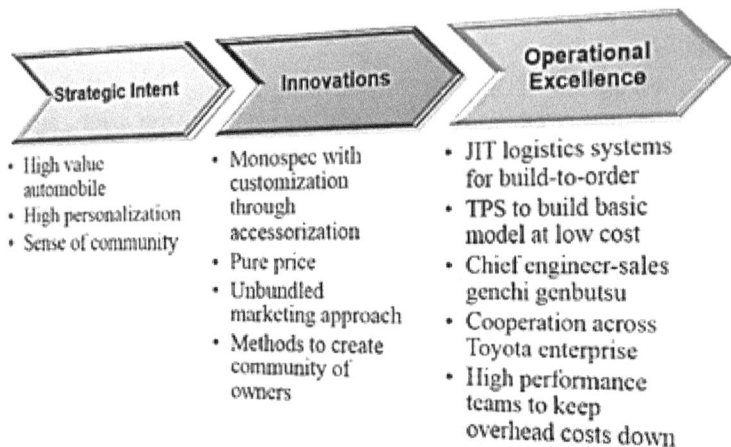

Figure 8-2. Relationship between Strategic Innovation & Operational Excellence.

Toyota Way Principles in Action

What were the key principles of The Toyota Way that we saw in action, which led to the success of Scion? The principles start with Respect for People, which means I respect the customer enough to really take the time to understand how they live, what they want from cars and what is really going to satisfy them. They also needed a problem solving process. The whole process of creating the Scion brand followed Toyota Business Practices. They began with a clear problem statement: the gap between the entry age they wanted for Toyota customers and the age they had. They had to grasp the situation and understand American youth through *genchi genbutsu*, through going and seeing. They broadly explored alternatives, going to wherever there might be a good idea like the interesting Chevy model, and then based on that they created the business model.

They needed to think long term, which meant accepting the strange idea that we will actually create a whole brand that might not make any profit for us as a company. The purpose of this particular brand was to bring new customers into the Toyota family. They then needed the process of Continuous Improvement. I have an initial system that I am going to modify based on feedback, and modify it to get closer and closer to what the customer wants. For example, in 2007, when sales declined, they needed to do a root cause analysis and solve the problem. The problem was mainly "we need new models."

To do all this, requires certain types of leaders who think in a certain way who follow the values of the company and are thinking first about the company and not about their own individual function or department needs. It was an opportunity for those leaders to grow their leadership skills. They grew their skills in problem solving, creative thinking, and working as a small team initially before growing larger. They learned more about leading horizontally, influencing other departments that they had no power over, such as engineering, manufacturing, and outside dealers who are independent business owners.

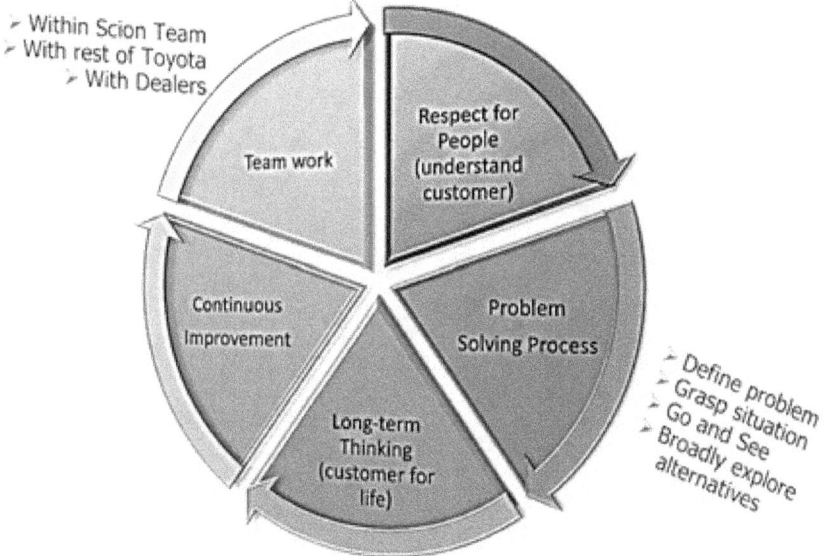

Figure 8-3. Principles in Action.

The Scion example is just one of many of how all these principles come together (see Figure 8-3). It gives you a big picture vision of Lean Leadership, from concept to product, to the product being built in the market, and then, continuing to connect with customers after the sales. Neither a good strategy nor operational excellence alone would have been enough for solving this problem. Strategy and operational excellence had to be directly connected.

That ends the story, but hopefully this has helped your vision of your long and exciting journey into Lean Leadership. It should be clear that developing a lean enterprise is a long-term process that affects all aspects. It is certainly not just a manufacturing thing. If there is one element that all parts of lean have in common it is critical and creative thinking. It starts with developing yourself. Then learn to become a teacher as you continue to be a learner. The journey never ends!

DEVELOPING LEAN LEADERS: For Further Reading

Throughout this book we have referenced various books that you might want to investigate more thoroughly. Here are some suggestions for further reading:

Freddy Balle and Michael Balle, *The Gold Mine: A Novel of Lean Turnaround*, (Cambridge, Mass.: Lean Enterprise Institute, 2005)

Michael Balle and Freddy Balle, *Lead with Respect: A Novel of Lean Practice* (Cambridge, Mass.: Lean Enterprise Institute, 2005)

Jim Collins, *Good to Great: Why Some Companies Make the Leap . . . and Others Don't* (New York: Harper Business, 2001)

Pascale Dennis, *Getting the Right Things Done: A Leader's Guide for Planning and Execution* (Cambridge, Mass.: Lean Enterprise Institute, 2006)

Robert Greenleaf, *The Power of Servant Leadership* (San Francisco: Berrett-Koehler, 1998)

H. Thomas Johnson, *Profit beyond Measure* (New York: Free Press, 2008)

Jeffrey Liker, *The Toyota Way* (New York: McGraw-Hill, 2004)

Jeffrey Liker and David Meier, *The Toyota Way Fieldbook* (New York: McGraw-Hill, 2006)

Jeffrey Liker and David Meier, *Toyota Talent* (New York: McGraw-Hill, 2007)

Jeffrey Liker and Michael Hoseus, *Toyota Culture* (New York: McGraw-Hill, 2008)

Jeffrey Liker and James Franz, *The Toyota Way to Continuous Improvement* (New York: McGraw-Hill, 2011)

Jeffrey Liker and Gary Convis, *The Toyota Way to Lean Leadership* (New York: McGraw-Hill, 2011)

Mike Rother, *Toyota Kata: Managing People for Improvement, Adaptiveness and Superior Results* (New York: McGraw-Hill, 2009)

Peter Senge, *The Fifth Discipline: The Art and Practice of the Learning Organization* (New York: Crown Business, 2006)

Richard Sheridan, *Joy, Inc.: How We Built a Workplace People Love* (New York: Portfolio Hardcover, 2013)

John Shook, *Managing to Learn* (Cambridge, Mass.: Lean Enterprise Institute, 2009)

George Trachilis, *OEM Principles of Lean Thinking*, http://lean101.ca

Taiichi Ohno's *Workplace Management: Special 100th Birthday Edition*, (New York: McGraw-Hill Professional, 2012)

www.ingramcontent.com/pod-product-compliance
Lightning Source LLC
Chambersburg PA
CBHW052104230426
43671CB00011B/1930